IDEAS

in

FOOD

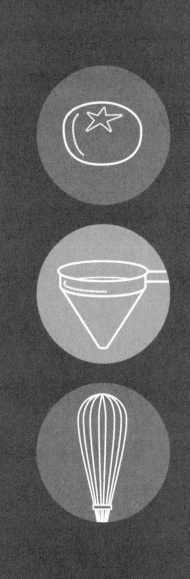

IDEAS

in

FOOD

GREAT RECIPES *and* WHY THEY WORK

AKI KAMOZAWA and

H. ALEXANDER TALBOT

Clarkson Potter/Publishers
New York

Published in the United States by
Clarkson Potter/Publishers,
an imprint of the Crown Publishing Group,
a division of Random House, Inc., New York.
www.crownpublishing.com
www.clarksonpotter.com

CLARKSON POTTER is a trademark and POTTER
with colophon is a registered trademark of Random House, Inc.

Library of Congress Cataloging-in-Publication Data
Kamozawa, Aki.
Ideas in food / Aki Kamozawa and H. Alexander Talbot.
p.   cm.
Includes index.
1. Cookery.   2. Chemistry.   I. Talbot, H. Alexander.   II. Title.
TX652.K325   2010
641.5—dc22   2010017633

ISBN 978-0-307-71740-5

Printed in the United States of America

Design by Claire Naylon Vaccaro
Illustrations on page 2 by Jonathan Correira

1   3   5   7   9   10   8   6   4   2

First Edition

For Aunt Marie

and Grandma Kitty,

our two biggest boosters,

and Amaya,

our greatest inspiration

CONTENTS

INTRODUCTION

We both love food. It's as simple as that. We love to eat and we love to cook, and we're lucky enough to be able to draw on those passions in our professional lives. This book is the result of years of eating, cooking, and studying food. We know that to take our food to the next level, we need to understand what's happening beneath the surface of what we experience in the kitchen. We enjoy juxtaposing science and creativity in the kitchen to create great food. We've learned to be methodical in our experiments with new ingredients, techniques, and equipment in order to maximize our results.

Our business, Ideas in Food, is about sharing our passion for food and experience in the kitchen with other food enthusiasts who want to push their boundaries and learn more. We are lucky enough to work with chefs and food companies from around the world in both educational and creative capacities. Our classes and hands-on workshops on cooking, whether in groups or one on one, are open forums for ideas, and while we present solid techniques and information, we always learn something new from everyone we work with. The crux of our philosophy in and out of the kitchen is that there's always something more to learn. This book describes many of the things we've discovered thus far.

We are comfortable walking into a room of skeptics. Our workshops are tailored toward each person or group, either focusing on an overview of ingredients and techniques or targeted to specific goals. In these sessions, we often face a mixed group of people, some of whom are excited about learning more and others who are dubious about the validity of what we have to offer. It is our job to illustrate why a deeper understanding of food and the ways in which it works are so important. Knowledge allows us to improve flavor, efficiency, and functionality in the kitchen. In a nutshell, it enables us to cook better.

What we find most interesting is how often people are opposed to the idea of something new simply because they are unfamiliar with it or because they've heard of it only in a negative context. We remember clearly when as kids we started reading the labels on candy boxes. Sightings of xanthan gum and carnauba wax often led to dramatic exclamations about the fact that we were eating car wax and other chemicals. Everyone remembers the story about Mikey and the Pop Rocks that exploded in his stomach when he ingested them with soda, right? The idea that manufactured foods can be dangerous to our health is a common one. Some of them, like trans fats, actually are. Still, even naturally occurring ingredients like salt, sugar, fat, and caffeine come under fire on a regular basis.

Many of the concepts that we teach in our workshops have been around for a long time. They were originally developed and tested extensively for the food service and food manufacturing industries, have proven themselves to work, and are now making the leap into restaurant and home kitchens. The big change is in the quality of the ingredients used and the inspiration of the cooks using them. Making cheese at home, for example, is not a new concept by any stretch of the imagination, but understanding how and why it works is. This information frees us to explore what's possible in our kitchens. Something as simple as adjusting the cooking temperature of a braise or flipping a steak as it cooks can make a huge difference in the final results. Appreciating why we do this and how it affects the meat allows us to improve our results. A better grasp of the ingredients and what happens when we use them is pivotal.

Our job is to strip away the hype and fantasy and talk cold, hard facts. We use the ingredients carrageenan, agar, and transglutaminase, for example, because they work. They allow us to gently manipulate the textures of our food and make it a cut above the ordinary. Rice bran oil is perfect for frying because it has a high smoke point and a clean neutral flavor. Gone is the smell of traditional fryer oil. Melting cheese slowly over low heat keeps it from breaking and gives far more pleasing results than melting cheese at high heat. No-knead bread requires minimal effort but lots of time to achieve the desired results. These are things we know to be true because we've tested them in our kitchen so you don't have to in yours.

The biggest barrier to using ingredients is unfamiliarity. You have to use something in order to understand how it works. We've spent hours and hours failing miserably with these ingredients. That means we can show other people how to use them, and perhaps more importantly, we can explain what happens when these ingredients aren't used properly. We all know that you learn more from the things that go wrong in the kitchen than from successes. Since we are intimately acquainted with most of the ways these ingredients and techniques can and will go wrong, we can help you figure out how things went awry and show you how to avoid the pitfalls in the first place.

So what is cooking? In our kitchen it's about great ingredients, well prepared to the best of our abilities. The rest is philosophy, creativity, and individual expression. With a handful of knowledge we exponentially increase our chances of enjoying a delicious meal.

We divided this book into two parts for ease of use. We believe that anyone can use both sections, but the part for professionals utilizes ingredients and equipment that require a little more of an investment of time or money from the home cook. We hope that everyone will read both sections and that we will inspire people to be a little more daring in their own kitchens.

IDEAS

for

EVERYONE

This section is focused on ideas for everyone. The ingredients are ones we all have in our kitchens and tend to take for granted. Why make vinegar? Because we can make something delicious with unique and exceptional flavors that is not available in stores. You could just let your leftover wine ferment on the counter. But understanding the science behind the process and having a path to follow allows you to produce consistent results and create new interpretations, like maple vinegar. Creativity requires a process. We are sharing our discoveries about kitchen processes so that you can take them and create new things in your kitchen.

In this section we build a foundation by covering ingredients and techniques that will be familiar to almost everyone. Many of the topics were inspired by questions that people have asked us over the years. Some are questions we've asked each other. Asking questions helps us all become better cooks. A great meal can be as simple as scrambled eggs but they should be the best darned scrambled eggs you can make. We're going to tell you how to do that and why our method works.

Many of the ideas may seem basic. Upon reflection, though, it's clear that a lot of mystery is still associated with many standard ingredients. Most of us know how to cook an egg. But how many of us have actually considered what is happening to the egg as it cooks? How does brine work to add flavor and moisture to your food? What is steam leavening? How does sourdough work? Why is lactic acid important to your starter? The answers to these and many other questions are in this section.

Cooking provides an opportunity for us to be both scientists and artists. We like to try new things just to see what will happen. The worst result is that we have to order pizza. But pizza dinners tend to occur at the end of our most illuminating days, because we learn more from failure than from success. Think of that. The more we know, the less pizza we order. Occasionally we even make our own. Delivery days never go completely out of fashion because there are always new questions to ask and mistakes to be made. That's what makes cooking fun for us.

The recipes in this section are given to illustrate the science and help you get a feel for how things work. They are also included because the food is delicious. We've listed ingredients by American volume measurements first and then by weight in grams to make them accessible to as large an audience as possible. We hope you'll try these recipes once as they are to see how they work and then use them as a jumping-off point for interpretation in your own kitchen.

SEASONING *and* PRESERVING

SALT

A little bit of salt makes food taste good. We have taste buds geared specifically for the flavor of sodium chloride, or table salt, because, in small quantities, it is essential for the proper functioning of our bodies. It regulates muscle contractions and fluid balance, carries nutrients to our cells, helps keep minerals soluble in the blood, is essential to digestion, and is a vital ingredient in blood plasma. Too much salt can be detrimental, but then again, too much of anything can have negative repercussions. In proper doses salt makes the world a tastier place.

Interestingly, as we have become more diligent about recording our recipes, we have noticed that our personal salt concentrations are very stable. Across the board, regardless of the recipe, we tend to season our food at a level of 0.5 percent of the weight of what we are cooking. There are a few exceptions where the level creeps up to 0.75 percent or down to 0.4 percent, but generally speaking, our palates are amazingly consistent. Now that we know this, when creating recipes we can calculate the necessary salt content based on the total weight of the ingredients, and we hit the bull's-eye every time.

Sodium chloride is what we all keep in our saltcellar. It is available in many forms, from sea salts of varying textures and hues to large granules of kosher salt, iodized crystals, and pickling salt. Sea salts also contain trace amounts of various minerals and impurities that give them their attractive colors and textures. Manufactured table salts often include anticaking ingredients and iodine. Whether or not you can actually taste different flavors in the different salts is a topic for debate. We believe that perception is 90 percent of reality, and since each salt is a totally different experience, it stands to reason that they are perceived differently, no matter what the scientists may tell us.

Salts are created when acids and bases react with one another. A transformation occurs when there is a partial or total replacement of a negatively charged atom with a positively charged metal atom, resulting in sodium. In nature, sodium hydroxide and hydrochloric acid react with one another to produce sodium chloride and water. The two main sources for salt are evaporated seawater and mineral deposits. Once the raw salt is obtained it is purified and refined before being sold to the general public. Salt has a cubic crystalline structure. In its pure form, it is water soluble and crystal clear. It has a characteristic flavor and no odor. Salt is known for enhancing sweetness and minimizing bitter flavors.

We use fine sea salt for seasoning proteins and vegetables. It appeals to us because it has a clean flavor free from chemicals and allows for consistency in our cooking. Its fine, delicate texture disperses quickly over ingredients for an even distribution. The salt's fine grain is extremely useful when seasoning salads and delicate greens because it is small enough to coat ingredients evenly and add the flavor we are looking for—to ensure consistent seasoning on every level. It's the perfect supporting player, enabling everything around it to shine in the spotlight.

We also use several finishing salts: fleur de sel, sel de Guérande, Hawaiian black and red salts, and our own homemade flavored salts. They give us a wide range of textures and underlying flavor notes. Fleur de sel, or "the flower of the sea," adds a delicate crunch to vegetable ragouts, foie gras *au torchon*, raw tuna, chocolates, and caramel. Sel de Guérande is a coarser, heartier salt. It is a salt with moxie. It has a larger mineral content and its petite pebbly structure guarantees that it gets noticed. Roasted and braised meats and fish, whole roasted vegetables, and confit potatoes benefit from the textures and flavors of sel de Guérande. Other salts we use are dish specific—from a fish or vegetable carpaccio to a particular foie gras or offal preparation. A variety of salts is like a painter's palette, and we enjoy playing with them.

Salt has many different roles in the kitchen. Salt in high concentrations is considered a preservative for meat and fish because it inhibits the growth of microorganisms and curtails the activity of the enzymes in the meat. At lower concentrations, salt increases the solubility of muscle proteins in water. In processed-meat applications, like charcuterie, this characteristic combines with salt's water-binding capabilities to form a stable emulsion of muscle fibers, proteins, and moisture. Salt inhibits fermentation and is well known for its negative interaction with yeast. Salt in bread dough strengthens the gluten bond and enhances browning during baking by reducing the breakdown of sugars.

Above and beyond all of these things, salt is important because it makes food taste good. At smaller concentrations it makes food taste more like itself. Of course, if you cross that line into overseasoning, food begins to taste like salt. It becomes minerally and sharp on the tongue to the point of being unpleasant to eat. It's as if our bodies know when a certain threshold has been reached and react accordingly to keep us from overdoing our intake.

In fact, the many varieties of salt have sparked our own interest in infusing salts. For our infused or flavored salts, we use fleur de sel for its texture and porous nature, which absorbs well and gently carries individual flavors. Our first flavored salt—now a standby—came about by an abundance of herbs gone to flower in our garden in Maine. We harvested and dried the flowers and then sifted them through a fine sieve to capture just the pollen—an intense focused essence of the herbs. Somehow combining all of the different herbs allowed them to fuse into one harmonious entity. We mixed the pollens with the salt and its intense aroma and flavor enabled us to taste the bounty of our garden all year long. We use it mostly as a finishing salt. It is wonderful with fish or vegetables that have been gently cooked and would benefit from the intense herbal accent. While this was our first flavored salt, we have since expanded our repertoire. Next we began smoking salt, again for an intense, focused delivery of the smoke flavor when applied to certain ingredients. Since then we have incorporated spices, citrus zests, mushroom powder, and even honey powder in our seasoned salts. Salt is important because it enhances the natural flavor of food. Our seasoned salts add more layers instead of simply disappearing into the background.

BEEF SEASONING

MAKES ABOUT 3 TABLESPOONS, ENOUGH FOR 2 LARGE STEAKS

We love the balance of salt, sugar, and pepper with the intense savory flavor of meat. Although we dubbed this Beef Seasoning, we use it on anything and everything, from hot smoked salmon to grilled eggplant, when we feel it's appropriate. It's a wonderfully balanced seasoning that brings out the inherent savoriness in food. We're not afraid to substitute different peppers either. Togarishi, a Japanese pepper blend, hot smoked paprika, green chile powder, and harissa powder can add subtle nuances to the finished blend. What's important when choosing your pepper is making sure it's one you feel passionate about.

2 tablespoons/27 grams packed **light brown sugar**

1 tablespoon/18 grams **fine sea salt**

¼ teaspoon/0.5 gram **cayenne pepper**

Blend the sugar, salt, and cayenne together. Use immediately or store in a lidded container.

VANILLA SALT

MAKES ABOUT 2 CUPS

Vanilla salt can add that mysterious sweet note that gives depth to many dishes without any actual sweetness. Its floral, fragrant aroma teases you into expecting sweetness and its deep flavor adds nuance to the background notes of a dish. We enjoy pairing it with fish, root vegetables, and other inherently sweet ingredients because this aromatic salt helps enhance their natural sweetness. Sometimes the flavor of vanilla can be overpowering and adding it this way can be just the right touch. We also use it for sweet preparations—for example, as a finishing salt for caramels, or lightly sprinkled on a chocolate tart.

1 Tahitian **vanilla bean**
2 cups/280 grams **fleur de sel**

Cut the vanilla bean in half and scrape out the seeds. Combine the vanilla seeds, the salt, and the scraped-out pod in a bowl and mix to disperse the seeds. Put the vanilla salt in a zip-top bag or lidded container for several days to let the flavors infuse before using. The vanilla bean itself will continue to perfume the remaining salt for as long as you have any left.

EVERYTHING CURED SALMON AND CREAM CHEESE

SERVES 6

This recipe is a play on the ubiquitous smoked salmon with cream cheese and a bagel. It was one of our favorite lazy Sunday breakfasts when we were living in New York. Once we moved away from the city, we found that we didn't always have access to great bagels or smoked salmon. We needed to find a good alternative that was readily available. "Everything" bagels—which typically contain onion, garlic, and several seeds—are our favorite, characterized by their crunchy coating of various seasonings. So we decided to use that flavor profile for cured salmon fillets and cream cheese that we could easily make at home.

6 tablespoons/108 grams **fine sea salt**

2¾ cups/285 grams **Everything Spice Blend** (recipe follows)

1¾ pounds/795 grams **center-cut salmon fillet**, with skin

7 ounces/200 grams **cream cheese**

1 cup/100 grams **Everything Spice Blend** (recipe follows)

½ teaspoon/3 grams **fine sea salt**

Grilled or toasted **bagels** or **bread**

Mix together the salt and the spice blend to make a cure.

Wet a 2-foot (60-centimeter) square of cheesecloth and squeeze it dry. Lay the cheesecloth flat on a counter and place the salmon in the center, flesh side down. Fold the cheesecloth around the fillet so the salmon is covered in one layer of cloth. This will make it easier to remove the cure later.

Lay two pieces of plastic wrap three times the length of the salmon fillet on the countertop so they just overlap to create a double-wide sheet of plastic. Place one-third of the cure in the center of the plastic wrap, shaping the mixture so it provides a wide base for the salmon. Lay the cheesecloth-wrapped fillet on the cure bed, skin side down. Sprinkle the rest of the cure over the salmon, allowing some of it to cascade off the sides so that the edges of the fish will also be coated in cure. Fold the long ends of the plastic wrap over the fish, followed by the wide ends. This should create a tight package of salmon that is evenly coated in cure and contained in plastic. To ensure a tight seal and even pressure, wrap the package in another length of plastic wrap. Place the salmon on a rimmed baking sheet and refrigerate for 24 hours.

Unwrap the fish, scrape off the cure, and carefully pull off the cheesecloth. Rinse the fish briefly in cold running water and then pat completely dry. Serve immediately or wrap in plastic and return to the refrigerator. The flavor will mature overnight. The fish will keep in the refrigerator for 3 to 4 days.

Place the cream cheese, spice blend, and salt in a food processor and puree until smooth. Refrigerate in an airtight container until ready to use. It will keep for up to a week.

To serve, remove the skin and bloodline from the fish. Thinly slice the fish and arrange it on a plate. Serve with everything cream cheese and the grilled bread.

EVERYTHING SPICE BLEND

MAKES ABOUT 3¾ CUPS

Clearly, toasted milk powder was not part of the original Everything Spice Blend. We add it here to give it depth of flavor. That milk proteins also help it stick to the fish is an incidental benefit. The real bonus is the toasty flavor it imparts, which adds to the perception of the toasted bagel flavor in the finished fish or whatever else you may season with it.

2 packets **nonfat dry milk** (enough to make 1 quart/1,040 grams milk)

¼ cup plus 3 tablespoons/47 grams **dried minced onion**

½ cup/60 grams **sesame seeds**

8 teaspoons/25 grams **poppy seeds**

3 tablespoons/20 grams **garlic powder**

4 teaspoons/10 grams **caraway seeds**

Preheat the oven to 350°F (175°C).

Combine the dry milk, dried onion, sesame seeds, poppy seeds, garlic powder, and caraway seeds in a shallow baking dish. Toast the mixture in the oven for 30 minutes, stirring every 5 minutes to ensure even browning. When the mixture is amber brown, remove it from the oven and let cool.

Process the mixture briefly in a food processor to break up any large chunks of milk powder that may have formed in the toasting process and to evenly distribute the spices. The spice blend will keep in an airtight container for a month.

BRINING

Brining is a popular technique for adding flavor and increasing the juiciness of food. Chickens and turkeys are popular candidates for brining because their lean, delicate flesh is greatly enhanced by a salt-water soak. We really enjoy the results of brining almost anything— meat, fish, and vegetables. Each has something to gain from the process. For us, brine is a vehicle for flavor, and while a simple salt-water solution has its place in our kitchen, we're not afraid to turn up the volume and add seasoned liquids, spices, and aromatics to the mix. Marinades are kissing cousins to brines, with sharper, more acidic profiles, and can be equally useful tools for amplifying flavor.

Brining is a method of passive transport where no energy is expended to make a change occur. When we brine, we surround a piece of meat or fish with a salt solution. Osmosis occurs as water moves through a selectively permeable membrane, in this case the cell walls, from areas of lower solute concentration to areas of higher concentration. Diffusion is when molecules, like salt, spread from areas of higher concentration to areas of lower concentration. Salt is hydrophilic, and in areas where salt has higher concentrations, it will draw available water toward itself until a state of equilibrium is reached. First the water will flow out of the protein and into the brine, because the brine's salt content is greater than that of the meat, giving it a higher osmotic concentration. Then diffusion causes the salt to be drawn into the meat. As the salt penetrates the meat, osmosis allows the water to be drawn back into the cells, still working toward a state of equilibrium.

Once the brine has been pulled into the cells, the salt begins to react with the meat's proteins, causing the bonds between the actin and myosin proteins to begin to break down, or denature. This allows the myofibrils, the main structural component of the muscles in the meat, to absorb the water in the form of the brine and swell. The myofibrils can expand to twice their normal size. The denatured proteins are able to interact with each other and create a water-holding matrix. This increases the meat's ability to absorb aromatics and flavors from the brine. The increased water-holding capacity that results from the denaturing of the proteins means that the seasoned meat contains a greater concentration of water in its cells and is able to retain a slightly higher percentage of it during cooking, resulting in juicier meat.

As the salt penetrates the meat, some of the myosin fibers actually dissolve. This creates more space between the muscle fibers, resulting in more tender meat. When the brined meat is cooked, this dissolved myosin forms a gel within the muscle fibers that helps them hold on to liquid, resulting in juicier meat. This reaction will occur when brining with salt solutions at concentrations beginning at 3 percent. The stronger the brining solution, the more quickly it will penetrate the inside of the meat. The larger the piece of meat, the harder it is to brine because the time needed to penetrate the interior will cause the outer layer to become increasingly salty. We like to use a 3 to 5 percent brine for our meats and keep the thickness to a maximum of three inches.

Brines are characterized by the presence of salt; marinades are defined by the presence of acid. Marinades are generally made up of an acidic component, a fatty component, and seasonings. They are meant to tenderize and season meats and fish. The acid in a marinade will partially denature surface proteins and create openings for flavor to penetrate the muscles. Marinades also improve the water-holding capacity of the meat. They work best on thinner cuts and smaller pieces of meat. This is because the reaction with acid limits the amount of time the meat or fish can remain in a marinade. If it is left for too long, the food "cooks," an effect used as a texture and flavor enhancement in the creation of ceviche and escabeche. This can result in meat or fish that becomes overly tender, to the point of being mushy. The slightly acidic kick of a marinade is a wonderful balance to rich proteins. It gives cooked meat and fish an increased depth of flavor that we find quite seductive.

A practical use for brining is as a preserving agent for seafood. We don't generally wash fish and seafood; instead we soak them in a 5 percent salt solution for ten minutes. This soak coagulates exterior proteins, firms the flesh, and extends the shelf life of the fish. We've also found that this saltwater bath results in fish and crustaceans that cook cleanly, without excessive amounts of albumen clinging to the surface. This is especially noticeable in lobster, which usually has a good amount of coagulated hemolymph adhering to the meat after cooking. The final result is a beautifully cooked piece of fish that has a clean, appealing presentation.

TWICE-COOKED SCALLOPS

SERVES 2 AS AN ENTRÉE OR 4 AS AN APPETIZER

These scallops are first cooked sous vide and then finished in a hot sauté pan. (Sous vide, or "under vacuum," is a technique where foods are vacuum sealed in food-grade plastic bags, then cooked slowly in a circulating hot water bath at precise temperatures; see a fuller discussion on page 199.) In all of our recipes using sous vide, we give you the option of substituting a zip-top bag for a vacuum-sealed one; as long as you are able to accurately control the temperature of your water bath, you will achieve a comparable result. It is important to squeeze as much air as possible out of the bag because this will affect how efficiently the heat is conducted through the food. The brining and first cook can be done as soon as you get the scallops into your kitchen. The first cooking seems to firm up the flesh and intensify the flavor. We utilize the first two steps even when we're planning to serve the scallops in a raw, marinated preparation. It makes them easier to work with and gives them a slightly firmer texture. When we sear the scallops just before serving, we find that they cook more evenly and do not exude as much liquid as raw scallops do.

> 4½ cups/1,012.5 grams **water**
> 2 tablespoons plus 2 teaspoons/48 grams **fine sea salt**, plus more
>   for seasoning
> 8 **U-10 scallops**
> 2 tablespoons/28 grams **olive oil**
> 2 tablespoons/28 grams cold **unsalted butter**

In a large bowl, combine the water and salt, stirring until the salt is dissolved. Remove the muscle from the scallops and place the scallops in the brine for 10 minutes. Remove and pat dry.

Preheat a circulating water bath or large pot of water to 122°F (50°C).

Set two sheets of plastic wrap on a work surface and arrange 4 scallops on each sheet, end to end, so they resemble scallop logs. Wrap the plastic tightly around the logs and then seal them in vacuum bags. Alternatively, you can place the logs in large zip-top bags and seal them, squeezing out as much air as possible. Place the bags in the water bath and cook the scallops for 30 minutes, then transfer the bags to an ice water bath and let cool. When the scallops are cold, transfer them to the refrigerator. They will keep for up to 2 days.

To cook the scallops a second time, heat a heavy-bottomed pan that is large enough to comfortably hold all the scallops over medium-high heat. Unwrap the scallops and season them with salt. Pour the oil into the pan and when it just begins to smoke, add the scallops. Sear the scallops on one side. When they have formed a dark golden crust, 2 to 3 minutes, flip them over and add the butter to the pan. Baste the scallops with the butter until it stops foaming. Remove the scallops from the pan, let rest for 5 minutes, and serve.

HONEY MUSTARD BRINE

MAKES 1 GALLON

This brine is wonderful with a pork shoulder or racks of lamb. We would brine the shoulder for forty-eight hours and the lamb racks for twenty-four. Whole chickens would also be great after twenty-four hours in the brine and a few hours on a rack to dry. You could even follow the Roast Chicken (page 218) procedure to finish them and have a meal to remember. For root vegetables like parsnips or celeriac, we peel them, cut them into bite-size pieces, brine them for a couple of hours, pat dry, and then roast or sauté them. The honey helps amplify their natural sweetness while the mustard provides a great contrasting kick of acid and spice. They are wonderful alongside salmon or any other full-flavored fish.

1 gallon/3,600 grams **water**

½ cup/144 grams **fine sea salt**

1 cup/330 grams **honey**

1 cup/260 grams **Dijon mustard**

Put the water in a large bowl. Stir in the salt until it is dissolved. Stir in the honey and the mustard until they are dissolved. Reserve the brine in the refrigerator until ready to use.

ROAST CHICKEN BRINE

MAKES 6 TO 7 CUPS

This may seem like an unorthodox flavor profile, but roast chicken brine is delicious. Just as chicken stock is used as the base for myriad soups, this roast chicken brine pairs well with a variety of vegetables and fish. Unsurprisingly, it is also amazing with chicken and turkey. We are lucky enough to be able to buy inexpensive chicken backs at our local Whole Foods. If you can't get backs or if wings are too expensive, chicken legs or thighs are sometimes an economical substitute. Even if you prefer to eat white meat, using dark meat for the brine will give you the most flavor.

3½ pounds/1,600 grams **chicken wings**

2 pounds/1,000 grams **chicken backs**

1 scant tablespoon/15 grams **fine sea salt**

6 cups/1,350 grams **water**

1 large **onion**, peeled and sliced

1½ cups/360 grams **red wine**

1 **head garlic**, peeled and separated into cloves

2 tablespoons/40 grams **soy sauce**

Preheat the oven to 425°F (220°C), or 400°F (205°C) with convection.

Season the chicken wings and backs with the salt. Roast them until golden brown, about 45 minutes.

Put the wings, backs, and pan drippings into a pressure cooker. Add the water, onion, red wine, garlic, and soy sauce. Cook on high pressure for 30 minutes. Let the pressure dissipate naturally.

Alternatively, place the wings, backs, and pan drippings in a large pot set over high heat. Add the water, onion, red wine, garlic, and soy sauce. Bring to a boil, reduce to a very gentle simmer, and cook for 4 to 6 hours, uncovered, skimming occasionally. If the water level gets too low, add some fresh water to the pot.

Strain the liquid, discarding the chicken and vegetables, and cool.

Skim the fat from the surface of the liquid and reserve for cooking. (It can be used to sear fish or chicken.) Use the brine to season chicken, fish, lobster, steak, and vegetables. Brining time depends on the thickness of your ingredients, ranging from about 30 minutes for shellfish and vegetables to about 1 hour for fish, steaks, and chicken parts, and 45 to 60 minutes per pound for larger pieces of meat. Once your ingredient has been brined, pat it dry and finish as desired.

VINEGAR

Vinegar is one of those ingredients that people tend to take for granted. It is mostly seen in salad dressings and pickles, which is a shame because there is a whole world of flavor just waiting to be explored. We both grew up in homes where vinegar was used mainly for salad and the occasional poached egg. As we matured in the kitchen we began using vinegar for cooking, realizing that its balanced and flavorful acidity had a lot to offer.

For years the word *vinegar* almost seemed synonymous with

balsamic, a sweet, dark brew that originated in Italy. After years of making overly sweet balsamic vinaigrettes in various restaurants, Aki was not a fan, and always resisted using it in our kitchen. Finally, at a local pizza joint, she had a salad with balsamic that was transcendent. It was balanced beautifully with peppery watercress, sharp arugula, sun-dried tomatoes, and sweet roasted peppers, where its rich, syrupy flavor was showcased to great advantage. It just goes to show that every vinegar eventually finds its place.

As professional chefs we see a lot of open bottles of wine at the end of an evening. Some restaurants have high-tech vacuum systems to preserve the flavor until morning, some use a simple gas spritz for the same purpose, and some recork and chill the bottles; still others let their staff finish any open bottles at the end of the night. While there are quality vintages that take well to an open bottle and bloom over time, the majority of bottles opened to pour by the glass do not. But fear not—because good wine makes good vinegar, and good vinegar is a stellar cooking ingredient. There's a certain cachet to housemade products, and wine vinegar is no exception. When we first began we went a little nuts, ordering small oak barrels for aging, which led to separate red and white vinegars, which led to Guinness vinegar produced from several cases of expired brew, which then begat maple, tequila, and a variety of other microvinegars to grace our pantry.

Vinegar is a living ingredient created through the process of fermentation. The final product will contain elements of the original batch, adding a depth of flavor that differentiates naturally fermented vinegar from a manufactured one. The term *vinegar* actually refers to the two-step process of fermentation from a carbohydrate to an alcohol to an acetic acid. (All acetic acids are not vinegar, although all vinegars are made from acetic acid.) Sugar is converted into alcohol, which is then fermented into vinegar. When creating a fruit-based vinegar, wild yeasts are added to convert the sugars into alcohol. Starch-based vinegars add an extra step wherein the starch is first converted into sugar for a triple fermentation process. Our Guinness brew is actually an alegar, not a vinegar, because it is made from sour beer. Strongly flavored beers that have expired and are no longer fit for consumption as á beverage can make delicious and complex alegars.

Vinegar stocks are made using a base material that is fermented with yeast to create alcohol. Brewer's yeast is used for cereals, grains, and molasses. Wine yeasts are used for fruit juices and honey. A sugar concentration in the range of 10 to 18 percent is considered ideal for making vinegar stock because it will transform into alcohol concentrations of 9 to 12 percent, which are considered optimal for vinegar production. Vinegar can be made from stock with alcohol concentrations as low as 5 percent, although these conditions can result in overoxidation; at higher concentrations, over 15 percent alcohol, acetobacters are inhibited by the amount of alcohol present and can even be killed off by it. Wine alcohol levels vary from 10 to 15 percent. If you're working with some leftover wine at the high end of that scale, say a California Cabernet clocking in at over 15 percent, just add a splash of water and let it ferment. It may take longer than something in the optimal range, but it will become vinegar eventually and you will be rewarded for your patience by the flavor in the end.

Acetobacter aceti is the bacterium used to produce vinegar from alcohol. It is widely found in nature. Acetobacters convert alcohol to acetic acid in the presence of oxygen. It is added to the vinegar stock, which is usually made from cereals, fruits, sugar syrups, or industrial ethyl alcohol, to begin the fermentation process.

A clean, sterilized container for storing your vinegar during the fermentation process is a must. Small oak barrels can be purchased online, although we've found that large glass cookie jars with loose-fitting lids are an economical alternative. Acetobacters need oxygen to function, so airtight containers will not work for the fermentation period. Pure soft water should be used for any dilution of the vinegar stock. The chlorine and fluoride found in municipal water can have an adverse effect on the fermentation process, so filtered water is recommended. Acetobacters also tend to be very temperature sensitive. They are happiest between 59°F and 94°F (15°C–34°C), with an optimum range of 80°F–85°F (27°C–29°C) for acetification, and they die off at temperatures over 140°F (60°C). Fortunately, this range is happily within normal room temperatures, although a warmer room is preferable to a cold one. Once the fermentation process has begun, the vinegar stock should be left alone in a dark spot (acetobacters are sensitive to UV light) for at least two to three weeks. The vinegar should not be stirred or agitated during the fermentation period.

When making homemade vinegars, a vinegar mother, or mat, will often appear in the container of liquid during the fermentation process. It is a combination of cellulose and acetic acid bacteria. This development is a good, though not a necessary, occurrence because the mother's appearance indicates a healthy environment for the vinegar's development. The vinegar mother can take on a variety of forms, ranging from transparent to dark in color and from delicate and leaflike in appearance to a solid mass floating at the top of the container. The largest mothers we experienced were from our beer vinegars— entire sheets of slippery, opaque cellulose that resembled creatures from the bottom of the sea. We've also seen mothers that were feathery and some that resembled forests of seaweed; the only constant is that the mother has looked different for every batch we've produced. Once the vinegar is completed, the mat should be removed and either used to create another vinegar or simply discarded. If the mother is left in the container for too long it can begin to rot and adversely affect the finished vinegar.

After a few weeks of fermentation it is time to test your vinegar. You will want to check the sugar, alcohol, and acetic acid levels and, of course, the flavor of your product. For a home brew you may simply wish to taste your vinegar and proceed accordingly. You may judge by looking for a complete absence of alcohol in the nose and on the palate. For a more scientific approach, you can purchase test kits from most home brewing or winemaking supply stores. You can use a pH meter or titration kit to determine whether or not the acetic fermentation is complete. We usually go by taste and thus far our palates have never led us astray.

When the acetic fermentation is complete, the vinegar should be strained and transferred to airtight containers to reduce the risk of spoilage. Once the alcohol disappears, in the presence of oxygen the acetobacters will continue to break down the vinegar into carbon dioxide and water, reducing the acid levels and leaving the vinegar open to the development of various undesirable microorganisms. Straining the vinegar and transferring it to an airtight container will safeguard it from deterioration.

The final step in your vinegar-making process is aging. Fresh vinegar has a sharp, intense flavor. The aging process allows the esters, chemical compounds created from the reaction between acids and alcohol that contribute to fragrance, to mature and the flavors to develop. If the vinegar is aged in wood, be sure to top off the barrel with additional vinegar on a regular basis. Otherwise simply storing it for several months in a sealed airtight container will do. A minimum of six months is generally recommended for maximum benefits. Once the vinegar has been aged you'll need to rack it—to pour the liquid into a clean bottle, leaving the sediment behind. It will keep almost indefinitely in a cool, dark spot in the cupboard.

You will be amazed by what you can transform into vinegar and by the amount of flavor in a handmade product. Store-bought vinegars are becoming increasingly fancy and expensive. We have found that with a few exceptions, the quality of what can be made at home rivals or exceeds that of any store-bought product. All it takes is a bit of patience and the space to store your brew. It's a terrific science project for children as it illustrates the fermentation process beautifully and with tangible results. Fruit juice vinegar is a wonderful first step into the kitchen laboratory for a budding chef.

EVERY WINE VINEGAR

*We use organic cider vinegar as a starter because it usually contains a
live mother. If you have friends who have made their own vinegar,
you can begin with their live vinegar instead. In either case, we start
with equal parts, by weight, of live vinegar (vinegar with mother) and
wine. Make sure there is enough room in the jar to add more wine as
the vinegar develops. Wrap the mouth of the vinegar jar with cheesecloth
to prevent vinegar flies from taking a dip and then place the lid back on
top. A little patience here will yield great results.*

3 cups/950 grams organic **cider vinegar**

4 cups/950 grams **red wine**

Combine the cider vinegar and wine in a large glass container with a
loose-fitting lid. Before replacing the lid, cover the opening with
cheesecloth to allow for ample airflow so oxygen reaches the vinegar
stock. Store the container in an undisturbed cool, dark place and leave
it alone for 1 week.

After a week, take the lid off and remove the cheesecloth. Smell.
The ingredients have changed. The wine and the live vinegar have
come together. The smell of wine is still prominent, but the smell of
vinegar cuts through the wine. A harmony is being created. Taste the
developing vinegar. You could use it now, but it will probably benefit
from another week of storage. At this point you may add another
2 cups (480 grams) of wine. If the cheesecloth is clean, you can reuse
it over the mouth of the jar; otherwise cut a fresh piece. Replace the lid
and store for another week.

After the second week, you should have something worth working
with in your kitchen. Pour off a portion for your pantry (leaving the
sediment behind) and feel free to add more wine to the base in your

jar. The vinegar in your pantry will continue to develop on its own, while the jar with the mother will continue as a work in progress until aging is complete. We enjoy the flavor of the developing vinegar. It's bolder than the wine vinegars you can get in stores, and has more nuanced undertones.

MAPLE VINEGAR

MAKES 7 TO 8 CUPS

Maple vinegar is a favorite of ours for its rich, nuanced flavor. Our version is not a product that can be found commercially, so there is a real reward in trying this recipe at home. Once you have it in your pantry, you'll easily find many different uses for it. It's wonderful drizzled over roasted squash or balanced with a touch of cayenne and butter and brushed over corn on the cob or a roasted chicken. It's amazing simply spooned over a rich, runny piece of brie, accompanied by crisp apple slices, or blended with diced apples and jalapeños as a condiment for meat or game. It also makes for a surprisingly balanced maple martini when combined with ice-cold gin or vodka. The possibilities are endless.

> 3 cups/936 grams **maple syrup**
> 2½ cups/800 grams **live vinegar** (we prefer red wine vinegar here, though cider vinegar works as well)
> 1⅓ cups/300 grams **dark rum**
> ⅞ cup/200 grams **water**

Combine the syrup, vinegar, rum, and water in a large glass container with a loose-fitting lid. Before replacing the lid, cover the opening with cheesecloth to allow for ample airflow so oxygen reaches the vinegar stock. Store the container in an undisturbed cool, dark place for at least 4 weeks.

After a month, test the vinegar for development; taste it. Once the alcohol has been completely fermented away, strain the vinegar and store it in sealed bottles or Mason jars. It may be ready at this first tasting or it could take an additional week or two. The finished pH for this particular vinegar tends to settle at 4.3. It can be used immediately and will improve with age.

PICKLING

Though the classic pickled cucumber has become ubiquitous enough to be simply dubbed a "pickle," a wide variety of fruits and vegetables are preserved using salt and acid. Every culture has its own specialties, ranging from the Mexican pickled jalapeño peppers to Korean kimchi. Pickles are often used as a flavor accent, garnishing a meal rather than acting as the main focus.

Fruits and vegetables are commonly pickled either in a brine, like dill pickles, or packed in sugar and salt mixtures, known as cures, like lime pickles. Quick pickles do not undergo the process of fermentation; they are simply acidified in a brine or cure over a short period of time. Traditional pickles are made by initiating an anaerobic fermentation process, usually by storing ingredients in a flavored brine. During fermentation sugars are transformed into lactic acids by *Lactobacillus plantarum*. The lactic acid gives pickles their characteristic tang and creates an inhospitable environment for bad bacteria by eliminating sugars and creating an acidic setting.

Salt acts as a preservative during the fermentation process by encouraging the growth of *L. plantarum*, the good bacteria. The level of salt is important because at too high a concentration, the *L. plantarum* cannot thrive, and at concentrations that are too low, other less beneficial bacteria have an advantage and can produce negative results in the final product. Although optimal concentrations vary for different fruits and vegetables, a 5 percent salt solution as the base for your brine is a good rule of thumb. Salt is also important because it draws the moisture from the fruits and vegetables being pickled, which adds to the brine and transforms the texture of the finished product.

Oxygen encourages the growth of negative bacteria, so it's important to keep it away from your developing pickles until fermentation is complete. For this reason it's better to leave your pickles alone and not stir them during the fermentation process. Acid is important because it helps prevent the growth of botulinum bacteria. The last critical factor for encouraging good bacteria and proper fermentation is temperature; optimum pickling temperatures fall in the range of 65°F–70°F (18°C–21°C). The warmer the area where you store your pickles, the faster fermentation will occur.

Here are a couple of tips for making pickles at home. Wash your fruits or vegetables before cutting to remove any microorganisms on the skin, and be sure to use uniformly sized pieces. Weigh your ingredients and follow a recipe. The proportions are very important for a safe fermentation process. Use canning or pickling salt because the anticaking ingredients in table salt will cloud your brine. Use soft or filtered water because iron and sulfur will darken your pickles, and calcium in tap water can interfere with fermentation. Use whole spices to infuse flavor because wiping ground spices off your pickles is tedious work. Avoid any soft or slippery pickles in the finished product, as these are signs of improper fermentation. Trust your instincts; if something feels wrong, it probably is.

If you plan to keep your pickles for longer than a week or so in the refrigerator you may want to consider low-temperature pasteurization. You simply need to hold them in a 180°F (82°C) water bath for 30 minutes. You can do this using a circulating water bath, a pot of water on the stove with a thermometer, or even a water bath in your oven if the temperature can be set low enough. The pickles can be pasteurized in

Mason jars or vacuum-sealed bags. It's very important to keep the water bath below 185°F (85°C) to preserve the texture of the pickles. At 185°F (85°C), the pectin in the pickles will begin to break down, resulting in soft pickles instead of crisp ones.

In our kitchen we usually rely on the quick pickling process. It's a wonderful way to use the abundance of produce available at different times of the year in a safe and delicious manner. Don't be afraid to pickle unusual ingredients like apples, corn, or zucchini. For every fruit or vegetable there is a corresponding pickle somewhere in the world, from chowchow to mostarda. Pickles make the world a tastier place.

INSTANT WATERMELON RIND PICKLE

MAKES ABOUT 1 QUART

Pickled watermelon rind is a classic summer condiment when the melons are in abundance. Here we've added our twist by using Japanese yuzu juice and rice wine vinegar to give the pickles a kick.

¼ cup plus 2 tablespoons/125 grams **rice wine vinegar**

½ cup plus 1 tablespoon/125 grams **yuzu juice** (see Sources, page 309)

¼ cup plus 1 tablespoon/100 grams **honey**

1 tablespoon/4.5 grams **juniper berries**

1¼ teaspoons/8 grams **fine sea salt**

18 ounces/500 grams diced **watermelon rind**, green skin removed

Mix the vinegar, yuzu juice, honey, juniper berries, and salt until the honey is dissolved. If you have a vacuum sealer, pour the pickling solution into a vacuum bag, add the watermelon rind, and seal on high pressure. (This can also be done in Mason jars in a chamber vacuum machine.) The watermelon rind will go from opaque to translucent and is ready to eat instantly, though it will mature over a few days.

Alternatively, you can combine the vinegar, yuzu juice, honey, juniper berries, and salt in a lidded jar, refrigerate, and age the rind for 3 days before using. The pickles will not be as bright and translucent as the vacuum-sealed pickles, but they will still taste delicious. The flavor will continue to improve over time.

RED CABBAGE KIMCHI

MAKES 4 QUARTS

When we think of kimchi we tend to picture the classic kind found in Asian supermarkets, which is made primarily with Napa cabbage stained red from the chili powder and pungent with garlic. Interestingly, although that is indisputably the most popular variation, kimchi can be made with a wide array of vegetables and spices, with regional variations that affect the ingredients used and levels of heat and spice. Here we've used red cabbage for two reasons. The first is because we like its sweet flavor and slightly sturdy texture. The second, more practical, reason is that these fermented pickles are generally deemed ready when enough lactic acid is produced to change the pH from 6.5 to approximately 3.5. Red cabbage juice changes color at this pH and becomes a bright reddish-purple, giving you a visual cue when fermentation is complete.

Kimchi is a surprisingly good condiment for grilled hot dogs. It is a great way to doctor up packaged ramen at home. In place of coleslaw on a sandwich, it can add an unexpected kick to anything from corned beef on rye to pulled pork on soft white bread. Its heat and tang are wonder-

ful for cutting through rich ingredients, and as a substitute for sauer-kraut in choucroute, it is utterly delicious.

1 large head **red cabbage**

1 cup plus 2 teaspoons/300 grams **fine sea salt**

6½ quarts/6,000 grams **water**

1 cup/200 grams **sugar**

2 bunches (4½ ounces **scallions**), root ends trimmed

2 bunches (11 ounces) **watercress**, root ends trimmed

1 large (1⅓ pounds/615 grams) **Korean radish**, peeled and grated

    (you may substitute **daikon** if you can't locate Korean radish)

6 (1¾ pounds) **Anjou pears**, peeled and grated

5¼ ounces/150 grams **ginger**, peeled and roughly chopped

3 **heads garlic**, peeled

½ cup/150 grams **fish sauce**

¼ cup/75 grams **shrimp paste**

4 teaspoons/8 grams **cayenne pepper**

5 teaspoons/10 grams **crushed red pepper flakes**

Cut the cabbage into quarters through its core. Cut the core out of each quarter. Cut each quarter cabbage into 4 sections lengthwise.

In a large bowl or plastic container, dissolve the salt in the water; then add the cabbage, breaking it apart as you add it to the brine. Use several plates to weigh the cabbage down so it is submerged in the solution. Let the cabbage soak for at least 6 hours and preferably overnight (10 to 12 hours).

Remove the cabbage from the brine and spin it in a salad spinner to remove the excess moisture. Place the drained cabbage in a large bowl and toss it with the sugar. Make sure the cabbage is evenly coated with the sugar.

Cut the scallions and the watercress into 1-inch (2.5-centimeter) sections and put them in a food processor. Process until finely minced. Combine the scallions and watercress with the cabbage, then add the grated radish and pears. Toss the mixture to thoroughly combine.

Put the ginger, garlic, fish sauce, shrimp paste, cayenne, and red pepper flakes in a blender and puree until smooth. Pour over the cabbage mixture, using a large spoon to stir until the puree and the vegetables are evenly combined. Pack the mixture into a nonreactive container and cover it loosely with plastic wrap or a lid. Let the cabbage sit at room temperature for 2 to 6 days, depending on the temperature of the room. (A cooler room will take more time; a warmer room will take less.) The kimchi will be ready when the mixture changes to a uniform purple color throughout. Bubbles will be visible in the kimchi and it will have a pH of 4.5 or lower.

When the kimchi is ready, pack it into jars and refrigerate. The kimchi will continue to mature and ferment in the refrigerator, though this will happen much more slowly in the cold environment. The kimchi should be eaten within 3 to 4 weeks.

LIME PICKLES

MAKES 2 QUARTS

These pickled limes use Vadouvan spice blend, sometimes labeled French curry, a combination of Indian spices often including curry leaves, fenugreek, mustard seeds, coriander, shallots, and garlic. The exact blend depends on who makes it. It is aromatic and gives a haunting depth of flavor to the finished pickles. They are wonderful with fish, pork, and roasted vegetables and add a subtle tang to sauces, rice pilafs, or creamy grits. Lime pickles can be finely chopped into a condiment, used whole in braises, or thinly sliced and gently fried. Once you taste them, a world of possibilities opens up before you.

15 **limes**

3 tablespoons/54 grams **fine sea salt**

3 **jalapeños**, cut into ½-inch (1.25-centimeter) slices

1 cup/100 grams **Vadouvan spice blend** (see Sources, page 309)

1½ cups/300 grams **rice bran oil**

Mason jars, sterilized

Wash and dry the limes. Cut each lime into 8 sections. Squeeze the juice from each section into a large bowl and add the lime as well. Add the salt and mix thoroughly.

Place the jalapeños, spice blend, and rice bran oil in a heavy-bottomed pot set over medium heat. Cook the mixture until the jalapeños begin to sizzle, about 5 minutes, then pour it into the bowl with the limes. Use a spoon to mix the ingredients thoroughly.

Put the mixture in pickling jars, packing the contents down to remove any air, and refrigerate for 2 weeks. After 2 weeks, the limes are ready to use. They will last indefinitely.

PICKLED CHORIZO

MAKES 1 PINT

Pickled chorizo is a harmonious blend of acid and fat that makes something more than the sum of its parts. The sweetness of the vinegars helps balance the heady spice blend of Spanish chorizo. It's wonderful folded into a ragout of chickpeas or giant lima beans. Pickled chorizo is an intriguing note with marinated raw seafood. It's delicious as an ingredient in soups and stews, softening the texture of the chorizo and permeating the liquid with its flavor. The resulting vinegar is a wonderful ingredient on its own, for salads and sauces, where that meaty, spicy note helps bring everything else into focus.

¼ cup plus 1 tablespoon/100 grams **sherry vinegar**

¼ cup plus 1 tablespoon/100 grams **rice vinegar**

¼ cup plus 1 tablespoon/100 grams **balsamic vinegar**

¼ cup plus 1 tablespoon/100 grams **soy sauce**

8 ounces/225 grams dried **Spanish chorizo**, cut into ⅛-inch
      (3-mm) rounds

One 1-pint Mason jar, sterilized

In a bowl, combine the sherry vinegar, rice vinegar, balsamic vinegar, and soy sauce. Add the chorizo to the vinegar mixture. Stir to combine and put the mixture into a 1-pint Mason jar. Screw on the lid and refrigerate for 2 days. The chorizo is then ready to use.

FREEZING

The term cryo-blanching *is being heard* in kitchens around the world. It may sound like something out of a science-fiction movie, reminiscent of when Han Solo was frozen and survived to fight another day. But in reality it refers to using the freeze-thaw cycle to effect changes in fruits and vegetables on a cellular level to enhance their color and subtly soften their texture. What matters most is the way the produce is handled during this process. There's a lot that can go wrong, as anyone who's ever experienced freezer-burned ice cream can attest.

Our technique of cryo-blanching evolved from our time working in isolated locations. To have access to the best ingredients available, we were forced to order minimum quantities that were still far more than we could use for our immediate culinary purposes. Once we developed a full pantry of pickles and preserves, we needed to find some different ways to utilize the food. Although the idea of cooking with frozen vegetables and proteins carries a bit of a stigma in the restaurant business, we thought that perhaps freezing our own would be something very different from buying frozen produce from big suppliers. With that in mind, we began to experiment with the vacuum sealer and the freezer.

The fatal flaw in this process is freezing things too slowly. The faster something is frozen, the smaller the ice crystals that are formed. We want to form many small crystals rather than fewer large ones because they do less damage. As ice crystals form, they poke holes in the cell walls. This causes a softening of the rigidity of the cell structure. Then when food is thawed and the ice melts, water seeps out of the holes. The larger the holes, the more moisture is lost. This accounts for the juices that collect when frozen fruits and vegetables are defrosted. If only small ice crystals are formed during the freeze-thaw process, then the food resembles lightly blanched produce.

A bit of history: Clarence Birdseye is considered a pioneer for his work developing commercial freezing techniques that did not appreciably alter the taste of the food. While working in Labrador he observed that in the Arctic temperatures, especially in the winter months, meats and seafood froze quickly, and when defrosted the foods retained their normal taste and texture. Returning to the United States, he experimented until he was able to reproduce those results with a technique that became known as flash freezing. It preserved the quality of the frozen food until it was thawed. From there he moved on to packing fresh food into cardboard boxes sized for the retail consumer and flash freezing them, thus making perishable foods available year round. Birdseye went on to develop a program leasing freezer display cases to retailers in order to market his frozen foods. In 1944 he began leasing refrigerated railroad cars. He is credited with creating the market for frozen foods in America.

The second step in the freeze-thaw cycle—storage of the frozen fruits and vegetables—is extremely important. Once the produce is frozen it is important that it remain solid until you want to defrost it. Fluctuations in temperature during storage can lead to melting and refreezing. Each time this happens, water, sugar, and fat crystals grow larger. This causes repeated and increasing damage to the cell walls, far beyond the intended results. You are left with overly soft fruits and vegetables with more liquid in the container than in the produce. Once vegetables have broken down, they cannot be re-formed and are better used for stews and purees than any lightly cooked or raw presentations.

Another critical factor is packaging. Improperly wrapped fruits and vegetables are vulnerable to freezer burn. Freezer burn, a process known as sublimation, occurs when the surface of the food oxidizes and dries out in the freezer. Sublimation is when a substance transforms directly from a solid to a gas. In this case ice crystals evaporate directly out of the frozen foods. Freezer burn causes discoloration and a change in texture. The process is encouraged by the circulation of cold air within the closed environment of the freezer. The food looks burned although it is actually dehydrated.

Interestingly, two modern improvements actually contribute to freezer burn. Self-defrosting freezers have heating coils that regularly melt the ice buildup on the refrigeration coils. This lowers the vapor pressure inside the freezer, which in turn encourages sublimation. It's a mechanical convenience that actually works against the food it is supposed to safeguard.

Individually quick-frozen fruits and vegetables are marketed as the best choice for consumers. As the label implies, individual pieces are frozen rapidly in order to preserve color and flavor by minimizing the formation of large ice crystals. This process backfires during shipping and storage, however, because the smaller pieces defrost more rapidly than larger blocks of frozen fruits and vegetables. This means they are more vulnerable during storage and more likely to show freezer burn when the package is opened. Fruits have more delicate cell walls than vegetables, so they are more susceptible to damage from repeated refreezing. With a few exceptions, like raspberries and blueberries, most fruits just do not survive the freeze-thaw cycle without a serious loss in texture and quality. This is why so many fruits are sugared and/or cooked before freezing. Pureed fruits retain more flavor and texture than raw ones after freezing.

For our purposes, we define cryo-blanching as using the freeze-thaw cycle to gently tenderize fruits and vegetables meant to be consumed relatively quickly. We don't plan on keeping them in the freezer for months at a time; in most cases we use them within a few days, perhaps a week or two at most. It gives us enough of a window to preserve the freshness of our produce for just long enough to be able to use it all.

Most frozen vegetables are first blanched to retain color and freshness. Instead of blanching to destroy or deactivate the enzymes present on the surface of the vegetables, which can cause browning and spoilage, we brine. We soak our cleaned and cut vegetables in a 3 percent salt solution for ten minutes. This seasons them and has a slightly inhibitive effect on the enzymes. By brining and then using the vegetables immediately once they are thawed, we have not had any major issues with browning. Peas and fava beans that are frozen in their skins are easily peeled when thawed. Since the vegetables are cryo-blanched before peeling, they retain a fresh flavor that is unparalleled. This technique allows us to truly highlight the flavor of the vegetables in their uncooked state in ways that we never could before.

PRESERVED LEMONS

MAKES ABOUT 1 QUART

Preserved lemons should be in everyone's pantry. They taste like sunshine, adding bright acidity and color to a dish. We often mince the preserved lemon and use it to season crab salads, enrich pan sauces for fish and meat, and flavor pastas like our preserved lemon noodles. Thinly sliced and fried, they can go sweet or savory depending on how you season them. Chopped up with fresh garlic and parsley, they make a wonderful replacement for classic gremolata. Create a tangy finishing sauce for grilled meat and vegetables by mixing them with olive oil and minced herbs . You can slide them under the skin of your roast chicken for an amazing lemon chicken. Even a simple bowl of noodles with butter and cheese is given unexpected zest with the addition of some preserved lemon.

4 organic **lemons**

1 teaspoon/6 grams **fine sea salt**

1 teaspoon/4 grams **sugar**

⅔ cup/150 grams **extra virgin olive oil**

Wash the lemons with warm water and pat dry. Slice off the ends, then cut the lemons into ⅛-inch (3-millimeter) slices. Sort through the lemons and remove any seeds.

In a medium bowl, combine the salt and sugar. Add the lemon slices and toss to coat evenly. Place the lemon slices in a vacuum bag and seal on high pressure. Alternatively, place the lemons in a zip-top bag, squeezing out as much air as possible. Place the sealed bag in the freezer for at least 8 hours and up to 24 hours.

When the lemons are frozen solid, remove the bag from the freezer and place it in the refrigerator to thaw. When the lemons are thawed, keep the bag sealed and place it back in the freezer. Let the lemon slices freeze solid a second time, at least 8 hours or overnight.

When the slices are completely frozen, remove the bag from the freezer and again place it in the refrigerator to thaw. When the lemons are thawed, remove them from the bag, discarding any juices. Place the lemons in a bowl and cover with the olive oil. Mix the slices to coat evenly with the oil, then place them in a clean plastic bag. Vacuum-seal the bag or use a zip-top bag, squeezing out as much air as possible, and freeze the slices one last time, at least 8 hours or overnight.

When the lemon slices have frozen for the third time, remove them from the freezer and let thaw in the refrigerator. The lemons are ready to be used, or they can be stored in the refrigerator covered in olive oil for up to a month.

CRYO-BLANCHED ASPARAGUS

SERVES 4

This technique produces a tender asparagus with all the flavor of the raw vegetable. It can be served as part of a salad to emphasize the fresh flavor or used in any recipe that calls for blanched asparagus. We like the way it emphasizes the meaty texture of the vegetable without requiring extended cooking time. The resulting asparagus will stand up to a very quick grill or sauté, achieving a tender bite while still retaining its grassy flavor and bright color.

3¼ tablespoons/60 grams **fine sea salt**

8¾ cups/1,968.75 grams **water**

2 pounds/907 grams **green asparagus** (2 bunches)

Dissolve the salt in the water. Rinse the asparagus and remove the small triangular scales that run the length of the stalk up to the tip. Leave the tip intact. Soak the asparagus in the brine for 10 minutes.

Remove the asparagus from the brine and place it in vacuum-seal bags. Seal the bags and place them in the freezer. Alternatively, place the asparagus in zip-top bags, squeezing out as much air as possible, and place them in the freezer. Freeze for at least 8 hours and up to 24 hours.

When the asparagus is frozen solid, remove it from the freezer, cut the bags open, and let the asparagus defrost in the refrigerator. Cut off the tough stem ends, then pat the stalks dry with a paper towel. The asparagus are much easier to clean after cryo-blanching. The asparagus is ready to be served or added to a cooked preparation.

DEHYDRATING

When Aki was a kid, every so often her family would go on weekend camping trips. As the youngest she was excluded from the festivities, but the only thing that really bothered her about that was not getting to try the food. Aki was fascinated by the myriad packets of dried foods, including the freeze-dried ice cream, that they took with them. Years later she discovered that camping wasn't her thing, but dehydrated foods are something Aki can really sink her teeth into.

The basic premise behind drying food (beef jerky, raisins, dried herbs) is simple. Air movement around food will cause moisture in food to evaporate. Evaporation speeds up as the temperature of the air increases. However, every increase of 59°F (15°C) doubles the amount of water the air can absorb. Temperatures that are too high will cause the food to cook before it dries out completely. Heat damage can occur in the form of oxidation, nutrient loss, enzyme destruction, and hardening. Temperatures that are too low may allow the harmful bacteria to grow and oxidation to occur before the food is completely dehydrated. On the other hand, in commercial situations, using extremely low temperature can be a good thing for dehydration because it results in freeze-dried food, arguably the highest-quality dried food on the market. The best temperature for drying food at home is 140°F (60°C).

Microorganisms in food are put in limbo when the food is dehydrated. They cannot multiply without moisture, though once the food is rehydrated they become active again. As a result, to be considered stable dehydrated foods must be protected from water especially and also from air, sunlight, and contaminants. Most foods are pretreated before drying to lessen the risk of bacterial contamination and to destroy any insects or larvae that may be present. At home this can be done by leaving the food in a freezer set at 32°F (0°C) for forty-eight hours or briefly heating the ingredients in a single layer in an oven set at 160°F (70°C) for thirty minutes.

Another type of pretreatment is used particularly with fruits to prevent oxidation. When oxidation occurs, the fruit can darken and look unappealing. The most effective treatment in commercially dried fruit is the use of sulfur. Sublimed sulfur, or sulfur powder, may be ignited and burned in an enclosed area so the fumes permeate the fruit. Alternatively, the fruit can be dipped in a mixture of water and food-grade sodium bisulfate, sodium sulfite, or sodium metabisulfate. Natural alternatives that can be used to treat fruit at home are ascorbic acid, fruit juices that are high in vitamin C, and honey solutions. These can all delay browning for shorter periods of time than sulfites. Some fruits are cooked before drying, either by blanching in syrup or by steam blanching. These processes change the texture of the fruit. They can make the finished fruit softer and more shelf-stable than untreated dried fruit.

All vegetables are blanched before drying. This is done to eliminate enzymatic browning. A side benefit is that it results in softened cell walls, which expedites the drying process. Vegetables can be blanched in water or steam. Steam blanching preserves more nutrients, but water blanching takes less time. Vegetables are then dried until they are brittle or crisp. This takes them down to about 10 percent moisture. Vegetables at this stage are much more fragile than fruit and must be carefully handled to avoid being broken into pieces.

Sun drying is a technique used in hot climates. Think of Italian sun-dried tomatoes. A minimum temperature of 86°F (30°C) with a humidity level of 60 percent or less is required. The fruits and vegetables are spread out in the fields and the natural radiant heat of the sun and the movement of the wind work together to dry them out.

Generally speaking, commercially dried foods are air dried, spray dried, drum dried, or freeze dried. Liquid ingredients are atomized into superheated air to create fine particles in spray drying. Drum-dried food is created by spreading liquid ingredients in a thin film on a heated drum. Freeze-dried foods have the advantage of concentrated flavor. They can be powdered and added to recipes to intensify flavor levels. They can be added to recipes in their dried form to introduce a new texture. Freeze-dried foods can be rehydrated with water and used in their original form. Their texture is similar to that of foods that have been flash frozen and gently rethawed. Freeze-dried foods can also be reconstituted with flavored liquids in order to introduce different seasonings to the original ingredient.

All dried foods have the ability to add concentrated flavor to a dish. We love to use dried fruits in braises to add sweetness and texture to the sauce. Freeze-dried fruits are an excellent addition to Rice Krispies Treats to add some tartness and extra vitamin C. We like to pulverize freeze-dried fruits and vegetables and add them to batters and doughs for flavor. Our daughter, Amaya, likes to eat them out of hand; their light crunchy texture and big flavors make them a fun and healthy snack.

In our kitchen we have a tray-style dryer. In addition to drying more traditional ingredients, we use it to create a variety of dried preparations that can be treated like tuiles and rolled into ribbons, spirals, and tubes to add flavor, texture, and visual appeal to a dish. Eating a crisp disk of onion glass or a pink rhubarb corkscrew is both fun and delicious. Although you can use your oven to dehydrate if you plan to work with this technique, it's worth purchasing a dehydrator. There are some relatively inexpensive ones available and you won't tie up your oven for hours on end.

ONION GLASS

This onion glass actually tastes like onion soup in a crispy form. The sheets are translucent with a deep golden brown hue. They can be broken into pieces and scattered in a salad. They are wonderful flavor accents on hors d'oeuvres. We like to break them up and use them as a final garnish on braised meats, where they start out crunchy and slowly dissolve back into rich bites of onion syrup. Last, well, we enjoy snacking on them just as they are.

3 medium **onions**, peeled

¼ cup plus 1 teaspoon/130 grams **liquid glucose** (see Sources, page 309)

¼ cup/60 grams **water**

3 tablespoons/45 grams **agave nectar**

¾ teaspoon/4 grams **fine sea salt**

Clear acetate sheets, available at most art-supply stores and JB Prince

Nonstick cooking spray

Combine the onions, glucose, water, agave nectar, and salt in a pot and bring to a boil over high heat. Reduce the heat to medium and simmer the mixture until almost dry, about 20 minutes. Transfer to a blender and puree until silky smooth. Strain into a metal bowl and cool in an ice bath. Refrigerate for at least 30 minutes.

Spray twelve 2 × 6-inch acetate sheets or foil strips with cooking spray and wipe them lightly with a paper towel to remove any excess. Use an offset spatula to spread the onion base as thinly and smoothly as possible on the strips of acetate or foil. Place them in a dehydrator and dry for 1 hour. The onion should be completely dry and come off the acetate cleanly with only a little help from an offset spatula. If it is not ready, continue drying until it reaches this stage. Alternatively, set your oven to the lowest possible temperature and let the sheets dry out for at least 2 hours until the desired texture is reached. Let the onion glass cool before storing in a lidded container or zip-top bag with parchment paper between the pieces. The onion glass can be used whole or broken into shards, as you prefer.

RHUBARB RIBBONS

MAKES AT LEAST 24

The sweet-tart flavor of these pink ribbons makes them a wonderful accent. They are fun with cheese courses where their crunch is a nice contrast to the creamy texture of the dairy. Their lightly tangy flavor is delicious with sweetbreads and game. They also make a beautiful garnish for a panna cotta, rice pudding, or slice of cheesecake. Sprinkle them with a little togarishi (a Japanese spice blend) before drying and use them to garnish crab salad. A hint of Old Bay seasoning can make them the perfect accompaniment for bay scallop risotto or fish cakes. Sprinkle them with sparkling sugar and they can become gorgeous tuiles to be eaten alone or perched on top of a sweet lemon tartlet.

> 1 pound/450 grams **rhubarb**
>
> 6½ tablespoons/90 grams **liquid glucose** (see Sources, page 309)
>
> ¼ cup/100 grams **grenadine**
>
> ½ teaspoon/3 grams **fine sea salt**
>
> Clear acetate sheets, available at most art-supply stores and
>   JB Prince
>
> **Nonstick cooking spray**

Combine the rhubarb, glucose, grenadine, and salt in a pot and bring to a boil over medium-high heat. Reduce the heat to medium and simmer until the rhubarb is tender and bright, about 10 minutes. Transfer to a blender and puree until silky smooth. Strain into a metal bowl to remove any rhubarb fibers and cool in an ice bath. Refrigerate for at least 30 minutes.

Spray 24 (1 × 4-inch) acetate sheets or foil strips with cooking spray and wipe them lightly with a paper towel to remove any excess. Use an offset spatula to spread the rhubarb base as thinly and smoothly as possible on the strips of acetate or foil. Place them in a dehydrator and dry for 1 hour. The rhubarb should be completely dry and come off the acetate cleanly with only a little help from an offset spatula. If it is not ready, continue drying until it reaches this stage. Alternatively, set your oven to the lowest possible temperature and let the sheets dry out for at least 2 hours until the desired texture is reached. Immediately shape the ribbons into coils around the handle of a wooden spoon, slide them off onto a baking sheet, and let cool. Store in an airtight container.

SMOKING

Almost everybody loves barbecue. There's something seductive about the transformation of meat or fish under the influence of smoke. At its best, hot smoking in particular yields meat of incredible succulence with deep layered flavors that make you want to lick your fingers and dive in for more. People may quibble over the nuances of beef versus pork, but good barbecue appeals to everyone.

Wood smoke is created using aged pieces of hardwood, usually in the form of chunks, although dust and compressed chips may also come into play. The combination of wood and fire is where all that great seasoning comes from. Hardwood has three main components—cellulose, hemicellulose, and lignin—that are responsible for producing that signature flavor. Cellulose and hemicellulose are the structural components of the wood. They are made up of aggregate sugar molecules and produce sweet, flowery aromas when burned. The cellulose burns at 500°F–590°F (260°C–310°C) and is responsible for the formation of aliphatic acids and aldehydes. The aliphatic acids, or acids of nonaromatic hydrocarbons, add a tart flavor to the smoke and provide some of its antimicrobial ability. The aldehydes are compounds containing a carbonyl group with at least one hydrogen attached. They are responsible for a variety of effects including the formation of skin in sausages, acceleration of the effects of nitrites, and surface color formation. Many aldehydes are also responsible for the fragrance of the smoke. Hemicellulose burns at temperatures ranging from 392°F to 500°F (200°C–260°C). The aldehydes produced from burning hemicellulose are important because they give smoke its browning capability, a reaction that happens more easily when the surface of the meat is dry and accelerates as the heat increases.

Lignin burns at temperatures ranging from 590°F to 930°F (310°C–500°C). Lignin produces phenolics and phenolic compounds, which give smoke a wide range of aromas and flavors. The phenolics are responsible for a lot of the smoke's antimicrobial and antioxidant properties.

Wood smoke is produced in two stages, gaseous and particulate. About 90 percent of the smoke volume occurs during the particulate stage. During this period smoke appears gray and cloudy and can contain unpleasant aroma and flavor compounds. The brief gaseous state is the most desirable for imparting positive flavors and aromas to the food. Because the components of the wood ignite at different temperatures, the quality of the wood smoke varies as it burns. Low, smoldering flames are best for smoking. This type of fire can be encouraged by soaking the wood beforehand and by limiting the amount of oxygen in the smoke chamber. High-temperature smoke tends to release more polycyclic aromatic hydrocarbons, which are suspected carcinogens.

Different types of wood have different flavor profiles. Softer woods burn more quickly and at lower temperatures, giving foods a more delicate smokiness. Generally speaking, it is best to use wood from trees that produce fruit or nuts. Fruitwoods, like apple and cherry, tend to impart a lighter, more subtle flavor. However, pine and fir, both soft woods, contain resins that create bitter, unpleasant smoke and should be avoided. Harder woods within the soft category burn for longer periods of time at higher temperatures, creating smoke with larger phenolic compounds and more robust flavors. Nut woods, like hickory and oak, tend to have a more assertive smoke flavor.

Hot smoking takes place at temperatures ranging from 165°F to 185°F (74°C–85°C). It falls into the category of slow and low cooking. Hot smoking results in food that has cooked all the way through. It is a very gentle process that allows the fat to render out and the proteins to firm up gently, without excessive dryness in the finished product. The Maillard reaction, when surface proteins on the meat combine with sugars and change color, helps compound flavor development in this and the following smoking techniques.

Cold smoking takes place at temperatures ranging from 59°F to 77°F (15°C–25°C). It is not so much a cooking process as a way to enhance flavor and preserve food. Therefore, foods that are to be cold smoked are often cured, fermented, or previously cooked.

Smoke baking and smoke roasting are relatively new terms in the smoking lexicon. They refer to cooking foods at higher temperatures with the addition of a smoke element. Smoke baking temperatures range from 185°F to 325°F (85°C–163°C). Smoke roasting occurs at temperatures from 325°F to 425°F (163°C–218°C). Depending on the recipe, there may be a bit of overlap in the temperature ranges for these techniques. Most Southern-style pit barbecue is cooked at temperatures ranging from 200°F to 250°F (93°C–121°C).

Liquid smoke is manufactured through a process of cold condensation and fractional distillation. First, the wood is superheated to create particulate smoke, which is then rapidly chilled. The drop in temperature causes the smoke to condense into a liquid, which is basically water filled with the smoke particles. The smoke water may be poured into wooden casks and aged to increase its depth of flavor. Finally, the smoke water goes through fractional distillation to remove carcinogenic compounds before it is bottled and sold. In this process the various components are distilled out of the liquid in a series of fractions based on their different boiling points and unwanted elements are removed. Liquid smoke is a very intense seasoning and should be used sparingly. Another product that is increasingly available is smoke powder. It comes in a variety of flavors corresponding to the wood used for smoking. It is begun in the same way as liquid smoke. In this case the condensed liquid is spray dried to create a powder that is often cut with starch to make a product that is free flowing and easy to use.

We love the flavor of smoke in measured doses. It multiplies and enhances all of those lovely umami characteristics in food, giving them a savory kick that can be found nowhere else. In addition to hot and cold smoking foods, we've also had great success smoking condiments. This is a great way to use smoke as a background note, taking advantage of its complex flavor while still allowing the ingredients themselves to stand at center stage.

At our house we use a Bradley smoker, which uses compressed wood bisquettes to generate the smoke. You can use a stovetop smoker or whatever brand you have at home. We turn the smoker on before assembling our ingredients so it has time to heat up and generate smoke. We use disposable aluminum pans to hold our ingredients for smoking because they are relatively inexpensive and we don't have to spend hours trying to scrub them clean afterward.

COLD-SMOKED FRIED CHICKEN

SERVES 4

This is the best fried chicken ever. The smoke permeates the meat, seasoning it from the inside out. Combined with the crunchy exterior and juicy meat, it is revelatory. Just remember to let it rest before eating. It's almost impossible not to dive in immediately, but when the chicken is too hot you can't fully appreciate the texture and flavors.

We use rice bran oil for frying because it has a high smoke point and a clean, neutral flavor, which means that fried foods tend to cook evenly without burning or absorbing any heavy flavors from the oil. It is pressed from the hull of the rice grain and is high in antioxidants. It costs about the same as good olive oil, and its slightly sweet, nutty flavor is good for baking, cold marinades, and dressings. Once you try it, it will be hard to go back to canola. You can substitute whatever your favorite chicken parts are for the thighs. If you use breasts we suggest cutting them in half crosswise for the proper coating-to-meat ratio. Whatever you do, just make sure you try this technique. It's a little bit of work for a big reward.

12 **chicken thighs**
1 quart/912 grams **buttermilk**
¼ cup/56 grams **Crystal hot sauce**
2 tablespoons/36 grams **fine sea salt**

2 cups/300 grams **all-purpose flour**
½ teaspoon/3 grams **fine sea salt**
¼ teaspoon/0.5 gram **cayenne pepper**
4½ cups/1,000 grams **rice bran oil**

Turn on the smoker, set it at the lowest possible temperature, and let it generate smoke for 10 minutes. Put the chicken thighs into one or two disposable aluminum containers that will fit in your smoker. Fill a third container with ice. Put the ice in the bottom of the smoker and put the chicken thighs on racks above the ice. Smoke the thighs for 1 hour and then turn them over. If the ice has melted, remove the container and replace with fresh ice. Smoke the chicken thighs for another hour.

Put the buttermilk in a bowl and add the hot sauce and 2 tablespoons (36 grams) salt. Stir to dissolve the salt. When the thighs are done smoking, place them in a large zip-top bag and pour the buttermilk mixture over them. Seal the bag, pressing out any excess air, and turn the thighs in the bag. Place the bag in the refrigerator and let the thighs brine for 24 hours. Occasionally turn the bag so that the thighs are fully submerged and coated in the buttermilk.

Set a baking rack over a sheet pan. Put the flour, ½ teaspoon (3 grams) salt, and cayenne in a bowl. Use a whisk to combine them evenly. Remove the chicken thighs from the buttermilk mixture and put them on the rack to drain. Dredge each thigh in the flour mixture and return it to the rack.

Put the rice bran oil in a deep, heavy-bottomed chicken fryer or other large skillet. Heat the oil over medium-high heat until it reaches 360°F (182°C). Turn the oven to 250°F (120°C). Take a second baking rack and put it on a sheet pan. When the oil is hot, add 3 or 4 thighs to the oil and fry until they are a rich golden brown, about 10 minutes. Maintain an oil temperature of 350°F (175°C). Depending on the size of your pot, you may have to flip the thighs once to brown them evenly. When the first set of thighs is browned, transfer them to the rack and put the rack in the oven to allow the meat to finish cooking and stay warm while you fry the remaining chicken. Repeat with the rest of the thighs, allowing the last batch to rest for 10 minutes in the oven before serving.

HOT-SMOKED MUSSELS

SERVES 2 AS AN ENTRÉE OR 4 AS AN APPETIZER

Packages of cold-smoked shellfish are often found on grocery shelves. It's not a new method of preserving the ocean's bounty. We decided to change things up and hot smoke our mussels instead. We use the grill instead of the smoker because we prefer the higher heat for cooking mollusks. The subtle smoke flavor is the perfect accent to bring out the sweet flavor of the mussels. As an added benefit you can pull any extra mussels from their shells and chill them in the leftover broth as a base for an amazing cold soup. You can use this technique with clams and even gild the lily by adding aromatics, like garlic, herbs, or curry, to the pan. We recommend that you try them straight up at least once to truly appreciate the flavors that blossom. We served these with a loaf of good bread, sweet butter, chilled white wine, and good company. Nothing more was needed.

3 pounds/2.2 kilograms **mussels**

1 loaf **crusty bread**

Turn a grill on high heat. Put wood chips—we like apple or hickory—in a disposable pie tin and set it on the grill. Give the wood chips time to begin to smoke; depending on the size of your chips this may take anywhere from 2 to 8 minutes.

Put the mussels in a large bowl and cover with cold water. Rinse them well and remove the small beard from each mussel. Drain the mussels and put them in a disposable aluminum lasagna pan.

Put the pan of mussels on the grill and close the lid. Cook for 5 minutes. Lift the lid and quickly stir the mussels. Close the lid and smoke for another 5 minutes. At this point the mussel shells should be open. If not, close the lid and cook for 2 to 3 minutes more. Do not overcook or your mussels will be tough and stringy.

Remove the pan from the grill and pour the contents into a large bowl. With the grill still on and the wood still smoking, cut the bread into thick slices and quickly grill each side. Put the grilled bread on a plate and serve alongside the smoked mussels.

SMOKED PASTA DOUGH

SERVES 4 AS AN ENTRÉE

This pasta dough has a wonderful texture with a bit of chew and snap. It is great served simply with butter and cheese, or it can be a vehicle for shrimp and asparagus, crabmeat and spinach, crème fraîche and caviar. It is decadent with classic carbonara sauce and can be used to mimic the flavor of bacon for vegetarian preparations.

> 2 cups/300 grams **smoked flour** (see page 62)
> 1 cup/160 grams **semolina flour**
> 1 teaspoon/6 grams **fine sea salt**
> ¼ teaspoon/0.5 gram **cayenne pepper**
> 4 large **eggs**
> 4½ teaspoons/25 grams **whole milk**

Combine the smoked flour, semolina, salt, and cayenne in a large bowl and whisk to blend. Whisk the eggs and the milk in a separate bowl until well blended. Pour the eggs into the center of the dry ingredients and use a wooden spoon or spatula to stir them together, working from the center of the bowl outward. Once the dough begins to stiffen, use your hands to bring it together. You may need to add a bit of extra smoked flour or water depending upon the size of your eggs.

Turn the dough out onto the counter and knead without any additional flour until the dough becomes smooth and silky. Wrap with plastic and let it rest, at room temperature, for at least 30 minutes before rolling out the dough.

NOTE: *For more information on mixing pasta dough see page 107.*

SWEET AND SOUR EGGPLANT

MAKES ABOUT 1 PINT

We love the complex flavors of this puree. We like to serve it with the Twice-Cooked Scallops (page 25). It also goes well with salmon, turkey, corned beef, and the Root Beer–Braised Short Ribs (page 226). The smokiness gives the mixture a rich meaty taste and enhances the sweetness of the dried fruits. Rest assured, though—even if you don't have smoked fruits, you can use the regular dried version and still enjoy something special.

1 large (about 1 pound/530 grams) **eggplant**, sliced
1 cup/250 grams **apple cider**
¾ cup/110 grams **smoked dates** (see page 62)
½ cup/70 grams **smoked prunes** (see page 62)
1 cup/45 grams **smoked dried apples** (see page 62)
½ cup/40 grams **candied ginger**
1 teaspoon/6 grams **fine sea salt**

Put 2 cups (450 grams) water in a pressure cooker. Place a trivet in the bottom that will support a bowl. In a metal bowl that will fit inside the pressure cooker, combine the eggplant, cider, dates, prunes, apples, ginger, and salt. Cook the eggplant mixture for 5 minutes on high pressure. Let the pressure dissipate naturally.

Alternatively, combine the eggplant, cider, dates, prunes, apples, ginger, and salt in a large pot over medium heat and cook for 1 hour until everything is very tender. Pour the cooked eggplant mixture into a blender and puree until smooth. Strain the puree through a fine-mesh strainer, then chill in a bowl set in an ice bath. Refrigerate the sweet and sour eggplant until ready to serve.

SMOKED CONDIMENTS

MAKES QUANTITIES LISTED BELOW

This is a mix-and-match recipe. You can smoke one or all of the following ingredients. Once you've tried the technique, we're sure you will come up with several more of your own. To fully utilize the smoker and maximize the smoke time, we recommend smoking numerous products in succession: dry goods and then liquids, finishing with extremely temperature-sensitive ingredients like dairy by themselves. When smoking dairy products we ensure that the ingredients stay cold by placing them in an open container on top of another vessel filled with ice. Smoked milk or cream can be used to make butter, crème fraîche, or cheese. A side benefit in using the ice is that it too picks up that essence of smoke and may be utilized as an ingredient for smoke-flavored brine or smoke-flavored bread.

3 cups/936 grams **maple syrup**

4½ cups/1,250 grams **Heinz ketchup**

1¾ cups/600 grams **soy sauce**

2⅞ cups/910 grams **balsamic vinegar**

4 cups/600 grams **all-purpose flour**

4 cups/235 grams **potato flakes**

2 cups/225 grams **dried fruit**

2 cups/452 grams **plain whole-milk yogurt**

1 pound/452 grams **unsalted butter**

2 cups/520 grams **whole milk** or **heavy cream**

1 pound/455 grams **cheese** (mozzarella, feta, ricotta, Cheddar, etc.)

Get your smoker going and set it to the lowest possible temperature. Have on hand an 8 × 10-inch disposable aluminum pan for each item to be smoked.

Pour each ingredient to be smoked in its own disposable aluminum pan. Cold smoke each ingredient for 2 hours. Stir them every 30 minutes to increase the amount of exposed surface area. If you are smoking dairy, fill one extra pan with ice for each container of dairy. Put each container of dairy on top of a pan of ice in the smoker. Remove them from the smoker and let any liquid condiments cool to room temperature before placing them in storage containers, putting any perishable items in the refrigerator.

NOTE: *We save the original containers and reuse them after smoking, simply labeling them "smoked," so that they are easily stored in our cupboards and refrigerator.*

BREAD

YEAST BREADS

The best lessons are rarely easy. One summer Alex and I were working as chef and pastry chef at a seasonal Italian restaurant. Several of the recipes that I was to execute belonged to the owner, a fabulous Italian cook. As it turned out, her focaccia became my Achilles' heel. I just could not make it work. The recipe ignored two basic bread-baking principles that I held dear by using a hefty amount of yeast and relying on a quick, warm rise. The dough was much thinner than I was used to, and I had to layer the top with sliced tomatoes just before baking. If the tomatoes were too thin, they burned. If the tomatoes were too thick, they didn't cook enough and weighed down the dough so that the end result was like pizza instead of focaccia. When the owner baked it, it was perfect every time. Invariably when I followed her recipe it was a small disaster. I *knew* I was a good bread baker and I couldn't figure out why I couldn't make this recipe work.

Finally Alex pulled me aside and told me to just change the darned recipe and make it taste like hers. It was like a lightbulb went off in my brain. I had been so caught up in trying to master her rules that it never occurred to me to circumvent them. It was time to get to work.

Good bread relies on a basic foundation of yeast and gluten. Baker's yeast, also known as *Saccharomyces cerevisiae,* is a live, single-celled fungus with two roles. Yeast adds flavor and creates the light texture in the finished bread. The slow fermentation of sourdough starters produces a distinctive tangy flavor that is prized by bread lovers around the world. Even with straight instant or active dry yeast, lacking a sourdough starter, the fermentation process produces a characteristic yeasty flavor in the finished bread. During the rising process the yeast consumes the sugar molecules in the dough. As it digests the sugars, it releases carbon dioxide and small amounts of ethanol, a type of alcohol. This is why overproofed bread can have an unpleasantly alcoholic flavor. The gases released by the yeast cause the dough to rise. During the fermentation process the complex starches in the bread flour slowly break down and release their sugars. The yeast consumes some of the sugars; the remainder add sweetness and facilitate a golden crust.

If the fermentation process is cut short, the final bread will be lacking in flavor. If it goes too long, the bread will overproof, resulting in unpleasantly yeasty and alcoholic flavors in the finished product. Placing the bread in a hot oven stops the fermentation process. The yeast responds to the elevated temperature with a rapid increase of activity, causing "oven spring," that initial dramatic rise, before it dies out having completed its job. The key to creating great bread is to use just enough yeast and allow it to rise for the right amount of time. It sounds complicated but in practice is relatively easy to master, especially with a few helpful tips.

Always use the minimum amount of yeast needed for your recipe. This will allow for a slower fermentation, which reduces the risk of the dough being affected by outside elements and rising too quickly for full flavor development.

Temperature is your friend. Yeast action accelerates in warm temperatures and slows down in cooler temperatures. If you're working in a hot kitchen, reduce the amount of yeast in your recipe and vice versa. If your dough seems to be rising too quickly, refrigerate it to slow the process. Adjusting the temperature of the environment around the dough is an easy way to make the yeast work on your schedule.

Bread can happily rise more than once. The trick is remembering to knock it down. Releasing the gas from inside the dough makes room for the yeast to refill the structure. As long as you continue to knock down the dough and there are sugars left for the yeast to consume, the dough will remain viable and continue to develop flavor. I've successfully knocked down dough up to four times, although I think more than that is pushing your luck.

The other key to bread making is the flour. Wheat flour can be made from hard or soft wheat. These designations are based on the protein content of the kernel, hard being high in protein and soft having lower levels. Hard-wheat kernels have a firmer texture and are higher in carotenoids than soft wheat, giving their flour a creamier color, more granular texture, and the ability to form strong gluten. Wheat flour is divided into three basic categories: whole wheat, clear (sifted once), and patent (sifted twice). Clear and patent are both considered white flours, which may be bleached or unbleached. Most white flours used in bakeries today are made from patent flour. Most bread bakers prefer unbleached flour because it is less processed and still contains beta-carotene, which gives the flour a slightly golden hue and adds flavor during the fermentation process. Gluten protein levels further break down white flours. Readily available in the retail market are cake flour at 6–7 percent gluten, pastry flour at 7.5–9.5 percent, all-purpose flour at 9.5–11.5 percent, bread flour at 11.5–13.5 percent, and high-gluten flour at 13–14.5 percent gluten protein. All-purpose, or AP, flour is exactly what the name implies. It can be used for everything from cakes to pizza dough with reasonably good results. On the other hand, if you are going to be baking on a regular basis, it pays to match your flour to your recipe. What all the different wheat flours have in common is that they create gluten and therefore provide structure in baked goods.

Alone in the kitchen, I started slowly, decreasing the yeast by half and relying on a slower rise. The results were immediate. That afternoon I finally got a compliment on the focaccia. It was such a small change, yet it altered my entire world. I quietly continued to tweak the focaccia and some of the restaurant owner's other recipes over the course of the summer.

By early July the owner would take a small piece of focaccia every evening, not to critique but simply because she enjoyed it. It was a turning point in my professional cooking career. I realized that I could change someone else's recipes and make them better for me, and better overall. I had crossed over from being only a cook to taking those first baby steps to becoming a chef.

FAIL-SAFE BREAD

MAKES ONE 13 x 18-INCH FOCACCIA

Before I get into this recipe I want to be very clear about something. While this is my fail-safe bread dough recipe, I don't guarantee that it will be a fail-safe recipe for everyone, although your probability for success is very high. I can make this bread in my sleep and fashion it into almost every flavor under the sun with a tweak here or a twist there. Substitutions for ingredients are provided in parentheses. Try it once the way it is written to get the hang of things and then have fun with the possibilities.

Any leftover rice or cooked grains can be added to the dry ingredients before mixing the dough. They will provide flavor and moisture to the finished product. A raw chopped onion mellows beautifully in the finished loaf. Chunks of cured meats, cheeses, olives, or herbs can be added when forming the loaves. Just flatten the dough into long rectangles. Sprinkle your chunks onto the middle three-quarters of the dough, leaving a space at the top and bottom. Roll up the dough,

lengthwise. Make sure the seam is on the bottom of your sheet tray.
Let proof and continue as the recipe indicates. Use your imagination
here because the dough is very forgiving and will accept most additions
with grace.

> 6½ cups/975 grams **all-purpose** or **bread flour** (you can
>   substitute any grain or meal of your choice for up to 50%
>   of the flour)
>
> 1½ teaspoons/4.5 grams **instant yeast** or 2¼ teaspoons/7 grams
>   **active dry yeast**
>
> 1 tablespoon/12.5 grams **sugar** (granulated or brown), **honey**,
>   or **maple syrup**
>
> 1 tablespoon/18 grams **fine sea salt**
>
> 2½ cups/562.5 grams room-temperature **water** (or milk, tea, etc.)
>
> **Extra virgin olive oil**, **corn oil**, or **clarified butter**
>
> **Semolina flour** for dusting the baking sheet

Combine the flour, yeast, sugar, and salt in either the bowl of an electric mixer or a large bowl. Add the water and mix to form a soft,
slightly tacky dough. If you are using a mixer, start with a paddle and
switch to a dough hook when the dough comes together. It will (mostly)
clean the sides of the bowl. You can either let the dough rest, covered,
for 15 minutes before kneading to improve water absorption or you
can go right into it. Depending on the day, I do what is convenient
(which I probably shouldn't admit, but it's true). Both versions are
good. Knead the dough for 5 to 7 minutes using a mixer on medium
speed or 10 to 15 minutes by hand. When it is done it will look cohesive
and silky. If you use a mixer, give it a few additional turns by hand.

Oil a large bowl and roll the dough around in the bowl to coat it
with oil. Cover the bowl with plastic wrap and set on the kitchen counter to rise. It will take up to 2 hours for the first rising, depending on
the temperature of your kitchen. Once the dough has doubled in size,
knock it down and let it rise again before shaping it into loaves. (This

step isn't absolutely necessary but results in a finer product.) The second rise will be much quicker than the first one, taking approximately half the amount of time, about an hour. If you are busy and can't get to the dough, just keep knocking it down or stick it in the refrigerator. Multiple proofings will actually improve the finished product as long as it doesn't overproof (deflate on its own). If you do chill the dough, for best results, bring it back up to room temperature before putting it in the oven.

Shape your loaves on a baking sheet rubbed with olive oil and sprinkled with semolina or lined with parchment paper. I usually get a half sheet pan of focaccia, 2 long loaves, or 12 to 14 dinner rolls from one batch. Spray or brush them with water and cover them with plastic wrap. The water will create a moist environment and prevent the wrap from sticking to the dough. Set the baking sheet aside and let the dough proof one last time for 15 to 20 minutes, or until the dough has risen and looks like a puffy marshmallow.

Preheat the oven to 450°F (230°C).

Remove the plastic from the baking sheet. If making focaccia, coat the dough with 1 tablespoon of oil and dimple the top with your fingertips. If making loaves or rolls, spray or brush them thoroughly with water. Put the baking sheet in the oven. Bake the focaccia for 25 to 30 minutes, rotating the pan once, until golden brown; bake loaves or rolls for 10 minutes. Rotate the pan 180 degrees and lower the oven temperature to 400°F (200°C). Bake for another 5 to 10 minutes for the rolls, 10 to 15 for the loaves. Once the bread has reached the desired golden to foxy brown color you prefer, take it out of the oven and let it cool. Set on a wire rack if you prefer a crisper crust.

NO-KNEAD
YEAST BREADS

Rustic, artisan breads were once thought to be the stuff of bakeries or lots of hard work. All that changed when no-knead bread hit the mainstream. Although this kind of bread has been around for hundreds of years, its current popularity can primarily be traced to Jim Lahey of Sullivan Street Bakery in New York City and food writer Mark Bittman. Sullivan Street Bakery is well known for its Italian-style breads, baked goods, and pizzas. Lahey developed a no-knead technique for the bread that he makes at his bakery. He shared the technique with Mark Bittman, who wrote about it in his Minimalist column for the *New York Times* in 2006. Readers were seduced by the idea of easy artisan bread and the technique took on a life of its own, spawning countless variations and several new books by various authors.

Strangely, we never even attempted the original recipe. Somehow the craze passed us by until we started researching this book. Bread making had fallen by the wayside in our home kitchen, supplanted by quick breads because they addressed our need for instant gratification and our lack of time for baking once our daughter Amaya was born. So as we attempted to unravel the mysteries of gluten, the idea of being able to make great bread with a minimal active time commitment became the carrot leading us forward.

Wheat flour is essential to most bread making because when combined with water it creates gluten, a superprotein built when the proteins glutenin and gliadin intertwine. The network they form creates the structure that holds the bread together when it rises in the oven and allows it to retain its shape. This process is activated when the starch granules in flour are hydrated. Common wisdom says that it is the kneading of the dough that dictates the strength of the gluten development. But what if the kneading simply dictates the shape of the network and not the actual power of the gluten itself?

The no-knead technique requires higher levels of hydration and smaller amounts of yeast. It also relies on a longer fermentation time to develop the gluten. Ingredients are stirred together just enough to form a cohesive, lump-free mass and then left alone for several hours, with only the occasional folding, until the dough is ready to bake.

Hydration occurs when the starch granules in flour swell in the presence of water and the proteins on the outside of the carbohydrate chain become sticky. This is what allows the glutenin and gliadin to adhere to one another. As the starch molecules are pulled apart, the proteins stretch between them, changing into the protein complex known as gluten. As the amount of water added to the flour increases, so does the mobility of the proteins in the starch. This allows more gluten to develop into the elastic sheets that will form the backbone of the finished dough.

As dough is kneaded, the gluten stretches into a uniform structure. During this process the dough's extensibility—its ability to stretch—first increases and then slowly decreases. On the other hand, elasticity, or the tendency for the dough to spring back to its original shape, only increases with continued kneading. Finding the balance between extensibility and elasticity during gluten development is the baker's challenge.

Folding instead of kneading is a classic technique used with wet dough to help gently release the fermentation gases, equalize the dough temperature, and, most importantly for this technique, stretch and align the gluten strands. It helps eliminate long kneading by accomplishing the same results with less active time and effort.

The easiest way to fold is to visualize the dough as a square, pulling in each of the four sides one at a time and gently pressing it into the center. You will have to stretch the dough with your hands to accomplish this. Wet fingers will help keep the dough from sticking. Once you've folded in each side to form a compact package, flip the dough over so the seams are underneath, cover it, and let it rest. The number of times dough is folded depends on how quickly fermentation is progressing and how uniform a crumb is desired in the finished bread. A large, irregular crumb is thought to have better flavor release than a small, finely textured one. Since folding causes much less oxidation than kneading, it preserves more of the carotenoids in the flour, resulting in an ivory, as opposed to white, crumb when using white flour. The slower fermentation results in a more complex and flavorful finished product. Common wisdom implies that these breads will have less oven spring and less overall volume than kneaded breads, but our experiments have shown that to be an old wives' tales. These types of breads can rise to more than double their original volume and achieve beautiful, light textures in addition to all of their other positive attributes.

When experimenting with no-knead breads, it is helpful to understand baker's percentages. In a baker's percentage, each ingredient in a recipe is expressed as a percentage of the total weight of the flour(s). This is because flour is the predominant ingredient. Flour is always designated as 100 percent, which means when adding together all the percentages in a recipe, they will always total more than 100 percent. These baker's percentages allow quick comparisons between recipes and easy calculations when multiplying the volume of a recipe. Once you get the hang of working with them, you will find that they make adjusting recipes very easy.

Our approach with no-knead bread was to take two of our favorite recipes, pizza dough and brioche, and adjust them to fit the parameters of the technique. We increased the liquid ratio for each recipe and then allowed the doughs to slowly ferment at room temperature for several hours. We are very pleased with the results. The pizza dough is light and flavorful with large, irregular bubbles, a crisp crust, and a tender crumb. The brioche, due to the high fat content, is incredibly tender and soft. When baked in a loaf pan the crumb is cakelike with small irregular holes. The flavor of the butter and the eggs permeates the bread like brioche on steroids. Best of all, the dough also makes some of the best sticky buns we've ever tasted.

NO-KNEAD PIZZA DOUGH

MAKES 3½ POUNDS OF DOUGH,
ENOUGH FOR 2 LARGE PIZZAS

Good pizza is all about the crust. In our mind great pizza is thin and crisp on the bottom. It has a tender crumb with a complex flavor from a long, slow fermentation. There are usually large, irregular air bubbles that hint of the resiliency of the crumb. Biting into a slice, you experience the contrast between the shattering crust, the soft chewy crumb, and the sweet, complex flavor.

6 cups/900 grams **all-purpose flour**

1 tablespoon/18 grams **fine sea salt**

1 tablespoon/12.5 grams **sugar**

½ teaspoon/1.5 grams **instant yeast**

3 cups/675 grams room-temperature **water**

Combine the flour, salt, sugar, and yeast in a large bowl. Whisk them together to thoroughly blend the yeast into the flour. Pour in the water and stir with a rubber spatula or wooden spoon until the water is absorbed and there are no lumps. Cover the bowl with plastic wrap and let rise at room temperature for 4 hours. The dough will rise to approximately one and a half times its initial volume.

Using a rubber spatula, gently loosen the dough from the bowl. Dampen your hands with cool water and, with the dough still in the bowl, slide one hand under one side of the dough. Fold that side of the dough into the center and press down gently so the dough adheres to itself. Give the bowl a quarter turn and repeat the folding process. Do this two more times. After the fourth fold, flip over the dough so the seams are on the bottom. Cover the bowl with plastic wrap and let it rise at room temperature for 3 to 4 hours until you are ready to make pizza. The dough will double in volume during this time.

Alternatively, after the first rising you can refrigerate the dough.

Gently deflate the dough once it has chilled and then you can leave it in the refrigerator overnight to use the next day. Let it come to room temperature for at least 1 hour before using. To freeze dough, rub it lightly with olive oil, wrap it securely in plastic, and put it in a zip-top bag in the freezer after the first rise. Defrost your dough in the refrigerator overnight and pull it out a few hours before you want to use it. Fold the dough and give it the second rising period before making your pizza.

NO-KNEAD BRIOCHE DOUGH

MAKES TWO 9 x 5-INCH LOAVES

Good brioche is an amazing thing. The bread is light, buttery, and full of flavor. It can be somewhat labor intensive in its original form, so we were immediately intrigued by the idea of creating a no-knead version. Normally the butter is beaten into the dough, but here we melt it and add it to the wet ingredients. The long resting period allows it to be fully absorbed into the dough without all that extra work. This may seem like a large recipe, but the dough can be used to make various sweet breads like the sticky bun recipe that follows, and the plain loaves freeze beautifully.

6½ cups/975 grams **all-purpose flour**

½ cup/100 grams **sugar**

3½ teaspoons/21 grams **fine sea salt**

½ teaspoon/1.5 grams **instant yeast**

8 large **eggs**

1 cup/225 grams room-temperature **water**

½ cup/130 grams **whole milk**

1 pound/452 grams **unsalted butter**, melted and cooled

Milk or **heavy cream** for brushing the loaves

Combine the flour, sugar, salt, and yeast in a large bowl. Whisk to thoroughly blend.

In a separate bowl whisk together the eggs, water, and milk. Once they are well blended, whisk in the butter. Pour the wet ingredients into the dry mixture and stir with a rubber spatula or wooden spoon until the liquid is absorbed and there are no lumps. The mixture will resemble muffin batter. Cover the bowl with plastic wrap and let it rise at room temperature for 3 to 4 hours. The dough will rise to approximately one and a half times its initial volume.

Using a rubber spatula, gently loosen the dough from the bowl. Dampen your hands with cool water and, with the dough still in the bowl, slide one hand under one side of the dough. Fold that side of the dough into the center and press down gently so the dough adheres to itself. Give the bowl a quarter turn and repeat the folding process. Do this two more times. After the fourth fold, flip over the dough so the seams are on the bottom. Cover the bowl with plastic wrap and let it rise at room temperature for 8 to 12 hours. The dough will double in size.

Repeat the folding procedure, ending with the seams on the bottom. The dough is now ready to use.

To Bake the Brioche

Divide the dough in half. Place each half in a greased 9 × 5-inch loaf pan. (You can also bake half and reserve half for the sticky bun recipe that follows.) Cover the pans with a towel or plastic wrap. Let the dough rest in the pans while you preheat the oven to 375°F (190°C) or 350°F (175°C) with convection.

Brush the loaves with milk and bake on the bottom rack of the oven for 1 hour. The loaves are done when they are a deep golden brown and sound hollow when tapped firmly with your finger. Cool for 10 minutes in the pan on a wire rack. Turn the loaves out of their pans and return them to the rack to cool completely.

STICKY BUNS

These sticky buns can be prepped in the skillet the day before, stored in the refrigerator, and baked in the morning for a decadent weekend breakfast indulgence—although they are so good that sometimes we just make them for lunch and ride the sugar high into the afternoon. Soft raisins make a big difference. If yours are dry you may want to soak them in water at least overnight. Instead of rolling out individual buns, we score the top of the bread for easy cutting and bake it as a whole. That way you can control the portion size and the bread itself cooks more evenly—no more doughy centers. We love that.

8 tablespoons/113 grams **unsalted butter**

1 cup/213 grams packed **dark brown sugar**

1 cup/150 grams whole **pecans**, roasted and salted

½ cup/70 grams **golden raisins**

½ recipe **No-Knead Brioche Dough** (page 75)

Preheat the oven to 375°F (190°C) or 350°F (175°C) with convection.

Cut the butter into thin slices and scatter them on the bottom of a 12-inch (30.4-centimeter) round cast-iron or other ovenproof skillet. Sprinkle the brown sugar evenly over the bottom of the pan, then sprinkle the pecans and raisins over the sugar. Put the brioche dough over the sugar mixture and gently press it to fill the pan. Use a sharp knife to lightly score (no more than ½ inch [1.25 centimeters] deep) the brioche into serving-size pieces.

Bake for 1 hour or until the brioche becomes a deep golden brown and sounds hollow when tapped firmly with your finger. Let rest for 5 minutes. Cut into pieces and serve warm.

NO-KNEAD WHOLE WHEAT
SWEET POTATO BREAD

We like to make whole wheat sandwich bread at home. We use a pain de mie bread pan, a French loaf pan that comes with a lid so the finished bread has perfectly square slices (although whether or not we use the lid depends on our mood). Sometimes perfect squares are desirable; sometimes we prefer a slightly bigger piece of bread. This dough will work either way. As for flour, we are partial to the King Arthur white whole wheat for its flavor, but you can use the whole wheat flour of your choice. This is a wet dough that will bake up into a moist, cakey loaf, excellent for toast and sandwiches.

6 cups/840 grams **white whole wheat flour**

1 tablespoon/12.5 grams **sugar**

1 tablespoon/18 grams **fine sea salt**

2 teaspoons/6 grams **instant yeast**

2 large **sweet potatoes**, roasted, skinned, and diced

1½ cups/375 grams **apple cider**

1½ cups/338 grams **water**

Unsalted butter or **nonstick cooking spray** for the pan

In a large bowl, combine the flour, sugar, salt, and yeast. Whisk to thoroughly combine. Add the sweet potatoes and toss gently with a rubber spatula to incorporate. Add the cider and water and continue to fold the mixture gently until all of the flour is absorbed and the mixture forms a wet dough. Cover the bowl with plastic wrap and let rise for 3 to 4 hours. The dough will rise to approximately one and a half times its initial volume.

Using a rubber spatula, gently loosen the dough from the bowl. Dampen your hands with cool water and, with the dough still in the bowl, slide one hand under one side of the dough. Fold that side of the dough into the center and press down gently so the dough adheres to itself. Give the bowl a quarter turn and repeat the folding process. Do this two more times. After the fourth fold, flip over the dough so the seams are on the bottom. Cover the bowl with plastic wrap and let it rise at room temperature for 8 to 12 hours. The dough will double in size.

Repeat the folding procedure. Gently turn the dough out onto a damp countertop. Shape it into a rectangle approximately the size of your loaf pan and roll up the dough lengthwise to make it easier to move it into the pan. Grease the inside of your pan with soft butter or nonstick spray and place the dough inside, gently stretching it to fit the inside of the pan. Cover it with plastic wrap and let it rest for 30 minutes.

While the dough is resting, preheat the oven to 400°F (200°C) or 375°F (190°C) with convection.

Remove the plastic wrap from the bread and put the pan in the oven. Bake for 20 minutes and then, without opening the oven door, turn the temperature down to 350°F (175°C) or 325°F (160°C) with convection. Bake for 45 minutes more. If the top of the bread starts to get too dark, tent the loaf with foil. The bread is done when the top feels firm to the touch and you hear a hollow sound when knocking gently on the bottom of the pan.

Remove the bread from the oven. Let it rest for 5 minutes in the pan, then turn it out of the pan and let cool completely on a rack.

SOURDOUGH BREADS

Sourdough. The word evokes images of crusty bread with a distinctive tang and a crackling crust. It brings to mind traditional bakeries with giant ovens and a constant flow of wooden peels loaded with loaves of bread rotated in and out of the ovens by muscular bakers à la Nicolas Cage in *Moonstruck*. For home bakers, sourdough bread tends to represent the ultimate in commitment and dedication. It's the creation of the starter that stops most of us in our tracks. Various recipes call for fruits or sweeteners, several days or weeks of feeding, a daily dose of time and flour to get things going. Then once you've got your starter it has to be fed. Daily. So either you continue to bake bread every day or it slowly threatens to take over your kitchen. You begin to have nightmares of a viscous flow of liquid dough creeping across the kitchen floor to consume you. Okay, perhaps we're overdramatizing here. Starter can be intimidating, but it really isn't as tough as all that.

Creating a starter can be as simple as combining flour and water. Yes, sugar in the form of fruit, honey, or sugar may help jump-start the project. Some claim that these ingredients add character to the starter; this is arguable. It's true that fruit may add different yeast cultures, and various strains have different flavors. On the other hand, whatever yeasts are in your flour and in the ambient air around the starter will have a greater impact, simply due to sheer volume, than any yeast riding in on the fruit. After all, your starter will be living in your kitchen and be fed daily with your flour, so those will be the things that have the greatest impact on your brew.

Potato water is sometimes added to starter to provide extra carbohydrates for the microorganisms to consume. Chlorinated water should be avoided. If your tap water is extremely hard or heavily chlorinated, filtered or bottled water is a good alternative. Unbleached flour provides more raw material for your starter than bleached, bromated flour. Rye flour is a good choice because it provides extra nutrients and sugars for the yeast. It can be phased out later if you like. Frankly, though, all you need to get started is a cup each of flour and water, thoroughly blended to encourage aerobic fermentation. This should be kept in a loosely covered glass or plastic container and stored at room temperature, which is hopefully somewhere close to 70°F (21°C). And you're on your way.

So, what's happening in your sourdough culture? You are creating a fermentation of wild yeasts and *Lactobacillus brevis.* The yeast and bacteria are already present in your flour and in the air. As the wheat flour hydrates, the enzyme amylase breaks down the carbohydrates into complex sugars. These complex sugars are further broken down into the simple sugars glucose and fructose, which provide food for the wild yeast. Yeast can ferment aerobically and anaerobically. Aerobic fermentation produces carbon dioxide, which is what makes your starter appear bubbly and full of life. Anaerobic fermentation produces alcohol, which normally separates and settles on top of the starter. Mixing your starter well every time you feed it helps aerate the culture and dissipate the layer of CO_2 that collects on the surface. Yeast fermentation also produces glutamate, the main ingredient in MSG, adding yet another level of savory flavor to your dough.

The *Lactobacillus brevis* bacteria are what give the ferment its acidic note, while the yeast provide leavening action for the dough. The bacteria consume glucose and produce lactic acid. Because of this, sourdough made with starter generally has a lower pH than dough produced with just baker's yeast. The presence of lactic acid produces dough with a pH of 4–4.5. This creates an environment that is unfriendly to pathogenic bacteria in both the starter and the finished bread. Although the pH of finished bread is always higher than that of the dough, sourdough breads are slightly more resistant to mold development as a side benefit of their tangy flavor.

You've got your mixture of flour and water, with or without any additional embellishments. Now find a home for your starter on the counter, because you want to keep it at room temperature and you don't want to forget about it. Leave it alone for twenty-four hours, give or take. It may separate into layers with the flour falling to the bottom, liquid collecting in the center, and a spongy layer forming on top. Don't be alarmed. Simply stir everything back together and then discard half, because otherwise you will end up with more starter than you can easily use. Feed the remainder by adding ½ cup flour and ½ cup water. The yeast will develop before the bacteria so it will look active before any acidity begins to evolve. Repeat this procedure for three days, discarding half and feeding the rest, after which time your starter should start to look alive, with bubbles and a clean sour smell.

The day before you want to bake, feed the starter 1 cup of flour and 1 cup of water without discarding any, and you'll be ready to go. The starter should look happy before you add it to your dough; it should be cohesive and slightly puffed at the center. If it looks like your starter has fallen flat and is beginning to separate, then it needs a little more love. Check the ambient temperature, make sure the room isn't too warm, and be sure to feed it regularly for a couple of days.

Your starter can live in the refrigerator during infrequent bouts of baking and will survive as long as you feed it every couple of weeks. When you're ready to bake again, feed it and leave it at room temperature for twenty-four hours to get things going again. If you're going on vacation or just need a break from the oven, you can freeze your starter or dry it out in a dehydrator or low oven. You'll just need to thaw it or revive it and feed it for a couple of days at room temperature to bring it back up to strength. Keep in mind that it will need to be brought back to life at room temperature with regular feeding for three to four days before it can be used again. Unless you are greatly attached to the flavor, it may be easier to simply use up or discard your starter and begin afresh when you're ready to start baking with it again.

When baking bread with sourdough starter, plan for a long, slow fermentation in order to let the flavors develop in the dough. All sourdough recipes are supplemented with a bit of baker's yeast to guarantee that the bread will rise appropriately.

Although you will need to feed the starter every day to keep it active, you don't have to bake bread all the time. Sourdough starter is a very useful ingredient to have around. It makes wonderfully light and flavorful pancakes and waffles. It can be incorporated into cake batters, fry batters, and fritters to add lightness and flavor to the finished product.

SOURDOUGH CIABATTA ROLLS

These are the perfect dinner rolls. Light and tangy, they are delicious eaten out of hand, dragged through a bowl of sauce, or slathered with good butter. Leftover rolls can be kept in a plastic bag and reheated in the oven or they can be split and toasted for breakfast. They can be sliced for bread pudding or diced for stuffing. If you prefer, you can shape the dough into two long loaves instead of small rolls, or you can shape it into the traditional wide, flat slipper loaf that ciabatta is named for. Either way, it makes for excellent sandwiches or grilled crostini.

½ teaspoon/1.5 grams **instant yeast**

¾ cup/200 grams warm **whole milk**, approximately 110°F (43°C)

1 cup/300 grams **sourdough starter**

1 tablespoon/14 grams **olive oil**

2¼ cups/338 grams **all-purpose flour**, plus more for kneading

1½ teaspoons /9 grams **fine sea salt**

1 tablespoon/14 grams **vegetable oil**

Cornmeal, for dusting the baking sheet

Put the yeast and milk in the bowl of a stand mixer and stir to dissolve the yeast. Add the sourdough starter and the olive oil to the bowl. Use the paddle attachment to stir the ingredients together. Slowly add the flour and then the salt. Mix for 3 minutes, then change the attachment to a dough hook. Scrape the sides and bottom of the bowl with a spatula, then knead the dough for 10 minutes on medium speed. Turn the dough out onto a lightly floured work surface. Knead the dough by hand until it is silky and smooth, about 5 minutes.

Alternatively, if you don't have an electric mixer, you can combine the yeast and milk in a large measuring cup. Stir to dissolve the yeast and add the starter. Combine the flour and salt in a medium bowl, stirring to blend them together, and then form a well in the center of the flour. Add the milk, starter, and olive oil to the well and stir them together using a wooden spoon, slowly incorporating the flour by working from the center outward. When the mixture forms a loose dough, turn it out onto the counter. Knead the dough with your hands, incorporating any additional flour from the bowl, until you have a soft, tacky dough that has the consistency of soft Play-Doh. Knead the dough for 10 to 15 minutes until it is smooth and silky with a loose, elastic texture.

Grease the inside of a bowl with the vegetable oil and put the dough inside, turning to coat with the oil. Cover the bowl with a damp towel and leave it on the counter. Let the dough rise for 1 hour and 15 minutes or until doubled in size.

Lightly dust a baking sheet with cornmeal. Put the dough on a floured work surface and roll it into a log about 18 inches (46 centimeters) long. Use a pair of scissors to cut the log into 12 equal pieces. With the palm of your hand, roll each piece into a ball. Put the balls on the baking sheet, forming an evenly spaced 3 × 4 grid. Cover the baking sheet with a damp towel and let the rolls rise for 2 hours.

Thirty minutes before the rolls are done rising, preheat the oven to 425°F (220°C).

Remove the towel from the baking sheet and put the rolls in the oven. Bake for 10 minutes. Rotate the baking sheet and bake for another 8 to 10 minutes until the rolls are a dark golden brown and sound hollow when tapped with your finger. Remove from the oven and allow to cool on the pan.

SOURDOUGH DOUGHNUTS

The tang of these doughnuts provides an excellent counterpoint to the cinnamon sugar that coats them. Beware; these doughnuts tend to disappear quickly, especially if there are people in the kitchen when they emerge from the fryer. The doughnuts can also be dipped in warm ganache made with equal parts chocolate and cream. We've even been known to turn these into bomboloni by filling them with vanilla pastry cream and serving them with chocolate dipping sauce. Lemon curd or good jelly, perhaps lightened with a little whipped cream, are also nice fillings. A little caramel sauce is never an unwelcome accompaniment, whether the doughnuts are stuffed or plain. But really, the cinnamon sugar does pretty well all by itself. Warm doughnuts are one of life's special pleasures, and once you experience them, you'll want to make these again and again.

½ cup/130 grams **whole milk**

8 tablespoons/113 grams **unsalted butter**, plus more for greasing the bowl

1 cup/300 grams **sourdough starter**

3 cups/450 grams **all-purpose flour**, plus more for dusting

¼ cup/50 grams **sugar**

1 large **egg**

1 teaspoon/6 grams **fine sea salt**

¼ teaspoon/0.75 gram **instant yeast**

1 teaspoon/4 grams **vanilla extract**

Rice bran oil or **canola oil** for frying

1¼ cups/250 grams **sugar**

1 teaspoon/3 grams **ground cinnamon**

In a saucepan set over medium heat, warm the milk and butter until the butter just melts.

Put the starter and flour in the bowl of an electric mixer fitted with the paddle attachment and mix on medium-low speed. Add the milk and butter, followed by the sugar, egg, salt, and yeast. Finally add the vanilla extract and knead the dough until it is soft and slightly tacky.

Grease a large bowl with butter and place the dough inside, turning to coat with butter. Cover with plastic wrap. Let rise for 6 hours at room temperature.

Using a rubber spatula, gently loosen the dough from the bowl. Dampen your hands with cool water and, with the dough still in the bowl, slide one hand under one side of the dough. Fold that side of the dough into the center and press down gently so the dough adheres to itself. Give the bowl a quarter turn and repeat the folding process. Do this two more times. After the fourth fold, flip over the dough so the seams are on the bottom. Cover the bowl with plastic wrap and let the dough rise a second time for 8 to 12 hours at room temperature.

Dust a work surface with flour and turn the dough out onto the flour. Lightly dust the top of the dough with more flour and pat it out so it is roughly ½ inch (1.25 centimeters) thick. Use a doughnut cutter or two different-sized round cutters to cut out a dozen doughnuts. You may be able to cut out a few extra holes. (Roll and cut the dough only once. You can fry the irregular cuttings for kitchen snacks.) Separate the doughnuts from the holes and lay them all on a lightly floured baking sheet.

Fill a heavy-bottomed pot halfway with rice bran oil and heat to 350°F (175°C). In a medium bowl, combine the sugar and cinnamon; set aside. Set a metal rack over a rimmed baking sheet.

When the oil is hot, test it with a doughnut hole or a dough piece. When the doughnut is golden on one side, use a metal spider or slotted spoon to flip it over. Set the tester on the rack to drain. Check the inside of the doughnut for doneness. Once the test doughnut is cooked, proceed with the doughnut holes.

Cook the doughnuts 3 or 4 at a time so the oil temperature does not fluctuate too much. Fry the doughnuts for 2 minutes on one side. Flip them over and fry for 2 to 3 more minutes or until golden brown. Drain the doughnuts and toss them in the bowl of cinnamon sugar while they are still warm. Place the sugared doughnuts on a plate and continue cooking the rest. The doughnuts are best warm but will keep up to 3 days in an airtight container.

SOURDOUGH SPAETZLE

SERVES 4 AS A SIDE DISH

Spaetzle is a German word meaning "little sparrow," an evocative description of these small dumplings that have a long, irregular shape. Traditionally, they are boiled, tossed with butter, and served alongside rich, saucy dishes. We like to fry spaetzle in butter because it gives them a delicate crispy edge to contrast their tender texture. They are a nice change of pace from traditional starches like potatoes and pasta. The sourdough spaetzle's light texture and tangy flavor are equally at home with meat or fish; they can be tossed with fresh peas or fava beans and finished with tarragon, sautéed with wild mushrooms, or combined with bite-size ratatouille for an interesting twist on a classic. Use them in place of rice or small pastas in your favorite preparations and you'll see what a difference they can make.

1 cup/300 grams **sourdough starter**

⅔ cup/100 grams **all-purpose flour**

1 large **egg**

½ teaspoon/3 grams **fine sea salt**

Olive oil

1 tablespoon/14 grams **unsalted butter**

In a medium bowl, mix the starter, flour, egg, and salt with a rubber spatula or wooden spoon to make a smooth, soft dough. Cover the bowl with plastic wrap and let the dough rest for 30 minutes.

Meanwhile, bring a large pot of salted water to a boil and prepare an ice bath. Push the dough through a spaetzle maker, perforated pan, or colander into the boiling water. Cook the spaetzle until they are floating and firm, about 2 minutes. Remove the spaetzle with a slotted spoon and transfer them to the ice bath. Once the spaetzle are cold, remove them from the water and pat dry. Finally, drizzle the noodles with a touch of olive oil to prevent them from sticking together and store them in a covered container in the refrigerator for up to 2 days.

To serve, melt the butter in a sauté pan over medium-high heat and cook the spaetzle, stirring occasionally, until just browned, 3 to 5 minutes. Serve immediately.

SOURDOUGH WAFFLES

SERVES 4

As long as there is starter on your counter, you can make sourdough waffles. These are an admirable way to start the day. Sourdough waffles are extremely light and crisp. They tend to soak up that butter and maple syrup as though they were meant for each other, while their distinctive tang helps balance the sugar and fat. Adding some crunchy bacon bits to the batter takes them up another notch. They make a wonderful base for fruit and ice cream sundaes, topped with chunks of fresh strawberries and bananas and creamy vanilla ice cream. If you want to try something different, serve sourdough waffles under poached eggs, crisp bacon, and hollandaise—it's the breakfast of champions in our house.

3 tablespoons/42 grams **unsalted butter**, plus more for serving

3 tablespoons/60 grams **maple syrup**, plus more for serving

2 large **eggs**

1 scant teaspoon/5 grams **fine sea salt**

4 cups/1,200 grams thick **sourdough starter**

1 teaspoon/5 grams **baking soda**

Put the butter and the maple syrup in a pan set over medium heat and stir until the butter is melted.

Whisk the egg yolks together with the salt, then stir them into the sourdough starter. Once the yolks are incorporated stir in the melted butter and syrup. Add the baking soda and stir the mixture to combine. Whip the whites to soft peaks and gently fold them into the batter.

Cook the waffles in a waffle iron until golden brown. Serve with butter and maple syrup.

FLATBREADS

Even if there are just a few people gathered at our house for dinner, we usually place some little tidbits on the table to enjoy with cocktails. Soft oozing cheeses, firm Cheddar, crisp apple slices, and flavorful crackers are one of our favorite ways to start a party. We like serving flatbreads at the beginning of the meal because they are a light way to provide a snack without filling up our guests and dulling their appetites. In other cultures the flatbread can be a major part of the meal, as with a Salvadoran pupusa made from masa harina and stuffed with meat or beans. Flatbread can also do double duty as the utensil used to scoop up the food, as with injera, an Ethiopian bread made with teff flour.

At their most fundamental, flatbreads are unleavened breads made with flour, water, and salt. By modern definitions, flatbreads are simply breads that are flat, usually less than two inches (5 centimeters) high, and yeast or chemical leaveners may be used in the dough. Flatbreads can be baked in the oven, cooked on the stovetop, or fried. Of course, there are also flatbreads that are perfectly flat, usually made without wheat flour, a prime example being corn tortillas. Flatbreads cover a wide range of textures and flavors, from matzoh to chapatis to focaccia.

Mixing together flour and a liquid creates basic batters and doughs. The mixing process incorporates air into the internal structure of the dough. Once the dough is put into a hot oven, any liquid is heated to a gaseous state and expands into the air pockets in the dough. This expansion causes the dough to rise. When the liquid in the dough is water, this process is referred to as steam leavening. Steam leavening works best at temperatures of 400°F (205°C) or higher because this optimizes the volume and pressure of the vapor molecules released. Once the liquid has evaporated and the air pockets have expanded, the proteins in the dough need to coagulate around these bubbles before they begin to collapse. While some of the steam will escape the dough during baking, enough will remain behind to significantly leaven the finished product. Some extreme examples of steam leavening can be found in puff pastry and choux paste. Puff pastry works by layering fat and flour to create a structured network of air pockets that expand when the steam is released by the heat of the oven. Choux paste actually relies on its high egg content rather than the flour alone to provide the structure for the steam leavening; the dramatic volume that can be achieved (imagine the hollow center of cream puffs) is a testament to the power of water vapor.

Steam leavening takes place anytime dough or batter is cooked. It can be amplified in two ways. The first is by increasing the amount of air introduced during the mixing/kneading process—the longer the dough is worked, the more air is introduced. Creaming together butter and sugar when making butter cakes is one method for adding air to the structure. Whipping eggs in a recipe is another. A more elemental technique is long kneading or beating of the dough itself. These methods all increase the amount of air in the dough, and the techniques can strengthen the structure, giving it more elasticity to expand around the air pockets as they are formed. Another way to increase the effect of steam leavening is to add an additional leavener, such as yeast or baking powder, which will increase the amount of gas released into the dough during the baking process to create a light texture in the finished product.

The protein that provides the strength and structure in many baked goods is found in the flour. Wheat flour, which contains two proteins known as glutenin and gliaden, is predominantly used in varying percentages for this reason. When mixed together and hydrated, these proteins intertwine in irregular coils to form gluten. As we knead the dough, these coils straighten out and the gluten becomes stronger, stretchier, and more elastic. The gliadin allows the dough to be stretched out while the glutenin is responsible for the strength of the dough and its tendency to snap back into its original form. Once the gluten is developed, the dough can be stretched thin, but the more the gluten is worked, the more elastic it becomes, resulting in a dough that shrinks after it has been shaped.

Dough relaxation refers to a rest period after stretching or shaping. This relaxation allows the gluten to adjust to its new shape and makes it less likely to spring back and recoil. When the gluten is overdeveloped, the final product becomes tough and chewy, with a dense crumb derived from an inability to rise in the oven. Once gluten has been overdeveloped, there's no fixing it. It's easy to tell when this has happened because the dough resists stretching and shaping no matter how long you let it rest. On the other hand, products with too little gluten are very "short." They lack the structure to rise properly in the oven and the finished baked goods are very crumbly and fall apart easily.

Unleavened flatbread recipes usually call for long periods of kneading. Because they do not use added leaveners, the development of gluten is key to help maximize the steam leavening. The kneading serves the dual purpose of incorporating air into the dough and developing the gluten to provide the structure needed to capture the steam pockets during baking.

Flatbreads are so much more than we give them credit for. What would life be like without cheese and crackers, quesadillas, and focaccia? They are a great way to get started if you've never baked bread and a good project for working with kids. We love them for their flavor, versatility, and the way they ignite our imagination.

ONION CRACKERS

MAKES 4 LARGE CRACKERS

These crackers combine the sweet flavor of onions in the dough with the taste of Old Bay, the ubiquitous seafood seasoning. The crackers are a great recipe for children because the dough is flavorful and easy to work with, and kids can have fun at the end breaking the large pieces into bite-size bits. They go well with cheese, seafood dips and salads, steak tartare, hummus, baba ghanoush, and of course, good butter.

½ medium **sweet or yellow onion**, peeled and roughly chopped

½ cup/113 grams **plain whole-milk yogurt**

1 teaspoon/6 grams **fine sea salt**

2 cups/300 grams **all-purpose flour**, plus more for dusting

2 teaspoons/10 grams **Old Bay seasoning**

Preheat the oven to 450°F (230°C).

In a food processor or blender, puree the onion, yogurt, and salt until smooth.

Put the flour in the bowl of a stand mixer fitted with the dough hook. Turn the mixer on low speed and pour in the onion mixture. Increase the speed to medium-low and mix until the dough forms a ball. Increase the speed to medium and knead the dough for 3 minutes. The dough will tighten around the hook and grow silky in appearance. Turn the dough out onto a clean counter and cut it into 4 equal pieces. Roll the pieces into balls and cover them with a towel. Let the dough rest for 10 minutes.

Lightly flour your work surface and dust the dough with flour. One ball at a time, roll the dough about ⅛ inch (3 millimeters) thick. Place the dough on the back side of a baking sheet; the flatbread will cook more quickly and evenly this way. Sprinkle the dough with ½ teaspoon (2.5 grams) of the Old Bay seasoning. Place the baking sheet in the oven and bake for 10 minutes, until the flatbread is dry and golden brown. Remove from the oven, let it rest for 5 minutes, and move the cracker to a wire rack to cool. Repeat with the remaining 3 balls of dough. When the flatbread is cool to the touch, break it into bite-size pieces.

CHEESE-STUFFED FLATBREAD

MAKES 1 LARGE FLATBREAD

This flatbread is a riff on the classic focaccia from Recco, Italy. Unlike the traditional yeasted focaccia, this bread is two layers of unleavened dough separated by cheese. The dough is made by first adding the oil to the flour, mixing it in to coat the starch, and then adding the water. This method keeps the flour from clumping and facilitates a well-blended dough. This flatbread is a great way to start a dinner party with everyone congregating in and around the kitchen, cocktails in hand as the flatbread comes out of the oven. It's a graphic illustration of the power of steam leavening. After the bread is cut it deflates into a truly flat bread. It's beautiful and delicious, a sure conversation piece as people relax and settle in for the evening.

> 1⅓ cups/200 grams **all-purpose flour**, plus more for kneading the dough
>
> 1 teaspoon/6 grams **fine sea salt**
>
> 3 tablespoons/42 grams **olive oil**, plus more for the pan and for brushing the bread
>
> ½ cup/112.5 grams lukewarm (105°F–115°F/41°C–46°C) **water**
>
> 3 cups/300 grams grated **Gruyère cheese**
>
> **Coarse sea salt** and **freshly ground black pepper**

In a medium bowl, mix the flour and salt. Pour in the olive oil and use your fingertips to evenly disperse it. The flour will take on the appearance of coarse sand. Stir the water into the flour with your fingertips and then knead the mass into a dough. It will be soft and sticky. Dust a work surface with flour, turn the dough out of the bowl, and knead the dough for 5 minutes until it becomes soft, smooth, and silky. Invert a clean bowl over the top of the dough and let it rest for 15 minutes.

Uncover the dough and knead it for another 5 minutes. Lightly flour the inside of the bowl and place the ball of dough inside. Cover the bowl with plastic wrap and set it aside in a warm spot for 1 hour and 15 minutes.

Using a rubber spatula, gently loosen the dough from the bowl. Dampen your hands with cool water and, with the dough still in the bowl, slide one hand under one side of the dough. Fold that side of the dough into the center and press down gently so the dough adheres to itself. Give the bowl a quarter turn and repeat the folding process. Do this two more times. After the fourth fold, flip over the dough so the seams are on the bottom. Cover the bowl with plastic wrap and let the dough rest for another 1 hour and 15 minutes.

Preheat the oven to 500°F (260°C).

By now the dough will have expanded by roughly 50 to 75 percent. Divide it in half and roll the pieces into balls. Cover the balls with a damp towel and let them rest for 20 minutes.

Put a silicone liner or sheet of foil on a baking sheet and brush it with an even layer of olive oil. Lightly flour a work surface and roll the first ball of dough into a rectangle the size of the baking sheet liner. Put the dough on the liner, then sprinkle the cheese over the dough, leaving a ½-inch (1.25-centimeter) border around the edges. Roll the second ball of dough into the same size rectangle and put it on top. Pull and stretch the doughs so their edges line up with each other. Fold the bottom edge up over the top dough in a continuous pinching and pleating motion, much like sealing the two edges of a double-crusted pie, around the perimeter. Brush the dough with olive oil, sprinkle with coarse salt, and grind black pepper over the top. Bake for 13 minutes, until the top is bubbly, golden, and crispy.

Remove the baking sheet from the oven and allow the dough to rest for 5 minutes. Slide the dough onto a cutting board and cut in half horizontally and then into 6 slices per half. Serve immediately.

QUICK BREADS

There's nothing like the fragrance of baking in the morning. It's instantly comforting, a wonderful way to ease into the day. Coupled with the scent of hot coffee and melting butter, that aroma can create a little piece of heaven in your kitchen. We love the idea of cinnamon rolls and sticky buns for breakfast. Unfortunately, they just can't satisfy our need for instant (or almost instant) gratification first thing in the morning. Let's not even talk about those refrigerated rolls of dough. Instead, we've become quick bread aficionados. From flour to table in just about half an hour, scones and biscuits are our go-to for those mornings when we need a little something special or want to feel pampered at home.

Quick breads, as opposed to yeast breads, have been a staple since chemical leaveners were discovered. Chemical leaveners release CO_2, or carbon dioxide, under specific conditions and are used in baked goods to create bubbles in the dough as it cooks. The heat of the oven causes moisture to evaporate out of the dough. As this happens, the proteins coagulate and the batter sets around the holes created by the bubbles, giving the final product a light texture. The two standard chemical leaveners are baking soda and baking powder. Baking powder contains baking soda, but the two products are not interchangeable. Baking soda is a pure product and four times stronger than baking powder.

Baking soda can be traced back to the discovery of carbonate materials in the 1780s. Potash, a material extracted by boiling wood ashes, was utilized for its potassium salts, which were used to make soap, glass, and dyes. Potash was further refined into pearlash, which was created by boiling the ashes of burned vegetables and weeds. In the mid-1700s bakers added pearlash to sourdough bread in order to counteract the acidic taste of fermented yeast. They discovered that the pearlash caused a reaction in the dough, resulting in lighter bread that rose more quickly in the oven. Hence the first chemical leavener in baking was discovered.

As wood sources declined, the search for a new source of carbonates began. In 1783 the French Academy of Sciences offered a prize for the best method to convert sodium chloride, or table salt, to sodium carbonate. Nicolas Leblanc won the contest using a two-step method that transformed sodium chloride to sodium sulfate using sulfuric acid, then treated the sodium sulfate with coal and calcium carbonate to create sodium carbonate. This was refined further using carbon dioxide to create sodium bicarbonate, otherwise known as saleratus, aerated salt—or baking soda. It is the weakest of all the sodium alkalis. Sodium bicarbonate releases carbon dioxide when it is heated above 122°F (50°C) or when it interacts with a weak acid. In fact, it was originally used as a medicine to treat acid stomachs. Later bakers realized that it was an effective, albeit expensive, alternative to pearlash as a chemical leavener for baking. Only mild acids are needed to activate the baking soda, and recipes using brown sugar, natural cocoa powder, honey, maple syrup, or buttermilk usually have enough acid to use baking soda as the sole leavener.

The development of commercially available cream of tartar was the next step in the evolution of chemical leaveners. Also known as potassium hydrogen tartrate, cream of tartar is an acid salt that is created when tartaric acid, a by-product of wine making, is partially neutralized with potassium hydroxide. It was combined with sodium bicarbonate to create the original baking powder, established by Alfred Bird, in 1835. The drawback to this kind of baking powder is that the reaction takes place as soon as the baking powder is added to a liquid. Once used, batters must immediately go into the oven in order to achieve optimal results. Calcium phosphate or disodium pyrophosphate can be used to create single-action baking powders that work more slowly than ones made with cream of tartar, although the window of opportunity is still brief.

Double-acting baking powder was created to slow down the process and increase leavening in the oven. It usually contains a blend of acid salts so the leavening reaction takes place twice. A small amount of the leavening, usually 20 to 30 percent, takes place during the mixing process, when the baking powder meets the liquids. The rest occurs when the batter is exposed to the heat of the oven. Four main acid salts are used in double-acting baking powder: monocalcium phosphate (a quick-acting acid), sodium acid pyrophosphate, sodium aluminum phosphate, and sodium aluminum sulfate. The last two aluminum compounds have fallen out of favor with bakers because they are believed to impart an unpleasant flavor to the finished products. The final ingredient in baking powder is a starch, usually cornstarch, which is used to keep the product dry and free flowing. It is also useful in separating the acids and alkalis during the storage process and acting as a filler for ease of measurement.

These days we are lucky to have our choice of leaveners. For most recipes a combination of baking powder and baking soda is employed. Many camps swear by homemade baking powder made with a 2:1 ratio of cream of tartar and baking soda. Baking soda is approximately four times as strong as baking powder, so you can use 1 teaspoon (6 grams) of baking powder or ¼ teaspoon (1.25 grams) baking soda to leaven 1 cup (150 grams) of flour. Baking soda has a stronger flavor that is neutralized by acid, which is also needed for leavening to occur, and works quickly. Baking powder has a slower reaction and can be used in batters that will not be cooked immediately. It has a milder flavor and only needs moisture to do its job. Double-acting baking powder will react a second time when exposed to high heat, guaranteeing leavening in the oven. Which leavener you choose for a recipe depends on your ingredients and your cooking method. Sometimes they are combined, in which case there is usually more baking powder because that is the primary leavener. The baking soda is used more to neutralize some of the acid and add tenderness.

It's important to note that baking soda and baking powder must be completely dispersed throughout the flour to work effectively. This is easily done by thoroughly whisking them into the flour before adding them to the liquids in a recipe. Too much of either chemical leavener can leave behind an unpleasant aftertaste. Also, if there is too much expansion of the air bubbles, they will burst before the dough can set, resulting in a flat, dense texture. Therefore, we like to use the least amount needed to achieve the right results.

BUTTERMILK BISCUITS

Buttermilk biscuits are a classic recipe that combines steam leavening and chemical leaveners to optimum effect. They are easily stirred together and rise dramatically in the oven. Slathered with cold butter and drizzled with cane syrup or honey, fresh biscuits are an easy and indulgent way to get your day started. Actually, they are pretty wonderful at any time of day. Buttermilk biscuits on the dinner table bring smiles to people's faces, and split open and covered with fresh fruit and sweet cream, they are a treat to remember.

> 2 cups/300 grams **all-purpose flour**, plus more for dusting
>
> 1 teaspoon/6 grams **fine sea salt**
>
> 2 tablespoons/25 grams **sugar**
>
> 2½ teaspoons/15 grams **baking powder**
>
> ½ teaspoon/2.5 grams **baking soda**
>
> 4 tablespoons/56 grams cold, **unsalted butter**, cut into small pieces
>
> 1¼ cups/285 grams cold **buttermilk**

Preheat the oven to 450°F (230°C) or 425°F (220°C) with convection.

In a medium bowl, whisk together the flour, salt, sugar, baking powder, and baking soda until well blended. Drop the butter into the flour and quickly rub it in with your fingertips until the mixture looks like coarse crumbs. Alternatively, you can freeze the butter in a chunk and grate it into the dry ingredients, stirring lightly so the butter is coated by the flour.

Pour in the buttermilk and stir with a wooden spoon or spatula until the mixture just comes together into a sticky dough. Turn it out of the bowl onto a floured work surface. Dust the top of the dough with flour and fold and turn it a few times to form a cohesive mass. Pat it out to a thickness of about an inch (2.5 centimeters) and use a sharp, floured cutter to punch out 2-inch (5-centimeter) rounds. The scraps can be re-formed and cut out one time.

Line a baking sheet with parchment or a silicone mat. Place the biscuits 2 inches (5 centimeters) apart on the baking sheet. Bake until golden brown and firm to the touch, 15 to 20 minutes. Let rest for 5 minutes before eating.

BANANAS FOSTER BREAD

MAKES 2 9 x 5-INCH LOAVES

We love the dark, rich flavors of the classic dessert bananas Foster. One time when we had an overabundance of bananas we decided that creating a bread featuring these flavors would be ideal. We used muscovado sugar, an intensely flavored sweetener, to help mimic the caramelized notes of the original dish. We combined baking powder and baking soda to maximize our leavening and ensure a light, tender bread. It's darned good all on its own, but we've also used it for French toast and bread pudding with fabulous results. Leftover bread can be toasted or grilled and slathered with butter for an excellent breakfast or snack.

> 6 cups/900 grams **all-purpose flour**
>
> 2½ tablespoons/45 grams **baking powder**
>
> ¾ teaspoon/4 grams **baking soda**
>
> 2 teaspoons/12 grams **fine sea salt**
>
> 7 medium ripe **bananas**, peeled
>
> 16 tablespoons/226 grams **unsalted butter**, plus more for the pans
>
> 1½ cups/300 grams **dark muscovado sugar**
>
> ½ cup plus 3 tablespoons/160 grams **dark rum**
>
> 5 large **eggs**

Preheat the oven to 375°F (190°C) or 350°F (175°C) with convection. Butter two 9 × 5-inch loaf pans; set aside.

Combine the flour, baking powder, baking soda, and salt in a large bowl.

Cut the bananas and butter into approximately ½-inch (1.25-centimeter) pieces. Place the bananas, butter, and sugar in a pot set over medium heat and bring to a slow simmer. Cook the mixture until the butter is fully melted and the bananas are falling apart. Remove from the heat and let cool to room temperature.

Pour the banana mixture into a blender, add the rum and the eggs, and puree until smooth. Quickly pour the banana base into the dry ingredients. Use a wooden spoon or rubber spatula to quickly mix the wet and dry ingredients together until they form a homogeneous batter. Do not overmix. Divide evenly between the loaf pans. Use an offset spatula to gently smooth the top and then run a finger around the edge of the pan creating a slight indentation in the batter to facilitate even rising.

Place both pans on the center rack of the oven and bake for 50 minutes. When the breads are done they will feel firm to the touch and a skewer inserted into the center should come out clean. Place the pans on a wire rack and let cool for 10 minutes. Remove the bread from the pans and return them to the rack to cool completely.

PASTA, GNOCCHI, *and* RISOTTO

FRESH PASTA

Making fresh pasta for someone you love or for anyone at all makes them feel special. It tells them that you care enough to go above and beyond the call of duty in creating their meal. Fresh pasta is simple to make, a blending of ingredients that goes back thousands of years. Noodles are one of the oldest recorded foods; in fact, archaeologists have uncovered a preserved bowl of noodles in China that scientists speculate could be up to four thousand years old. That's a lot of history for a ubiquitous comfort meal.

Making fresh pasta can be as simple as mixing two ingredients, either flour and water or flour and eggs. Wheat flour is preferred because its unique proportions of the proteins glutenin and gliadin are what give the finished dough its extensibility and elasticity. It makes noodles that are slightly sweet and absorb other flavors well. Other types of flour, like buckwheat, can be used to make pasta but they don't have the right protein structure to achieve the same type of results on their own. Instead, noodles made from nonwheat flours tend to be short in texture, breaking easily, and emphasize the flavor of the grain. Soba noodles made from buckwheat have a wonderful nutty flavor, but the higher the percentage of buckwheat flour, the less resilient the noodle.

The type of wheat flour used to make the dough will have an impact on the finished noodles. Asian noodles are made with softer flours with lower protein content to minimize gluten development. Baking soda is sometimes added to Asian noodle dough. The increased alkalinity of this dough improves moisture retention by hydrating the starches, weakening the proteins in the flour, and producing stretchier dough. Noodles made with baking soda or other alkaline salts are firmer than noodles made without it. This helps improve the texture of the finished noodles, giving them added bite in spite of the softer flour. Asian noodles are notable for their texture; cooked noodles have a unique springy feel that is sometimes referred to as bounciness on the tongue. This texture is part of what makes slurping up ramen noodles such a pleasurable experience.

Italian noodles, on the other hand, are more tender and toothsome. This type of pasta is usually made from durum flour or semolina, either alone or combined with all-purpose or Italian-style flour. Italian 00 flour has a superfine texture. It is widely thought that 00 refers to protein content, but in fact it refers to the refinement process; the protein content can range from high to low. Italian-style pasta dough is generally made with higher protein flours or flour blends so the resulting pasta will have a firmer texture and hold its shape. In both Italian and Asian pasta dough the flours are often blended to achieve optimal results in the finished product. As you work with fresh pasta dough you will find out what you like the best. Pasta made with all-purpose flour is delicious, but for those of us who like to tinker, it's important to know the effect that different ingredients have on the dough.

Interestingly, there are a wide variety of Asian pasta dough recipes and many of them include eggs or egg yolk in small quantities. They are usually added to provide texture in the finished noodles.

Salt in pasta dough is a personal decision. Some recipes season the dough and others rely on the cooking water to add salt to the pasta. Salt provides flavor. It also toughens the gluten structure. So if you are trying to formulate firm dough, it may be helpful to add salt and baking soda to your recipe. On the other hand, if you prefer soft, delicate pasta sheets that seem to melt on your tongue, you will let the cooking water and the sauce season your noodles.

Once you've mastered basic pasta dough, you will probably want to branch out and try adding different flavors. Pureed vegetables are sometimes added to dough for extra color and flavor. Herbs can be rolled into the pasta layers and various spices added for flavor. The flour itself can be smoked. Various vegetable flours can add flavor. Tomato, onion, and garlic powders can all add a subtle background note and increase umami. Fresh pasta dough is a blank canvas simply waiting for the chef's inspiration.

Once you've decided on your components it's time to mix the dough. In many ways pasta dough is very similar to bread dough, although pasta dough has a significantly lower water content. In both cases kneading the dough produces a homogeneous mixture where the gluten strands cross-link to form a more stable structure. Once the dough is completely kneaded it assumes a soft, velvety texture, a tactile confirmation that the necessary changes have occurred. Then the dough rests so that the gluten bonds can align. When this happens the dough becomes more extensible and less elastic. This means that it can be stretched into a thin film without snapping back into its original shape and with minimal breaking and tearing. The rolling process further strengthens and aligns the gluten network and presses any air bubbles out of the dough.

The resting period allows the flour to hydrate, or fully absorb the liquid in the dough. If the dough is too moist, it becomes too difficult to roll out. If it is too dry, it is hard to work with and will crack and tear easily. One way to use less liquid in the dough is to give it a longer resting time to allow the starch in the flour to hydrate. A faster method is to make a drier dough and vacuum seal it. This sounds a little extreme, but it produces wonderful results. The pasta is put in a vacuum bag in the machine and the oxygen is removed from the vacuum chamber. When the air is returned to the vacuum chamber, the storage bag collapses around the dough and the available water is forced into the empty spaces in the cells that used to contain oxygen. This takes seconds and leaves you with perfectly hydrated dough that is ready to roll. This method also intensifies the color of any additional ingredients in the dough, such as herbs or vegetable purees.

Once the pasta dough is rolled out, it can be cooked immediately. Alternatively, it can be rolled out, frozen, and cooked directly from the freezer. Many recipes call for drying pasta at room temperature, but there is a significant risk of contamination by mold and other bacteria with this method, especially in warm, humid temperatures. Since freezing pasta causes no loss of texture and flavor, that is the method we prefer for keeping fresh pasta on hand.

EGG YOLK PASTA

SERVES 4 AS AN ENTRÉE

This Italian-style pasta dough makes golden noodles that have a great silky texture. It is wonderful cut into noodles or used to make ravioli. A simple pan sauté is all you need to finish the pasta. Who needs bottled pasta sauce? Depending on the season, we like cherry tomatoes with artichoke hearts and basil, wild mushrooms with thyme, zucchini with fresh garlic, or sweet corn with green onions and cayenne. Once the vegetables are cooked, the hot pasta is added to the pan and tossed with a few spoonfuls of the pasta cooking water to make a delicious and flavorful sauce. A little freshly grated cheese and perhaps a touch of freshly ground pepper, and you're ready to eat.

1½ cups/225 grams **all-purpose flour**, plus more for kneading and rolling the dough

8 large **egg yolks**

1 tablespoon/14 grams **olive oil**

2 tablespoons/30 grams **whole milk**

4 tablespoons/56 grams **unsalted butter**

Fine sea salt and **freshly ground black pepper**

Mixing by Hand

Place the flour in a large mixing bowl and form a well in the center. Put the egg yolks, olive oil, and milk in the center of the well and gently whisk them together with a fork. Once the wet ingredients have been combined, begin stirring from the center outward, gradually incorporating the flour until the mixture forms a soft dough (not all of the flour will be incorporated). Turn the contents of your bowl out onto a work surface and knead the dough with your hands, pulling in more flour from the excess, and adding more as needed, until you have a smooth, silky dough.

Mixing by Machine

Combine the flour, egg yolks, olive oil, and milk in a food processor and pulse to blend. Once the mixture comes together into a rough dough, turn it out onto a lightly floured work surface and finish it by hand. Knead the dough, adding more flour as needed, until it becomes smooth and silky to the touch.

Resting the Dough

Cover the dough with plastic wrap and let it rest for at least 30 minutes before rolling out. Alternatively, you can put it in a vacuum bag, seal it, and let it rest for 10 minutes before rolling. (This will leave you with moister dough than resting in plastic wrap.)

Rolling the Dough

Uncover the dough and cut it in half. Keep one half of the dough wrapped loosely in the plastic. Lightly flour a work surface and, using a rolling pin, begin to roll out the other half of the dough. Dust the surface of the dough lightly with flour and continue to roll from the middle to the edges, turning the dough a quarter turn and flipping it over every couple of rolls. Continue to roll the dough until it is ⅛ inch (3 millimeters) thick and roughly 10 × 12 inches. Dust the dough generously with flour and fold the top third down and the bottom third up, as you would fold a letter. Dust the dough with flour and, using a sharp knife, cut it crosswise into ribbons ¼ inch (6 millimeters) wide. Unfold each noodle, and dust with flour. Sprinkle a baking sheet with flour and loosely nest each batch of noodles on the pan in a single layer. Cover them with a kitchen towel and repeat with the other half of dough.

Alternatively, you can roll out the dough with a pasta maker following the manufacturer's instructions, using the cutter of your choice.

When all the dough is rolled, refrigerate the noodles until ready to use. If using within a few minutes, simply cover with a kitchen towel.

Cooking the Pasta

Bring a large pot of water to a boil. Generously salt the water, then add the noodles. Cook for 3 to 4 minutes.

Meanwhile, in a separate pot large enough to hold the noodles, melt the butter over medium heat. Drain the cooked noodles and put them in the pot with the butter. Coat the noodles evenly with the butter and season with salt and pepper to taste. Serve immediately.

BLOND MISO NOODLES

SERVES 4 AS AN ENTRÉE

Miso has become a common ingredient in the supermarket. It is a fermented soybean paste that is traditionally seasoned with salt and koji, *which are grains, usually rice, fermented with* Aspergillus oryzae *molds.*

Miso is classified by color (white or blond, red or brown), flavor (sweet or salty), and ingredients (barley, soybean). In this pasta dough we like the delicate taste of blond miso, which is fermented with a high percentage of rice koji. It is the sweetest and mildest of the miso varieties and adds a savory depth of flavor with a lighter touch than a darker miso.

Traditionally, flavored noodles are often served simply buttered, as they are in this recipe. Chopped sautéed watercress, freshly cooked clams, sautéed ground pork, braised baby radishes, or pan-seared calamari would all complement this pasta and create a satisfying meal.

3 tablespoons/55 grams **blond miso paste**

1 large **egg**

⅓ cup/75 grams **water**

1½ cups/225 grams **all-purpose flour**, plus more for kneading
and rolling the dough

4 tablespoons/56 grams **unsalted butter**

Fine sea salt and **freshly ground black pepper**

In a small bowl, combine the miso, egg, and water and mix well.

Put the flour in a medium bowl and make a small well in the center. Pour the wet ingredients into the well and, using a fork or your fingertips, begin stirring the wet ingredients from the center outward, gradually incorporating the flour. The dough will be a bit sticky and crumbly. Use your fingers and then your whole hand to squeeze and then knead the dough. Once the dough forms a large mass, turn it out onto a lightly floured work surface. Knead the dough for 5 minutes, dusting with flour if it is sticky. Once the dough develops a soft, velvety texture, wrap it in plastic and let it rest for at least 30 minutes.

Unwrap the dough and cut it in half. Keep half of the dough wrapped loosely in the plastic while you work with the other half. Alternatively, you can put the dough in a vacuum bag, seal it, and let it rest for 10 minutes before rolling. (This will leave you with moister dough than resting in plastic wrap.) Lightly flour a work surface and, using a rolling pin, begin to roll out the dough. This process takes time. Dust the surface of the dough lightly with flour and continue to roll from the middle to the edges, turning the dough a quarter turn and flipping it over every couple of rolls. Continue to roll the dough until it is ⅛ inch (3 millimeters) thick and roughly 10 × 12 inches. Dust the dough with flour and fold down the top third of the dough. Dust the dough with flour again, and fold the bottom edge of the dough up over the third of dough you just folded down. Dust the dough with flour and, using a sharp knife, cut it lengthwise into ribbons ¼ inch (6 millimeters) wide. Unfold each noodle, and dust with flour. Sprinkle a baking sheet with flour and loosely nest each batch of noodles on the pan in a single layer. Cover them with a kitchen towel and repeat with the other half of dough.

When all the dough is rolled, refrigerate the noodles until ready to use. If using within a few minutes, simply cover with a kitchen towel.

Alternatively, you can roll out the dough with a pasta maker following the manufacturer's instructions, using the cutter of your choice.

Bring a large pot of water to a boil. Generously salt the water, then add the noodles. Cook for 3 to 4 minutes.

Meanwhile, in a separate pot large enough to hold the noodles, melt the butter over medium heat. Drain the cooked noodles and put them in the pot with the butter. Coat the noodles evenly with the butter and season with salt and pepper to taste. Serve immediately.

POTATO CHIP PASTA

SERVES 6 AS AN ENTRÉE

We love potato chips. We use them in a variety of preparations, from stuffings to ice cream, so making the leap to pasta dough wasn't as crazy as it may sound. After all, potato chips go with almost anything. Think of all those dips. Although we originally tried to make this with actual potato chips, the dough was too greasy. Using toasted, ground potato flakes gives it that nutty flavor without the added fat. The potato flakes, sometimes labeled "instant mashed potatoes," are easily found in the supermarket. It doesn't take much effort to toast the flakes and grind them into flour, and the results will make you feel like a kid again. The dough can be cut into noodles or used to make ravioli. The potato chip pasta is delicious tossed with brown butter, parsley, and lemon, perhaps served alongside soft-shell crabs or sweet Maine lobster.

1½ cups/100 grams **potato flakes**

2 cups/300 grams **all-purpose flour**, plus more for kneading and rolling the dough

1½ teaspoons/9 grams **fine sea salt**

6 large **eggs**

4 large **egg yolks**

6 tablespoons/84 grams **unsalted butter**

Fine sea salt and **freshly ground black pepper**

Preheat the oven to 350°F (175°C).

Put the potato flakes on a baking sheet and bake for 20 minutes, or until they are a deep golden brown. Stir them once during baking to ensure even browning. Place the baking sheet on a wire rack and let the flakes cool completely, stirring them occasionally to speed the process, about 30 minutes. Pour the flakes into a blender and pulverize them into a fine powder.

Combine the potato powder, flour, and salt in a bowl and whisk together. In a separate bowl, whisk the eggs and yolks. Pour the eggs into the flour mixture and slowly mix them together, working from the center of the bowl outward. Once you have a cohesive dough, turn it out of the bowl and knead it on a lightly floured work surface, adding more flour as necessary until the dough is silky and dry. Wrap the dough in plastic and let it rest for at least 30 minutes. Alternatively, you can put it in a vacuum bag, seal it, and let it rest for 10 minutes before rolling out your pasta. (This will leave you with a moister dough than resting in plastic wrap.)

Unwrap the dough and cut it in quarters. Keep 3 pieces of the dough wrapped loosely in plastic while you work with the first piece. Lightly flour a work surface and, using a rolling pin, begin to roll out the dough. This process takes time. Dust the surface of the dough lightly with flour and continue to roll from the middle to the edges, turning the dough a quarter turn and flipping it over every couple of rolls. Continue to roll the dough until it is ⅛ inch (3 millimeters) thick and roughly 10 × 12 inches. Dust the dough with flour and fold down the top third of the dough. Dust the dough with flour again, and fold the bottom edge of the dough up over the third of dough you just folded down. Dust the dough with flour and, using a sharp knife, cut it lengthwise into ribbons ¼ inch (6 millimeters) wide. Unfold each noodle, and dust with flour. Sprinkle a baking sheet with flour and loosely nest each batch of noodles on the pan in a single layer. Cover them with a kitchen towel and repeat with the remainder of the dough.

When all the dough is rolled, refrigerate the noodles until ready to use. If using within a few minutes, simply cover with a kitchen towel.

Alternatively, you can roll out the dough with a pasta maker following the manufacturer's instructions, using the cutter of your choice.

Bring a large pot of water to a boil. Generously salt the water, then add the noodles. Cook for 3 to 4 minutes.

Meanwhile, in a separate pot large enough to hold the noodles, melt the butter over medium heat. Drain the cooked noodles and put them in the pot with the butter. Coat the noodles evenly with the butter and season with salt and pepper to taste. Serve immediately.

DRIED PASTA

In this case we are talking about semolina pasta, common to countries around the world and a staple on supermarket shelves everywhere. As with any other ingredient, there is a wide range of quality, from the readily available Barilla and Ronzoni to artisan pastas, which are dried slowly to emphasize the flavor of the grain. Dried pastas may contain additional ingredients like eggs and various seasonings. Although pasta encompasses several varieties of noodle, there are noodles from other countries that are not classified as pasta. Asian noodles are created from a wide variety of flours, including rice and mung bean. Although the oldest pasta specimen was found in China, Asian noodle dishes bear little more than a passing resemblance to Italian pasta dishes. In Italy regulations require that any dried pasta, or *pasta secca,* must be made with 100 percent durum flour or durum semolina flour and water.

Dried pasta is an inexpensive, portable, and versatile food. It's no wonder that it gained popularity around the globe. There are shapes to suit any fancy, from couscous to rigatoni. Quality depends on several factors—the quality of the durum wheat, the purity of the water, and the temperature involved in drying the pasta. No pantry is complete without it, and we love to play with the many different shapes and sizes. From alphabet soup to noodle pudding, dried pasta can be found in sweet and savory dishes around the world.

Durum is the hardest variety of wheat. It has dense kernels with a high protein content and high gluten strength. Pasta dough made with durum wheat flour and water is very stiff, which is what gives dried pasta its unique resilient texture when cooked. The density of the flour helps ensure even cooking. The durum wheat kernels are ground through steel rollers, which separate out the bran and the germ and then crack the starchy endosperm into pieces. Semolina, a slightly coarser flour, is made from the middlings of durum wheat flour production. The finest particles in this category are designated as durum wheat flour and the coarsest pieces are used to make farina.

Water used for making pasta must be of drinking quality. Any impurities in the water will affect the taste of the dough. The purer the water, the better the finished pasta.

Pasta dough for commercially produced dried pasta is mechanically mixed for twenty to thirty minutes. Imagine trying to do that at home. The dough is rolled through a laminator, which flattens it into sheets, and then flattened further in a vacuum mixer. This process removes air bubbles and excess water from the dough. Dough to be pasteurized is then taken through a steamer where it is heated to 220°F (104°C). The finished dough is either cut with rotating blades or pushed through extruders to form the different shapes. Artisanal pastas employ bronze dies on their extruders. This results in pasta that is extruded more slowly, creating a rougher surface that allows sauce to cling to it so that each bite tastes that much better. Artisan pasta makers also emphasize slower drying times in the open air. Dried pasta dough has an optimum moisture level of 12 percent. Pasta that is dried too quickly breaks easily. Drying conditions are closely monitored because drying that occurs too slowly can result in microbacterial contamination. Care is taken to avoid browning at high temperatures and thus preserve the flavor of the flour. There are so few ingredients and techniques involved in making dried pasta that each one has a profound impact on the finished product.

Dried pasta comes in a wide range of shapes and each one has a recommended application. Generally speaking, the smaller shapes are meant for soup. Longer strand-style pastas like spaghettis and linguine are used with sauces. Thicker shapes like penne and gemelli are meant for casseroles. Larger shells and tubular pasta may be stuffed. And so on. In Italy these designations are even more precise, stipulating tagliatelle or fettuccine with Bolognese sauce and linguine with pesto or seafood-based sauces. Of course, most modern kitchens are not constrained by traditional applications; pasta salad, for example, is a nontraditional use of dried pasta that has taken deep roots.

Once you get your pasta home, all you have to do is cook it in ample amounts of boiling salted water, right? Not exactly. Let's consider what happens when we cook pasta. The starch in the flour has to hydrate in the water and then gelatinize from the heat. When you put dry noodles in hot water, the surface starch hydrates and becomes sticky. Some of it washes off into the boiling water and some of it stays on the surface of the pasta. This means that if you don't remember to stir the pasta when it starts to cook, these starches will adhere to one another and your noodles will clump together. This is not a happy thing. People think that if you have a large pot of boiling water, it will return to a boil rapidly, and there will be plenty of room for the noodles to move around to prevent sticking. However, you still need to stir the pasta in the beginning. Theoretically you will need to stir it less because the motion of the boiling water will move the pasta around, and it will cook more quickly and evenly without clumping or adhering to the pan than it will in smaller amounts of water. Unfortunately this is more theory than reality.

In February of 2009, Harold McGee published an article in the *New York Times* demonstrating that you can cook pasta in just enough water to cover it. We're sure that many home cooks have known this, without realizing it, for years. Aki has always cooked capellini pasta for herself in the smallest available pot, adapting the technique from years of cooking packaged ramen noodles. This initially earned her much ribbing from Alex, who, after a few good meals, became a convert. You don't need a large pot of boiling water. Admittedly, cooking pasta in a smaller amount of water requires a bit of extra effort because it tends to stick more easily. But it takes significantly less time to heat the water, and paying attention to your cooking is never a bad thing. Cooking pasta in less water is more efficient and the results are comparable. The only trick is making sure there is enough water for the pasta to fully hydrate.

Harold's experiments reignited our interest. We knew about hydrating starch from our work with potatoes and rice (see page 120). It made sense to apply the idea to pasta. Many large restaurants parcook their dried pasta before service. They take it to a very al dente texture, shock it, and coat it with neutral oil. Then they can finish dishes quickly in the heat of service. We've never been enamored of this method because things go wrong. The pasta easily gets overcooked. If there isn't enough oil it can stick together or continue to absorb any available moisture and become swollen and flabby in the storage container. Finally, the pasta itself adds unnecessary oil to the cooking water or to the sauce it is finished in. Was there another way to prep the pasta for efficiency?

The answer was a cold-water soak. This technique almost completely separates the hydration and cooking processes. We know that starch needs water to cook properly. A cold-water soak, at a 4:1 ratio of water to pasta, allows the starch to slowly absorb the water that it needs to gelatinize. The time spent soaking depends on the size of the pasta. We soak linguine for an hour and a half, fettuccine for two hours, and rigatoni for four hours. We soak it in a baking pan or zip-top bag. The pasta hydrates to a texture similar to just before al dente, becoming pliable while retaining a pale, opaque color. Once the pasta is done soaking, we drain off the water and store it in the fridge in a sealed zip-top bag. When we do this the surface starch is rinsed off the pasta, which minimizes sticking during the cooking process. Refrigerated, the soaked pasta will easily keep for up to three days.

If fully hydrated, the pasta begins to cook as soon as it comes in contact with boiling water or hot pasta sauce. It's an amazing visual transformation. You can actually see the hydrated pasta change color as it finishes cooking. You'll have a meal on the table five minutes after the pasta is heated, and there's only one pan to clean up. It's a beautiful and delicious process.

Taking ideas one step further is always our motto. We don't always plan far enough ahead to soak our pasta in advance. Since the hydration process washes off the surface starches, we wondered what would happen if we gave the pasta a brief soak in cold water. Say for the amount of time it takes for a small pot of water to come to a boil. We put our dried pasta in a bowl of cold water while we heated the cooking water. Once the water came to a boil, we rinsed off the pasta and dropped it into the pot. The cold water washed off the surface starch and the individual pieces didn't stick to each other or to the pan, even though we cooked the pasta in a minimal amount of hot water. It's these small steps that make a big difference, allowing us to cook smarter and more efficiently.

Once we figured out the best ways to cook our pasta, the next question was how to add flavor to the noodles before saucing them. Since we were cold soaking the pasta in water, it seemed logical to then substitute other seasoned liquids. The caveat here is that they have to be water based for the pasta to properly hydrate. Thin tomato sauce or juice was a good starting point and worked nicely. Soaking linguine in clam broth led to a transcendent linguine with clam sauce. A dried mushroom broth spiked with soy gave fettuccine a major flavor punch. The darker color of these soaked noodles led us to the next evolution.

Roasted pasta was fashionable in restaurants about ten years ago and has since fallen back into obscurity. We always enjoyed the flavor produced by this technique and decided to see if it would affect the hydration process. We roasted a box of dried linguine in a 350°F (175°C) oven for twenty minutes to give the noodles a rich, toasty flavor. Then we hydrated the pasta for two hours because of the roasting time and finished it in a simple butter emulsion. The difference was fantastic. The pasta had a deeper flavor and we immediately thought of several uses for it, the first one being linguine with clam sauce.

The roasted pasta was so good that we couldn't resist putting some dried pasta in the smoker. We cold smoked the dried pasta for two hours. We then soaked the pasta in milk to make macaroni and cheese. In this case we reserved the milk with the surface starch in it to help thicken and emulsify the sauce. These experiments were successful in creating something deliciously different that was fun to eat.

As with many of our ideas, we wanted to road test these techniques.

We asked friends, both in and out of the restaurant business, to try them, and they were all pleased with their results. It takes a bit of planning, although if you eat pasta on a regular basis, as we do, keeping some hydrated pasta in the refrigerator is a no-brainer.

BBQ RIGATONI

SERVES 4 AS AN ENTRÉE

We love the flavor of barbecue sauce. Here we've added the sauce to the pasta instead of the other way around. The pasta is simply tossed with butter, ready to be paired with sautéed jumbo shrimp, breaded pork chops, or sausage and peppers. These rigatoni could also be stuffed with raw shrimp sausage and then gently simmered in a blend of barbecue sauce, butter, and white wine to cook the pasta and the shrimp.

> 6½ cups/1,462.5 grams **water**
>
> One 17.6-ounce/500-gram jar **barbecue sauce**
>
> 1 pound/453 grams **dried rigatoni**
>
> 6 tablespoons/84 grams **unsalted butter**

Stir together the water and the barbecue sauce. Submerge the rigatoni in the barbecue water and refrigerate for 4 hours. Drain the pasta from the liquid, reserving the barbecue water, and store the hydrated rigatoni in a zip-top bag in the refrigerator.

In a large pot, combine the reserved barbecue water and enough clean water to equal roughly 4 quarts (4 liters). Bring to a boil over high heat, then add the soaked rigatoni. It will cook in less than 3 minutes. Taste for texture. When cooked to your satisfaction, drain the pasta and toss with the butter. Serve immediately.

ROASTED CACIO PEPE

Cacio pepe *literally translates as "cheese and pepper." It is a classic
Italian pasta dish that centers on the flavors of grated cheese and
freshly ground black pepper. The simplest versions we have seen are
made with abundant cheese and pepper, melted and moistened only
with the cooking water. More indulgent recipes add olive oil or butter
as we do below. Most recipes call for Pecorino Romano, a hard sheep's-
milk cheese, although Parmigiano Romano also crops up here and
there. In our version the roasted pasta adds a deeper, more savory flavor
to the finished dish. It is simple to make but it's important to get the
balance right so that your pasta is silky and flavorful. It's the perfect
meal for when the pantry is almost bare but the body needs something
delicious to satisfy it.*

> 1 pound/453 grams **dried bucatini**
>
> 8¾ cups/1,968.75 grams **water**
>
> 2 tablespoons/28 grams **extra virgin olive oil**
>
> 3½ ounces/100 grams fresh **pecorino**, grated
>
> **Fine sea salt**
>
> **Freshly ground black pepper**
>
> 3½ ounces/100 grams **Pecorino Toscano**, grated

Preheat the oven to 350°F (175°C).

Arrange the bucatini on a baking sheet in an even layer two bucatini deep. Toast in the oven for 10 minutes, until the noodles are a
deep golden brown. Remove the bucatini from the oven and let cool.
When the pasta has cooled completely, place it in a large zip-top bag
and add the water. Close the bag, pushing out as much air as possible,
and put it in the refrigerator. Let the bucatini hydrate for 2½ hours.
(Roasted pasta takes longer to hydrate than normal dried pasta.)

Remove the bag from the refrigerator and pour out the water. Return the pasta to the bag and refrigerate it until needed. (You can store the pasta for up to 2 days.)

Bring a pot of water to a boil and add 2 teaspoons salt per quart of water. Add the hydrated pasta to the water and cook for 1 minute. Drain the pasta, reserving some of the cooking liquid, and return it to the pot. Add the olive oil and stir in the fresh pecorino. Crack some pepper into the pasta and stir. A quick sauce will form. Add half of the Pecorino Toscano and stir to combine. Scoop the pasta into a serving bowl and top with the remaining Pecorino Toscano and some more pepper.

GNOCCHI AND RISOTTO

We do love our starch. Rice and potatoes are the quintessential side dishes that occasionally make it to the center of the plate. For their moments in the spotlight they often appear as either gnocchi or risotto. These are dishes that can be a little intimidating because the starch that makes them creamy and wonderful can easily morph into a sticky, gluey mess. As chefs we are always looking for ways to "idiot proof" our techniques, and it's easy to understand why risotto and gnocchi were at the top of our list of recipes looking for improvement.

First, a little technical background. When we cook rice or potatoes in hot water, the starch granules soak up the water and swell to the point of bursting, or gelatinize. The more water is absorbed, the lower the gelatinization temperature. If the starch does not cook long enough to absorb enough water, it will not completely gelatinize.

Think of a half-cooked potato. It is usually a bit tender and sticky on the outside and rock hard on the inside. While some of the starch on the outer layer may be partially gelatinized, the spud will not be completely soft until it absorbs enough water to hydrate all of the starch contained in its cells. Once the starch in the potato has gelatinized, it forms a gel that is contained inside the cells. If the cells are ruptured, say when you beat them for mashed potatoes, the gel leaks out, forming a sticky mass that is unpleasant to eat and to clean off your dishes. Take our word for it.

In his seminal book *The Man Who Ate Everything*, Jeffrey Steingarten details the process of isolating potato starch for mashing potatoes. He states that at 140°F (60°C), the starch granules begin to absorb water. By the time it reaches 160°F (71°C), the starch has absorbed enough liquid to swell many times its original size, although the cell walls are still too strong for mashing. At 180°F (82°C) the cells have weakened enough to separate easily but have not yet broken— this is the temperature he suggests for cooking mashed potatoes. Steingarten also says that if you precook the potatoes at 160°F (71°C) and then chill them, you will hydrate the starch and then trigger a process known as retrogradation, which strengthens the cell walls of the starch. Here we need a brief primer on starch.

All starches are polysaccharides synthesized by plants through photosynthesis. This means that they form chains of glucose. There are two types of glucose in starch molecules, amylose and amylopectin. Amylose is a straight chain while amylopectin has a branched structure. As a basic rule of thumb, amylopectin acts as a thickener, while amylose forms gels. Since all starches contain both, their differences depend on the ratio of amylose to amylopectin and the size and shape of the molecules.

Generally speaking, amylopectin makes up 75 to 80 percent of starch by weight, and amylose makes up the remainder. The exact ratio depends on the source of the starch. Amylopectin is not soluble and because it is a thickener, starches higher in amylopectin form softer gels that tend to be translucent and stringy in texture. Roots and tubers are higher in amylopectin than cereals and grains. Waxy corn and rice contain mostly amylopectin. Short-grain rice, like the types used for risotto and sushi, contains almost no amylose; the high concentration of amylopectin is responsible for the characteristic sticky texture.

Observation of starch molecules under a light microscope illustrates that amylopectin looks very similar to the growth rings inside a tree trunk. Following that imagery, picture a starch granule as a series of concentric circles drawn closely together. The branched amylopectin forms a lattice that holds the granule together in the shape of the rings, while the amylose lives in the area between the circles. Hydrogen is the glue that holds the two together. Amylose is soluble, so it swells and breaks out of the starch structure more easily than amylopectin. Its linear shape makes it easy for the amylose to then wrap itself around fats and aromas. For example, potato starch has very long amylose molecules. Its soluble nature enables it to thicken quickly and efficiently in soups and sauces. On the downside, it tends to be stringy and grainy when first activated, but continued cooking easily breaks down the starch into a smoother and more refined texture.

Starch granules are not considered water soluble because the molecules are too large to form true solutions. Starch must be heated in order to effectively absorb water. When a starch granule is heated to its gelation range—133°F–167°F (56°C–75°C) depending on the type of starch—the bonds between the molecules are loosened. This allows hydrogen bonds to form between the water and the starch, allowing the starch to absorb copious amounts of water and gelatinize. The granule continues to absorb water until it ruptures, allowing the amylose to leak out and absorb any available water. This happens at a lower temperature for root and tuber starches than for grain starches. You can actually observe the process happening because the mixture becomes more translucent. As the freed amylose disperses in the hot water, it becomes viscous and eventually forms a gel. Imagine the white cornstarch slurry that is added to a pot of strawberries being cooked for a pie filling. The berries and starch form an opaque pink mixture that gradually thickens and becomes shiny and translucent as the starch cooks in the juice.

Once starch has reached its maximum thickening point, it begins to break down. Imagine a long-cooked roux. It starts out as a sandy liquid that eventually comes together as a cohesive paste. As you cook it, the paste slowly thickens; then after continued cooking it begins to break back down into a thinner consistency, as seen in a dark roux. The process of stirring and simmering causes the starch granules and their components to fragment and break down into smaller pieces. This allows the starch to almost disappear into its cooking medium.

As the temperature decreases after gelatinization, the starch undergoes retrogradation, which makes it harder for the starch to break out of the cells. Once the starch cools to below 100°F (38°C), a gel can form. The amylose forms hydrogen bonds that hold everything in place and the mixture begins to congeal into a soft, yet solid mass. Imagine hot and sour soup from a Chinese restaurant. It has a fluid, viscous texture when hot that transforms into something resembling brown mayonnaise as it cools down. Stirring during the setting process will break the bonds and weaken the gel. The amylose bonds will continue to re-form for several hours and set into a crystalline structure that is actually stronger than the original network within the starch granules. At this point the starch has formed a stable gel, although over time the hydrogen bonds continue to tighten. The gel will eventually begin to exhibit syneresis as the water is slowly squeezed out of the structure.

This means that after retrogradation, the cell walls inside the potato starch have been reinforced and are much less likely to burst and release amylose. Without amylose to thicken the available liquids, there is no danger of gummy mashed potatoes. The potatoes can be cooked a second time, put through a ricer or mashed while they are still hot, and thickened fearlessly with hot milk and butter to creamy perfection. It's one small step that makes a huge difference in the finished product.

Let's go back to Jeffrey Steingarten's mashed potatoes. Steingarten stated that parcooking sliced potatoes at 160°F (71°C) for twenty to thirty minutes, cooling them, finishing the cooking process by steaming or boiling, and then mashing the potatoes produced the best results. We tried his method and have to agree that it works beautifully. After working with his technique for a while we decided to start parcooking whole potatoes instead of sliced ones to improve the flavor of the cooked tubers. Some research turned up the information that the gelatinization range for potatoes is actually 136°F–150°F (58°C–66°C). This made us wonder why we would parcook them at a temperature above the gelatinization range, which risks rupturing the starch cells. So we turned down the heat to see what would happen, and we were very happy with the results.

Potatoes need to be parcooked long enough to gelatinize all of the starch inside them. This means that cooking times vary depending on the size of the potato, ranging from half an hour for small new potatoes to up to two hours for large russets. Then when the potatoes are completely cool and the starch cells have been strengthened by the crystallization of the amylose, we finish cooking them at temperatures above 185°F (85°C) to break down the pectin. The resulting potatoes will not become gummy because the starch will no longer swell until it ruptures. We were very pleased with the results of these two adjustments and wholeheartedly embraced a technique that made perfectly cooked potatoes almost bulletproof.

Now we have the ability to make flawlessly cooked potatoes that really taste of what they are instead of being just a vehicle for butter and salt. We discovered that we could take the parcooked potatoes, cook them a second time, rice them, and cool them down again. This enabled us to finish potato puree to order. We realized that we could use the cooked potatoes for other applications. They made beautiful potato gnocchi. Potato pancakes were light and crisp. French fries fried after parcooking were never hollow. Smoking cut potatoes for home fries after parcooking was a revelation. The parcooked potatoes do not oxidize as readily as raw potatoes, finally making cold smoking a viable technique. A secondary benefit is that, because the starch has been stabilized, the potatoes do not stick to the skillet, resulting in beautiful, crispy home fries.

As always, the wheels kept turning in our brains, and Alex decided to see what would happen if he parcooked rice for risotto using our immersion circulator. We took Carnaroli rice and wrapped it loosely in cheesecloth so that water could circulate through the grains but the rice was still contained. We set the immersion circulator to 150°F (65°C) and parcooked the rice for thirty minutes. Then we cooled it in cold running water, allowing the surface starch to wash away. We patted the grains dry for storage. The dried rice will keep in the refrigerator for up to three days. The parcooked rice can be added to boiling seasoned stock; bring the stock back to a rolling boil and the rice will be fully cooked in seven minutes. As it turns out, the gelatinization range for rice is 130°F–175°F (55°C–79°C). Short-grain rice tends to fall in the lower end of that spectrum. So a little extrapolation and sheer dumb luck came together to create a pretty nifty new technique.

The parcooked rice makes beautiful risottos. It also works for rice puddings. It frees the cook from the tyranny of having to stir constantly and it allows us to finish a dish to order in a reasonable amount of time. An added bonus is that risotto made using the parcooked rice has a much longer service window. It does not become gluey and overcooked if it has to sit for an extra ten minutes while the guests are corralled and brought to the table.

RANCH-FLAVORED POTATO GNOCCHI

SERVES 4 AS AN ENTRÉE OR 8 AS A SIDE DISH

One summer we worked as private chefs on a ranch in Montana. One of our jobs was to oversee the chefs in the employee kitchen. We watched as they lamented the crew's love of ranch dressing, culminating one evening when a guy poured it on his lasagna. We were fascinated by how much people loved the flavor of ranch and slowly began to weave it into our repertoire just for fun. These gnocchi were one of our first experiments and are still one of the best.

7 medium **russet potatoes** of approximately equal size

Kosher salt

2 tablespoons/26 grams/½ lightly beaten **egg**

3 tablespoons/40 grams **Ranch Spice Blend** (recipe follows), or finely ground **store-bought ranch seasoning**

⅔ cup/100 grams **all-purpose flour**, plus extra for dusting

Preheat a circulating water bath or a large pot of water set over medium heat to 152.5°F (67°C).

Place the potatoes in the water and lower the heat to 149°F (65°C). Cook the potatoes for 2 hours in the water bath. Transfer the potatoes to an ice bath and cool completely. This cooking and cooling process must be followed in order to hydrate, gelatinize, and isolate the starch in the potato.

Preheat the oven to 350°F (175°C).

Prick the potatoes with a knife to create vent holes. Line a baking sheet with a layer of kosher salt approximately ½ inch (1.25 centimeters) thick. Place the potatoes on the salt and bake until they are cooked through, about 1 hour. Cut the potatoes lengthwise and open them up to release the steam. Brush off any salt that sticks to the skin. Press the potato flesh through a tamis or large strainer. The skins will not pass through the mesh sieve. Discard the potato skins and put 3 cups (500 grams) of potato in a bowl.

Sprinkle the egg over the potato mixture. Fold the potatoes on top of the egg until the egg is incorporated.

In a small bowl, whisk together the ranch seasoning and the flour. Dust this mixture over the potatoes. Fold and knead the dough so that the flour-ranch mixture evenly coats and combines with the potatoes. If the dough is still wet and tacky, add more flour. The finished dough should be soft, silky, and dry to the touch. Shape the dough into a ball, cover it with a dry cloth, and let it rest for 20 minutes.

Fill a medium pot with water, salt it generously, and bring to a boil over medium heat.

Uncover the dough and cut it into five sections. Roll each section into a log ½ inch (1.25 centimeters) thick. Cut each log into ¾-inch (2-centimeter) sections and then roll these sections across a butter board to add ridging. Alternatively, you can mark each one with the back of a fork.

Once all the gnocchi are formed, cook them in small batches in the boiling water. The gnocchi will sink to the bottom at first and then begin to float. As they float, lift one out to test it. When the gnocchi feel firm and set, 3 to 5 minutes, they are cooked. Serve immediately with the sauce of your choice or, to serve later, transfer the gnocchi to an ice bath and let cool completely. Remove them from the ice bath, pat dry, and place in a container large enough to hold them in one even layer. Dress the gnocchi lightly with olive oil so they do not stick. They will keep in an airtight container in the refrigerator for up to 2 days.

RANCH SPICE BLEND

While you can certainly buy ranch spice blend in the super-market, we prefer to make our own. It just tastes fresher and we can fine-tune the seasoning exactly the way we like it.

⅓ cup/40 grams **buttermilk powder**

4 teaspoons/9 grams **dried minced onion**

4 teaspoons/9 grams **garlic powder**

2 teaspoons/12 grams **fine sea salt**

2 teaspoons/12 grams **freshly ground black pepper**

½ teaspoon/2 grams **dried lemon peel granules**

¼ teaspoon/0.75 gram **smoked paprika**

¼ teaspoon/0.5 gram **cayenne pepper**

¼ teaspoon/0.5 gram **dried parsley**

Put the buttermilk powder in a small bowl. Combine the onion, garlic powder, salt, black pepper, lemon peel, paprika, cayenne, and parsley in a spice grinder or blender and grind to a fine powder. Add the spices to the butter-milk powder and whisk to combine. The spice blend can be stored in an airtight container for up to a month.

SEVEN-MINUTE RISOTTO

SERVES 4 AS AN ENTRÉE OR 8 AS A SIDE DISH

This is an excellent technique for a dinner party or any occasion when you want to spend time with your guests instead of standing over the stove. The risotto will be firm and toothsome, but you can treat this as traditional risotto and finish it with a dollop of extra virgin olive oil or butter and some freshly grated cheese for added creaminess. It's a nice change of pace served with sautéed chicken with a quick pan sauce of white wine and fresh herbs, crispy skate in brown butter with capers, or a garlicky stir-fry of seasonal vegetables.

> 17½ ounces/500 grams **Carnaroli rice**
> Seasoned **vegetable** or **chicken stock** (2½ to 3 parts stock:1 part parcooked rice)
> **Extra virgin olive oil** or **unsalted butter**
> Freshly grated **Parmigiano** or **Piave Vecchio cheese**

Preheat a circulating water bath or a large pot of water set over medium heat to 152.5°F (67°C).

To parcook the rice, loosely wrap it in cheesecloth, leaving room for the rice to expand, and tie the package with butcher's twine so the rice is securely contained. Just make sure there are no holes in the package for the rice to escape. Put the rice in the water and turn the heat down to 149°F (65°C). Cook the rice for 30 minutes.

Set up an ice bath. Put a large strainer in the ice bath and empty the parcooked rice into it. Stir the rice to expedite cooling. Once the rice is completely cool, remove the strainer and run cold water through the rice to rinse off any remaining surface starch. Let the rice drain, then pour it out onto paper towels and pat dry. Place in a zip-top bag and store in the refrigerator for up to 3 days.

To cook the risotto, use a ratio of 2½ parts seasoned stock to 1 part rice. If you want softer rice, use a 3:1 ratio. Put the stock in a saucepan set over medium-high heat. Bring to a boil, add the rice, and cook for 7 minutes. For softer rice, increase the cooking time to 10 minutes. Remove the pan from heat, add a generous splash of olive oil or a few tablespoons of butter, and stir to combine. Add cheese as desired and stir it into the rice. Serve the risotto, garnishing each serving with another sprinkle of cheese.

APPLE AND CHEDDAR RISOTTO

SERVES 4 AS AN ENTRÉE OR 8 AS A SIDE DISH

This is comfort food at its finest. It blends Italian risotto with the idea of American macaroni and cheese to create a dish that is more than the sum of its parts. And because we love the crisp juicy flavor of apples with our Cheddar cheese, we decided to take things a little further and use cider to deepen the flavors of our risotto. That hint of tartness balances out the richness of the dish. If you happen to have them around, fresh chives are a wonderful finishing garnish.

9¾ cups/2,437.5 grams **apple cider**

2 medium **onions**, sliced

1 **head garlic**, split in half crosswise

1 pound/460 grams **sharp Cheddar cheese**, cut into chunks

18 ounces/510 grams **bacon**, diced

2 medium **onions**, diced

¾ teaspoon/4.5 grams **fine sea salt**

17½ ounces/500 grams **Carnaroli rice**, parcooked (see page 129)

10 ounces/287.5 grams **sharp Cheddar cheese**, grated

3 **jalapeños**, seeds removed, diced

Pour the cider into a pressure cooker. Wrap the sliced onions, garlic, and Cheddar in cheesecloth and tie it with butcher's twine. Add to the pressure cooker and cook for 5 minutes on high pressure. Let the pressure dissipate naturally. Open the pressure cooker, discard the cheesecloth package, and strain the liquid into a container to cool. Cheddar fat will rise to the top and should be skimmed off. (The fat has a wonderful flavor and can be kept, refrigerated, to add flavor to baked goods, sauces, or soups.) Reserve the stock to make the risotto. This makes a bit more stock than is needed for the recipe; the extra stock may be used to reheat leftover risotto, cook other vegetables, enrich a soup, or braise meat.

Put the bacon in a large, cold sauté pan and set over medium-low heat. Cook the bacon slowly, rendering the fat, until the bacon is browned but still slightly chewy. Strain the bacon and the fat through a mesh strainer set over a bowl. Reserve the fat. Transfer the bacon to paper towels, let drain, and pat dry. Put the bacon in a lidded container and store in the refrigerator.

Set a clean sauté pan over medium heat. When the pan is hot, pour in most of the drained bacon fat; discard the sediment. Add the diced onions and the salt. Slowly cook until soft and translucent. You do not want the onions to take on any color, so adjust the heat as necessary. Transfer the onions and fat to a heatproof container and store in the refrigerator until you are ready to finish the risotto.

To make the risotto, put 7 cups (1,600 grams) of the apple-Cheddar stock in a large pot and bring it to a simmer.

In a separate large pan over medium heat, cook the onions and bacon fat until they just begin to sizzle, about 1 minute. Increase the heat to medium-high and add the rice. Stir the rice to coat it evenly with the fat. Increase the heat to high. Pour all of the hot stock into the pan, stirring the rice so it does not stick. Bring to a boil. Adjust the heat so the rice boils gently but does not scorch and stick to the bottom of the pan. Cook for 6 minutes.

Add the grated Cheddar, jalapeños, and reserved bacon pieces. Stir for 1 minute, then turn off the heat. The rice will be cooked and can be served immediately, although it benefits from a short (1 minute) rest in the pan. If you prefer softer rice, simply cook it for an extra minute or two.

NOTE: *If for some reason you need to delay the serving of this risotto, do not worry. Heat up a bit more stock and stir it into the finished risotto when the time is right. The rice will not become gummy or gluey, even after resting and reheating.*

EGGS

PERFECT EGGS

Eggs are a wonderful source of complete protein. They contain all of the essential amino acids the human body needs, a combination of fats, and thirteen vitamins and minerals. One large egg contains about 75 calories. Beyond their nutritive boost, eggs are one of the most useful ingredients in your refrigerator. Delicious on their own, eggs also provide structure in baked goods, facilitate the formation of foam, and provide the stability in custards.

The largest portion of an egg is the white. It is often referred to as the albumen, which is the term for a simple water-soluble protein. Egg whites are composed primarily of water and albumen, encompassing approximately forty different proteins. When you crack open an egg it is immediately obvious that the white has two parts, thick and thin. The thick albumen surrounds the yolk and protects it. The innermost thick layer actually attaches to the yolk via a twisted cord known as the chalaza. This cord loses strength as the egg ages. The inner white is visibly thicker than the outer albumen, often illustrated in fried eggs, where the high center white surrounding the yolk slowly thins and spreads out along the edges. The thick albumen is an excellent source of protein and riboflavin.

Eggshells are porous, containing upwards of 17,000 pores over their surface area. They are a semipermeable membrane made up mainly of calcium chloride. This porosity is why eggs left uncovered in the refrigerator can pick up off-scents from their surroundings. There is also an air pocket in each egg. There are two thin protein membranes, which protect against bacterial invasions, between the shell and the white. After an egg is laid the air pocket appears between these membranes. As the egg ages, moisture evaporates through the eggshell, the egg inside shrinks, and the air pocket grows progressively larger. As the egg continues to lose carbon dioxide through the shell, its pH slowly increases from 7.9 to as high as 9.3. This can affect the creation of egg foams because the whites whip better at a lower pH, which is why cream of tartar and lemon juice are often added when whipping egg whites.

Now that we understand what we're eating, we can concentrate on the best ways to cook our eggs: scrambled or fried, over easy or sunny-side up. At fancier places the menu expands to include poached eggs and their classic companions, while our favorite diner serves up bacon and cheese omelets with their own special flair. Our daughter is a huge fan of eggs, so we've been working through our repertoire to keep things interesting at the table. Although almost everyone has cooked an egg, how often do we think about the right way to achieve the best results?

When cooking eggs it's important to understand that the whites and yolks coagulate at different temperatures. Egg whites coagulate at temperatures ranging from 140°F to 150°F (60°C–65.5°C). At the lower end of the spectrum the whites achieve a jellylike mass. They do not form opaque solids until they reach the higher end of the temperature range. Egg yolks coagulate at temperatures ranging from 149°F to 158°F (65°C–70°C). At 149°F (65°C), the yolks just begin to thicken. They do not hold their shape until 158°F (70°C), the coagulation temperature for whole eggs. To understand what is happening, think of the egg proteins as small coils. As heat is applied, the protein coils are denatured, and they unfold into shapes that resemble wavy lines. These lines bind together to form a network resembling a fishing net. At their optimal levels these structures hold everything in a stable network. As the proteins continue to coagulate with further cooking, the strands of protein tighten up and shrink in upon themselves. Picture the net tightening around its contents. This gradually forces all of the liquid back out of the structure, resulting in curdling, or syneresis. The speed of coagulation increases as temperatures increase.

The results of overcooking eggs are most visible in the yolks. Imagine the differences between a runny poached egg; a creamy, just-set over-easy yolk; and a greenish, chalky, hard-boiled yolk. These last effects are caused by a reaction between the sulfur in the white and the iron in the yolk. As the pH of the egg increases with age, it facilitates this reaction between the white and the yolk. The change that occurs in egg whites is much more subtle. Just-cooked whites have a soft, tender texture that becomes firmer and more rubbery as the proteins continue to coagulate. Imagine the crunchy, chewy edges of a fried egg versus the tender whites of a soft-boiled one. Understanding how the textures change as the parts of an egg are cooked will help you troubleshoot issues that may come up in your egg cookery down the line.

Making perfect eggs is a balancing act. As with all cooking, it's important to pay attention to the details. On the other hand, once you master your perfect egg, you always have a great meal in your back pocket.

NOTE: *For all of the following recipes, we specify large eggs (58 to 62 grams per egg), and any variation in size will affect your results.*

SOFT SCRAMBLED EGGS

SERVES 2; AERATED, SERVES 4

By far the quickest and easiest egg dish to put on the table is scrambled eggs, which are warm, comforting, and softly luxurious. Scrambled eggs can resemble soft curds or a dry sponge depending on how they are treated. They are a good example of why cooking with gentle heat can be a good thing. Higher heat leads to a higher coagulation temperature, but it also increases the rate at which the eggs scramble. By lowering the heat, we slow down the cooking process, thereby upping the possibility of perfectly cooked results. Here we've taken the process one step further by using a hot water bath to cook the eggs. By controlling the temperature of the cooking medium, we can guarantee that the eggs will not overcook. While the eggs are cooking, your hands are free to prepare the rest of breakfast so that everything is ready at the same time.

6 large **eggs**

¼ cup plus 2 teaspoons/75 grams **whole milk**

¾ teaspoon/4.5 grams **fine sea salt**

3½ tablespoons/50 grams **unsalted butter**

Heat a circulating water bath or a pot of water set over medium heat to 162.5°F (72.5°C).

Whisk the eggs together with the milk and salt. Cut the butter into small chunks and stir into the eggs. Pour the egg mixture into a vacuum or zip-top bag and seal. Place the sealed eggs in the water bath and cook for 25 minutes. Remove the bag from the bath and shake the contents. This will bring the butter into the eggs and create the small scrambled curds familiar in scrambled eggs. Serve immediately.

For a more decadent preparation, pour the contents of the bag into a whipped cream canister and aerate with one nitrous charge. Shake the contents thoroughly and then extrude the eggs.

HARD-BOILED EGGS

MAKES 1 DOZEN EGGS

We decided to try cooking hard-boiled eggs at 158°F (70°C), hypothesizing that cooking them at slightly above their coagulation temperature would give us the best results. This did not work as we had planned because by the time the whites were fully set to our satisfaction, the yolks were overdone. We then cooked eggs at 167°F (75°C) and pulled them from the water at fifteen-minute intervals. At fifteen minutes the whites were just set, opaque yet without enough structure to hold them together. The yolk held together and was very pliable, resembling softened Play-Doh in texture. At thirty minutes the whites were firm enough to be peeled but still a bit soft for our taste.

In cooking eggs at this temperature we found that even eggs cooked for as little as thirty minutes produced some hard-boiled-egg characteristics. Knowing this, we can produce a range of hard-boiled eggs with yolks at varying degrees of firmness, depending on the desired results.

12 large **eggs**

Heat a circulating water bath or a pot of water set over medium heat to 167°F (75°C).

Lower the eggs into the water and cook for 1 hour. Transfer the eggs to an ice water bath to cool. When the eggs are ice cold, gently crack the shells and peel the eggs.

SOFT-BOILED EGGS

MAKES 8 EGGS

A beautiful soft-boiled egg, warm and served from its shell, perhaps with crisp fingers of buttered toast, is enough to make the heavens sing. We have been lucky enough to experience different versions of this egg at Per Se, Elements in Princeton, and Momofuku Ko. Each preparation and presentation inspired us and raised the question of how to consistently prepare and serve this elusive culinary delight.

Alex began by weighing our eggs to see if all large eggs were the same size. They were close, with about a two-gram differential in our sample. We bought a pot of water to a boil and added the eggs. We cooked the eggs for five minutes and fifteen seconds in gently boiling water and then placed them in an ice bath. The eggs were cooked the way we wanted them and were relatively easy to peel. It may seem finicky to specify a cooking time in minutes and seconds but the devil is in the details. Deciding which details are important and paying attention to them is essential to consistent cookery.

8 large **eggs**

Fine sea salt and **freshly ground black pepper**

Bring a large pot of water to a boil. Set a timer for 5 minutes and 15 seconds, gently lower the eggs into the pot, start the timer, and turn the heat down so that the water boils gently.

While the eggs cook, prepare an ice bath. When the timer rings, transfer the eggs to the ice bath. Let them cool completely, then gently crack the shells and carefully peel the eggs. This is a delicate process and takes practice since the egg is still soft on the inside. The peeled eggs can be kept in the refrigerator for up to 2 days.

To serve, bring a pot of water to 140°F (60°C). Place the eggs in the water for 10 minutes to just heat them through. Transfer the eggs to egg cups or small bowls and season with salt and pepper before serving.

THIRTEEN-MINUTE ONSEN EGGS

MAKES 8 EGGS

Onsen *means "hot springs" in Japanese, and the original onsen eggs were cooked in natural hot springs and served for breakfast. They are famed for their soft, silky texture. We've been chasing the perfect onsen egg for years. By increasing the temperature of the cooking water from the modern standard of 147°F (63.8°C) to a more traditional 167°F (75°C), we shortened the cooking time and produced both whites and yolks with the textures we prefer. The results are tender, just-cooked whites paired with a warm, liquid yolks. This version is a great stand-in for the poached eggs in eggs Benedict because the eggs can be cooked ahead of time and then warmed when you are ready to serve.*

8 large **eggs**

Heat a circulating water bath or a pot of water set over medium heat to 167°F (75°C). Lower the eggs into the water and cook for 13 minutes.

While the eggs cook, prepare an ice bath. Transfer the cooked eggs to the ice bath to cool. The eggs can be stored in their shells in the refrigerator for up to 2 days.

To serve, place the eggs in either a circulating water bath or a pot of water heated to 140°F (60°C) for 10 minutes to just heat them through. Remove the eggs and crack them into a shallow bowl. The thin white will still fall free from the egg. Use a slotted spoon to pick up the egg, pat it on a paper towel to remove any loose egg white, and place in a dish to serve.

EGG FOAMS

One of the best parts of walking into a diner is the dessert case right by the front door. There are always tall layer cakes and homemade pies piled high with golden-tipped meringue. That gorgeous meringue is a classic example of an egg white foam. Other egg-based foams include marshmallows, sponge cakes, and soufflés. They are highlighted by the light spongy textures unique to these particular creations. Egg foams are relatively simple to create; in a nutshell, you are beating air into a protein structure. Upon closer inspection, we realize there's a lot more going on here than meets the eye.

Foams are a mass of bubbles of air or gas in a matrix of liquid film. They are a two-stage system, generally beginning as a liquid and transforming into a semisolid as gas is introduced in the form of bubbles. There are dry foams such as meringues and stabilized foams such as sponge cakes and marshmallows. Fundamentally, egg foams, whether made of whites, yolks, or whole eggs, are whipped or shaken to form a stable system of tiny air bubbles. Eggs have the benefit of providing elasticity so that when these foams are placed in the oven, they can expand before the proteins coagulate and set the structure. Popovers are a great example of what the combination of a foam system boosted by steam leavening can accomplish. In stabilized foams, this system is given extra support by the addition of ingredients that strengthen the structure of the foam. For example, many marshmallows contain gelatin or xanthan gum to provide stability in the finished confection.

As with our other egg-cooking techniques, foams are created by denaturing, or breaking down, the proteins, mostly through the whipping process. As air is introduced to the eggs, it forms bubbles. These bubbles are coated with a protein film or membrane. The smaller the bubbles, the more stable the foam. As you continue to whip the eggs, more bubbles are introduced and they become increasingly smaller, creating a more solid foam. Imagine stirring egg whites with a fork.

At first you simply create large air bubbles on the surface of the eggs. Switch to a whisk and, as more air bubbles are introduced, the whites become opaque and start to stiffen. Continue whisking and you will achieve soft peaks, where the foam will loosely hold its shape. Beat them for a bit longer and you'll reach stiff peaks, where the meringue holds sharp edges and precise forms. Finally, you'll cross the line, overworking the whites, and they will begin to curdle and lose their elasticity.

Sugar is often added to egg foams. It helps by slowing down the process of unwinding the proteins. A minimum of 1½ tablespoons (18.75 grams) of sugar is needed to stabilize one large white, 2 tablespoons (25 grams) are considered optimal, and 4 tablespoons (50 grams) are the maximum that can be absorbed. Once sugar has been added to the foam, it will lead to a longer whipping time. It's important to add sugar slowly and make sure that it dissolves completely into the egg white so that it doesn't weigh down the foam structure. For this reason superfine sugar works best. It should be added to the whites at the soft peak stage. It will stabilize the meringue and give it a glossy appearance. Sugar has a hygroscopic effect, meaning it will hold on to water, which helps stabilize the foam and add elasticity.

A small amount of acid, usually in the form of cream of tartar or lemon juice, can also be added to egg white foam. The acid is used to help bind the available water, prevent coagulation, and increase the volume of the foam by bringing the whites closer to a neutral pH, which is where they can achieve optimal foam. Another option is to whip your egg whites in a copper-lined bowl. The positively charged copper ions in the bowl migrate to the whites and form a complex with the proteins to help stabilize the foam and reduce the whipping time.

Fats will destroy any egg white–based foam system. They are like kryptonite for the egg whites, rapidly causing them to lose strength. Fats work by destroying the surface tension of the liquid, which is necessary for the stability of the foam matrix. Fats will coat the protein molecules and inhibit their bonding action. If the proteins don't stick together, there is no structure to hold the air bubbles, and no foam can be created. When using fats with an egg white–based foam, add them at the very end of the mixing process. Or, as with many cake and pancake recipes, you can add the egg white foam to the fat-based batter just before baking.

To create a baked meringue, the egg white foam is cooked. This process is a delicate balancing act between evaporation and coagulation. As the foam cooks, the air bubbles expand and the protein sets into a stable system. The moisture needs to migrate out of the center of the meringue before the outside sets completely. If the meringue center is too moist, the sugar in the structure will dissolve, causing syneresis, or a "weeping" meringue. The meringue needs to be set top to bottom to ensure that it keeps its shape after cooling. Slow cooking that veers toward dehydration is also an effective cooking process for meringues. They will be dry and crunchy in texture and almost weightless in the palm of your hand.

Whole eggs and egg yolks can also be used to create egg foams. These foams will be softer and rise less than egg white foams. Egg yolk proteins do not have the same capability for foam creation as egg whites, though they will double or triple in volume when whipped with sugar. They are usually incorporated into batters as a leavening agent. Yolk foams need the addition of liquid and heat to really take off. Think of a classic Italian zabaglione. Egg yolks are combined with sugar and sweet wine and whipped over a warm water bath to create an incredibly light sauce that still maintains a rich, satiny mouthfeel from the yolks.

Whole egg foams are most often seen in sponge cake recipes. Genoise is a classic example of a whole egg sponge. Foams created with whole eggs fall somewhere between egg white and egg yolk foams. The foaming action of the whites is inhibited by the presence of the egg yolks unless they are whipped separately and then combined. Cakes made with these foams tend to have a slightly rubbery texture with a coarser crumb. Whole egg sponge cakes take well to soaking with flavored syrups because they don't fall apart. For this reason they are often used to build individual desserts and layered cakes common to classic European pastries. As with egg yolk foams, whole egg foams will reach higher volumes if they are whipped over a hot water bath to help encourage the proteins to unwind. They will achieve optimal results at 110°F (43°C).

CRISPY CHOCOLATE MOUSSE

MAKES ABOUT 2 DOZEN COOKIES

These light cookies have the texture of brownie edges, crisp with a touch of chew and a surprisingly big chocolate flavor. They bake for five hours at 200°F (95°C) in order to achieve this texture. On the bright side, you can set a timer and forget about the cookies until they are done— although it's hard to ignore them as the scent of chocolate slowly fills your home. Fortunately, they can be eaten as soon as you pull them from the oven.

> 4 large **eggs**, separated
> 3½ tablespoons/45 grams **sugar**
> 10 ounces/285 grams **64% cacao bitter chocolate**, chopped
> 6 tablespoons/84 grams **unsalted butter**
> 1 teaspoon/4 grams **vanilla extract**
> ¼ teaspoon/1.5 grams **fine sea salt**
> **Nonstick cooking spray**

Preheat the oven to 200°F (95°C).

Put the egg yolks and the sugar in a metal bowl and whip them with an electric mixer until they form a thick ribbon, about 5 minutes.

Put the chocolate, butter, vanilla, and salt in a glass bowl and microwave on high for 3 minutes, stopping every minute to stir the mixture. Be careful that the chocolate does not burn. When the chocolate and butter are fully melted, stir them until well blended. Gently fold this mixture into the whipped egg yolks in three additions.

Put the egg whites in a clean bowl. Using an electric mixer (make sure that the beaters are clean and dry), whip the whites until they form soft peaks. Fold the egg whites into the chocolate-yolk mixture in three additions, making sure the whites are fully incorporated.

Line a baking sheet with parchment paper and spray it lightly with nonstick cooking spray. Transfer the chocolate mixture to a pastry bag fitted with a large star tip. Pipe the mousse into circles approximately 2 inches (5 centimeters) in diameter. Alternatively, use a small offset spatula to spread the chocolate mousse onto the parchment in circles ½ inch (1.25 centimeters) thick. Bake the mousse cookies until dry and crisp, about 5 hours.

OMELET SOUFFLÉ

SERVES 1

This is a recipe for a classic omelet soufflé. It's a simple yet decadent preparation that shows off the beauty of an egg foam on the plate and the palate. Perfect for breakfast, it also makes a satisfying evening meal when paired with a green salad and some crusty bread.

3 large **eggs**

Scant ¼ teaspoon/1 gram **fine sea salt**

1½ tablespoons/18.75 grams **unsalted butter**

½ cup/50 grams grated **Gruyère cheese**

Preheat the broiler.

Separate the eggs into two bowls, the yolks in a small one and the whites in a bowl large enough to contain them once they are whipped. Whip the egg whites until they reach soft peaks. Add the salt to the yolks and whisk together. Fold one-third of the whites into the yolks, folding quickly to combine. Fold the yolk-white mixture into the rest of the whites.

Set an 8-inch ovenproof sauté pan over medium-high heat. When the pan is hot, add the butter and swirl it around until it covers the bottom of the pan. When the butter begins to foam, add the whipped egg mixture to the pan. Tap it gently to evenly distribute the egg. The bottom and edges of the omelet will begin to cook. Sprinkle the cheese over the eggs. Place the pan on the middle rack of the oven and broil to melt the cheese and finish cooking the eggs, 3 to 5 minutes. The mixture will puff a bit. When the cheese is melted and the eggs are just set, the omelet is done. Remove the pan from the oven and gently fold the omelet onto a plate.

GINGERBREAD SOUFFLÉ

MAKES 8 INDIVIDUAL SOUFFLÉS

We love the indulgence of individual soufflés straight out of the oven. These are the perfect winter dessert; the spicy gingerbread flavors permeate every delicate bite. You can top them with a small scoop of vanilla ice cream and enjoy the play of hot and cold, spicy and sweet. Or you can pour on a little hard sauce or crème anglaise or even eat them plain. If you love gingerbread, you will be very happy with these light, airy soufflés.

3 large **egg yolks**

2 tablespoons/12 grams **tapioca flour**

1 **vanilla bean**

1 cup/260 grams **whole milk**

½ cup/106.55 grams packed **dark brown sugar**

1 teaspoon/2.5 grams **ground ginger**

½ teaspoon/1.55 grams **ground cinnamon**

¼ teaspoon/0.75 gram **sweet smoked paprika**

⅛ teaspoon/0.25 gram **cayenne pepper**

½ teaspoon/1.25 grams **grated nutmeg**

2 tablespoons/28 grams **unsalted butter**, melted

¼ cup plus 2 tablespoons/75 grams **granulated sugar**

4 large **egg whites**

Put the egg yolks and tapioca flour in a blender and blend on low speed to form a light-colored paste.

Cut the vanilla bean in half and scrape out the seeds. Put the seeds and pod in a small saucepan. Add the milk, brown sugar, ginger, cinnamon, paprika, cayenne, and nutmeg. Bring the mixture to a simmer. Turn off the heat, cover the pot, and let the spices infuse for 15 minutes.

Remove the lid and take out the vanilla bean. Bring the mixture back to a boil, then remove from the heat. Turn the blender that contains the egg yolks and tapioca starch back on low. Quickly and carefully pour the hot liquid into the blender, then increase the speed to medium. The hot liquid will cook the egg yolks and thicken the tapioca. Strain the mixture into a bowl set over an ice bath and let it cool completely. When the mixture is cold, you can refrigerate it until you're ready to make the soufflés.

Preheat the oven to 350°F (175°C).

Brush the inside of eight 8-ounce ramekins with the melted butter. Put 1 tablespoon (12.5 grams) granulated sugar into the first ramekin and spin it around the inside to coat the interior. Tap out the extra sugar into the next ramekin and coat the inside of that one, continuing through all 8 containers, adding more sugar as needed until ¼ cup (50 grams) has been used or all the ramekins have been coated. When the final ramekin is coated, discard any extra sugar.

Put the egg whites in a bowl and beat them with an electric mixer on medium-high. When the whites become foamy, sprinkle in the remaining 2 tablespoons (25 grams) sugar and continue to whip until they reach soft peaks. Fold the whipped whites into the gingerbread base in three additions. Fill each ramekin two-thirds full. Run your finger lightly around the inside of each ramekin, trying not to dislodge the sugar, to form an exterior edge around the soufflé mixture.

Put the ramekins on a baking sheet and bake for 18 to 20 minutes. The soufflés will be tall and hold their shape. Serve immediately.

BROWN BUTTER HOLLANDAISE SAUCE

MAKES 1½ CUPS

We love the bit of heat and piquancy that is added by the Lime Pickles in this recipe. You can also buy prepared lime pickles if you're in a pinch. This hollandaise can be substituted for regular hollandaise in almost any preparation where you want to change things up a bit. It is wonderful with vegetables, as a sauce for steaks and chops, or paired with steamed or grilled whole fish like snapper or branzino. Of course, the real star is the nutty flavor of the brown butter. This hollandaise sauce is so good you could just eat it with a spoon.

16 tablespoons/226 grams **unsalted butter**

2½ tablespoons/35 grams **lemon juice**

2 tablespoons/30 grams **Lime Pickles** (page 40)

¼ teaspoon/1.5 grams **fine sea salt**

2 whole **eggs**

1 large **egg yolk**

Melt the butter in a small sauté pan set over medium-high heat. Cook, stirring occasionally, until the milk solids have turned golden brown. Let the butter cool for 5 minutes.

Combine the lemon juice, lime pickles, salt, eggs, and egg yolk in a blender and puree until smooth. While the blender is running, slowly drizzle the brown butter into the mixture, creating a rich and creamy sauce.

EGG CUSTARDS

Custards are some of our favorite preparations. From baked custard cups to savory bread puddings to creamy butterscotch pudding, great custards are silken and velvety. They are divided into two categories, stirred custards and baked custards. Stirred custards are still pourable when finished. Baked custards set completely in the oven. Once eggs coagulate into a gel, this effect is irreversible.

Understanding how different ingredients affect the eggs in your custard will help you troubleshoot and get closer to achieving perfect results every time. There are two main types of egg proteins, albumen and globulin. Albumen is water soluble; globulin is soluble in weak salt solutions. Therefore, salt must be present for egg proteins to coagulate into a custard. When using dairy ingredients, the natural salt contained in these products is enough. When making water-based custards like Japanese chawan mushi, salt must be added. However, too much will result in curdling. Sugar slows down the action of the proteins, thus slowing both coagulation and curdling. It increases the translucency of the finished custard and, in extremely high concentrations, sugar can prevent the eggs from coagulating completely. Fats or lipids coat the protein molecules and also slow coagulation. Acid works by increasing the rate of coagulation without accelerating the breakdown of proteins. However, too much acid will result in custard that is curdled instead of set into a smooth gel. Finally, starch can be added to slow the coagulation process, as with pastry cream or cornstarch puddings. Starch acts by blocking the proteins from binding to one another until a higher temperature of 212°F (100°C) is reached. Although it feels counterintuitive to let any custard boil, at this temperature the starches and proteins all bind together to form a gel.

The coagulation temperature of whole eggs is 158°F (70°C). As eggs are diluted with other ingredients, coagulation temperatures increase. Custard bases have much higher coagulation temperatures than pure eggs. When making custards, as the temperature increases so does the firmness of the gel until an optimum point is reached, after which your custard scrambles, becoming tough and leaking juices.

Custards can be made with whole eggs, just yolks, just whites, or any combination thereof. When creating a recipe, it is important to keep the finished product in mind. Consider the experience of savoring a hard-boiled egg. The whites are soft, tender, and slightly rubbery. The yolks have a creamy, dense texture. When you add some mayonnaise or sour cream, as with egg salad, the yolks melt into it, creating a smooth, creamy emulsion while the whites remain separate and are coated by the yolk mixture. The whites have longer protein strands and set into a firm, tender gel. The yolks have shorter protein strands and set into a softer, more delicate custard with a richer mouthfeel. Flans usually have a high proportion of yolks and a luxurious, silky texture. Egg white custards are generally used as low-fat substitutions and have a much lighter texture than flans, while recipes like classic custard pie made with whole eggs walk the line between the two. Whole egg custards are more common than egg white custards and are lighter, with a more resilient texture, than those made with only yolks.

Most egg custards are cooked in the oven in a water bath. The water insulates the custard cup, provides a moist environment, and helps ensure even cooking. It's important not to overcook custards. They continue to cook after they are pulled from the oven, and once the mixture has scrambled and the egg proteins have coagulated, there's no saving them. The advent of the immersion circulator and the CVap, with their precise cooking temperatures, have made the process close to foolproof. For the circulator, seal the custard base in a vacuum bag and let it cook in the water bath until it is the same temperature throughout, about 30 minutes. The CVap, or controlled evaporation system, is available for home kitchens; it resembles an oven and allows you to control the temperature and rate of evaporation. When using the CVap, you have the added advantage of being able to use custard cups or molds when cooking your custards. Custard bases cooked at 180°F (82°C) are perfectly done in either piece of equipment. At home, a stovetop steamer can be used to achieve similar results with a little more effort. The key is controlling your flame and keeping the water at a very gentle simmer while your custard cooks.

CLAM CHAWAN MUSHI

MAKES 6 INDIVIDUAL CUSTARDS

While most custard is made with eggs and dairy, classic Japanese chawan mushi is made using stock. There's no real equivalent to chawan mushi. It is a light and deeply savory custard. The egg-to-liquid ratio is 3:1, designed so there is slightly more liquid than the eggs can hold.

This way, as you dip the spoon into the custard, it releases some of its juices and creates its own sauce. Here we've used fresh clams to make the broth. Its buttery flavor speaks of our American heritage. We've garnished the custards with the clams, celery, and jalapeño instead of cooking them inside the custard, as would be traditional; this preserves the texture of the littlenecks. As with all steamed custards, it's important to keep a close eye on things because the time difference between a smooth, silky custard and a grainy, scrambled mess is less than you might think.

1 **fennel bulb**, sliced

1 medium **onion**, sliced

2 **celery ribs**, sliced

5 large **button mushrooms**, quartered

1 cup/250 grams **dry vermouth**

2 dozen **littleneck clams**

3 large **eggs**

1 tablespoon/20 grams **soy sauce**

¼ cup/60 grams **dry vermouth**

3 tablespoons/42 grams cold **unsalted butter**, cut into pieces

1 **jalapeño**, seeded and diced

1 **celery rib**, diced

Celery leaves

In a medium saucepan, combine the fennel, onion, celery, mushrooms, and vermouth. Bring the mixture to a simmer and cook until the liquid is reduced by half. Add the clams, increase the heat to medium-high, and cover the pot. Cook for 5 minutes. Remove the lid and check to see how many clams are open. Transfer any open clams to a plate to cool and put the cover back on. Check the clams at 1-minute intervals, removing the cooked clams as they open. Continue to cook until all the clams are open. If after another 5 minutes some clams have not opened, discard them.

Strain the contents of the pot through a fine-mesh strainer, reserving the broth for making the chawan mushi. If there is less than 1½ cups (340 grams) of liquid, add water to reach that amount. Remove the clams from their shells and transfer them to the refrigerator.

Place a steamer over high heat and bring to a full simmer. Use a fork to lightly blend the eggs and soy sauce in a medium bowl. Stir in the clam broth and then strain the mixture through a fine-mesh strainer. Some egg particles will be caught in the strainer and can be discarded. Pour ½ cup (125 grams) of the base into each of 6 ramekins. Place the ramekins in the steamer and immediately turn the heat down to low. Cook the custards, covered, for 13 minutes, until they are firm to the touch and still jiggle. The custards will be a strange gray color if you open the steamer before they are fully cooked. Remove the custards from the steamer and set them in a warm place to rest while you finish the garnish.

Put the vermouth in a small sauté pan set over medium heat, bring to a simmer, and cook until reduced by half. Swirl the butter into the vermouth to thicken it. Add the jalapeño and celery, then gently stir in the steamed clams. Heat the clams and the vegetables until very warm. Spoon 4 clams and some vegetables on top of each chawan mushi. Tear a few celery leaves into pieces and sprinkle them on top of the clams. Serve immediately.

BURNT SUGAR PUDDING

SERVES 6

Pudding is one of Aki's favorite desserts. Classic American puddings are made with either flour or cornstarch. We substitute tapioca flour in our stirred custards because it gels at a lower temperature and still provides the right texture in the finished dessert. This pudding was inspired by classic butterscotch pudding, which gets its flavor from brown sugar and a hint of vanilla. Burnt sugar is a slight misnomer because although the dark caramel we make here does have a slightly bitter edge, it is not the unpleasantly acrid taste of fully burnt sugar. We recommend that, if possible, you let the pudding rest for several hours or overnight before eating it. This gives the intense caramel flavor time to soften and mellow.

4 large **egg yolks**

4½ tablespoons/27 grams **tapioca flour**

1 cup/260 grams **heavy cream**

2 cups/520 grams **whole milk**

1 teaspoon/6 grams **fine sea salt**

1 teaspoon/4 grams **vanilla extract**

1 cup plus 2 tablespoons/225 grams **sugar**

8 tablespoons/113 grams **unsalted butter**, cut into pieces

Put the egg yolks and tapioca flour in a blender and blend on low speed until they form a light-colored paste.

Combine the cream, milk, salt, and vanilla in a saucepan set over medium heat and bring to a simmer, stirring frequently.

Put the sugar in a heavy-bottomed pot set over medium-high heat and cook until the sugar becomes a dark reddish brown, just shy of burnt. Remove the sugar from the heat and slowly pour the hot cream mixture into the sugar. This process creates a lot of sputtering and steam and should be done very carefully.

Return the mixture to the heat and bring to a boil. Stir to make sure all the caramel is dissolved. Remove the pot from the heat and turn the blender containing the egg and tapioca mixture back on low. Quickly and carefully, pour the hot caramel mixture into the blender and increase the speed to medium. The hot mixture will cook the egg yolks and allow the tapioca to thicken to the consistency of thick mayonnaise. With the blender running, add the butter in stages so it is emulsified into the pudding. When all the butter is added, strain the pudding into a serving bowl (or 6 individual bowls) and let it cool to room temperature before transferring to the refrigerator to cool completely.

CHOCOLATE PUDDING

SERVES 6

This is the classic pudding of our childhood. Chocolate pudding is the ultimate comfort food, and this version is decadent without being over-powering. Use your favorite good-quality chocolate here because it will make your pudding that much better. A dollop of unsweetened whipped cream or lightly sweetened heavy cream poured over the top takes this to yet another level, although Aki has been known to eat it straight out of the container with a spoon. Jell-O pudding has nothing on us.

4 large **egg yolks**

¼ cup plus 2 tablespoons/36 grams **tapioca flour**

½ cup plus 2 teaspoons/108 grams **sugar**

1 cup/260 grams **heavy cream**

2 cups/520 grams **whole milk**

1 teaspoon/6 grams **fine sea salt**

1 teaspoon/4 grams **vanilla extract**

12 ounces/340 grams **66% cacao dark chocolate**, chopped

Put the egg yolks and tapioca flour in a blender and blend on low speed until they form a light-colored paste.

Combine the sugar, cream, milk, salt, and vanilla in a saucepan set over medium heat. Bring the mixture to a boil, then remove it from the heat. Turn the blender containing the egg and tapioca mixture back on low. Quickly and carefully, pour the hot milk mixture into the blender and increase the speed to medium. The heat will cook the egg yolks and allow the tapioca to thicken to the consistency of thick mayonnaise.

With the blender running, add the chocolate in stages so it is emulsified into the pudding. When all the chocolate is added, strain the pudding into a serving bowl (or 6 individual bowls) and let it cool to room temperature before transferring to the refrigerator to cool completely.

DAIRY

HOMEMADE CHEESE

The word cheese *encompasses* a large range of products that run the gamut from fresh curdled cheese to aged blue-veined Cheddars and everything in between. Generally speaking, we are a nation of cheese lovers, and we are extremely lucky to have access to a huge variety of incredible dairy products.

As chefs we understand the importance of process. To that end we wanted to begin making some simple cheeses at home. Mozzarella and ricotta are universally considered good starter cheeses for any cook because they are relatively easy to make and can be consumed immediately. Even better, we can use the leftover whey from making the mozzarella for braising pork shoulder. It's amazing what you can produce from a few gallons of milk, some rennet, acid, and salt.

Everybody knows the saying that milk does a body good. Cow's milk is the milk of choice in America. Kids are raised drinking it to promote strong bones and teeth. It's available in four different fat levels—whole, 2%, 1%, and skim milk. We also find half-and-half and different levels of cream in the markets. Our milk of choice comes in glass bottles from a local farm store. In spite of the fact that clear glass is supposed to rob milk of its nutrients and flavor, we find the taste of this milk to be head and shoulders above the rest. Because of this, it is consumed quickly, and we theorize that this makes up for the exposure to light. Other dairy products that commonly appear in our kitchen are butter, cheese, sour cream, crème fraîche, condensed milk, evaporated milk, buttermilk, and yogurt. Frankly, our culinary repertoire would require some major retooling if we were to eliminate cow's milk from our diets.

Milk is a liquid composed mainly of water, lactose, fat, proteins, minerals, and vitamins. It is a complicated liquid. Milk is a liquid colloidal system of evenly dispersed milk proteins that are too large to dissolve; a solution of lactose, enzymes, salts, vitamins, and minerals; and an emulsion of fat globules.

Lactose is the major carbohydrate in milk. A disaccharide, lactose is responsible for drawing water into the mammary glands when milk is being produced. Lactose is broken down by the enzyme lactase into the simple sugars glucose and galactose. It is what gives milk its lightly sweet flavor. It adds body to the texture of milk. Finally, lactose is responsible for the browning and the caramelized flavor that develop in cooked milk products.

Casein and whey are the major proteins found in milk. Casein is a phosphoroprotein that accounts for 80 percent of the proteins found in milk. Acids or rennet can coagulate it. When this happens, the protein settles out of the solution, separating into curds and whey. Curdling can be prevented during cooking by thickening the milk with starch. Whey proteins are also known as serum proteins. They are found in the liquid left after fat and casein have been removed from the milk. They are coagulated by heat. The pasteurization process denatures most enzymes contained in milk.

The fats in milk are extremely complex. Over four hundred different fatty acids are found in milk. The fats are emulsified into the liquid with a thin coating of protein around each globule. Untreated milk is in suspension when it comes out of the cow. As it sits, the fat droplets collect in clusters whose low density allows them to break free and float to the surface. This process is known as creaming and was common back in the days when the milkman brought the bottles to your doorstep. Cream is defined as milk with an extra-high fat content. Most commercially produced milk is now homogenized to prevent creaming. This is done by breaking down the fat particles to a size that will remain uniformly distributed.

Riboflavin is the most prevalent vitamin in milk. It is light sensitive and has a greenish tint that is detectable only when there is no fat present, as in skim milk. The other three vitamins naturally found in milk are thiamine, niacin, and vitamin A. The calcium and magnesium ions in milk are what keep casein micelles stable. Micelles are groups of molecules found in colloidal systems like milk. Casein micelles reflect light and give milk its opaque white color. When the pH of milk is lowered, the acid removes the calcium ions from the micelles as the casein curdles and the whey separates out. The curdled casein is collected and pressed together and becomes cheese.

The basic ingredients for cheeses are essentially the same. You begin with milk, a bacterial starter, rennet, enzymes, and salt. Cheese making relies on the fermentation of lactose into lactic acid by lactic acid bacteria. This lowers the pH of the cheese curds, which in turn helps coagulation occur, encourages the separation of curds and whey through syneresis, prevents spoilage, discourages bacteria, develops flavor compounds, affects texture, and improves the cheese's shelf life. There are many different strains of lactic acid bacteria and they are typically sold as starter cultures for the different cheeses. The type of bacterial culture makes all the difference in the finished product. Bacteria grow at different rates and temperatures. Each batch of bacteria requires different enzymatic partners to work effectively. They process the raw materials in the cheese as it ages and gains flavor and character. There is a secondary group of cultures that do not begin working until after the cheeses are formed. These fermentations occur during storage and are responsible for the complex flavors and unique textures that can develop during the aging process. Some of them even produce carbon dioxide, which is responsible for the holes that develop inside cheeses like Swiss and Jarlsberg.

Lipase is sometimes added to cheese to improve the flavor. It is a water-soluble enzyme that reacts with lipids. Lipases modify the triglycerides in the milk fat, which frees the fatty acids. Pasteurization deactivates the lipase naturally present in milk. Lipase is added back to pasteurized milk before the rennet, so that it can help break down the milk fats and increase flavor in the finished cheese. Lipase decreases rennet's potency, so if you add it to cheese, you must increase the quantity of rennet in the recipe.

The cheese-making process begins by introducing the starter, a process also known as inoculating the milk. After the bacteria are introduced, the milk is held at 77°F–86°F (25°C–30°C) to ripen. This ripening period ensures that bacteria are alive and flourishing in the milk.

The next step is coagulating the casein proteins in the milk. This can be done in one of three ways. The first and most common way is through the use of enzymes. Rennin (commercially sold as rennet), obtained from the fourth stomach of milk-fed calves, is the easiest to obtain. Rennin can also be obtained from pigs, plant sources, and genetically engineered bacteria. Once the rennet is added, the milk is generally held at 72°F–95°F (22°C–35°C) to provide the best possible environment for fermentation to occur and curds to form. Calcium chloride is sometimes added to speed up the process and increase the uniformity of the curds. Normal coagulation under these conditions generally takes less than an hour. During this process the whey separates out. Due to the high pH levels, most of the calcium remains trapped in the curds and helps hold the casein micelles together. Rennin coagulation results in firm, elastic curds that readily compress and expel whey.

The second method for coagulating the proteins is known as acid coagulation. Cheeses made from this method include cream cheese, quark, and fromage blanc. These types of cheeses are considered fresh and are sold well before sixty days of aging. In the simplest method, acid is added to the milk and it is left to coagulate naturally. Pasteurized skim milk is most commonly used because it produces delicate cheeses with high acidity levels that discourage the growth of bacteria necessary for aging firmer types of cheese. Be careful to avoid ultrapasteurized milk for any cheese making as it does not curdle properly. Nonfat milk is a good choice for these cheeses because unhomogenized whole milk will cream during the long coagulation period, which leads to uneven quality in the finished curds. The standard setting temperature for acid-coagulated cheeses is 70°F (21°C), although temperatures as high as 90°F (32°C) can be used. Higher temperatures and increased starter result in shorter coagulation periods. It takes anywhere from four to sixteen hours to form curds. One-quarter to one-half the calcium is lost to the whey during this process. Because of this, acid-coagulated curds are much softer, weaker, and wetter than curds produced from enzymatic fermentation. Texture is directly related to pH; as acidity increases, the curds become firmer and more compact. Rennet may be added simply to improve syneresis, resulting in firmer curds. Once the curds are fully formed, at a pH of 4.6 to 4.7, the acid whey is drained from the cheese using filtration or centrifugal separation.

The final method is acid-heat coagulation, which is used to make ricotta and queso blanco. *Ricotta* means "twice cooked." In its earliest forms it was produced as a way to use up the whey left over from cheese making. While ricotta can be made from whey alone, most versions call for a combination of milk and whey to maximize yield and to produce a creamier, more delicately flavored cheese. Because rennet coagulates only the casein proteins in the milk, the by-product of these cheeses is sweet whey. When additional milk or cream is added to the sweet whey, the combination of casein and whey proteins is precipitated using a combination of acid and heat. The heat denatures the whey proteins, which then interact with the casein proteins. When acid is added the casein coagulates with the whey. During normal rennet coagulation, only 76 to 78 percent of the protein is coagulated. Up to 90 percent of the proteins are coagulated using the acid-heat method. The remaining whey is referred to as acid whey and can be filtered to produce dry whey or the whey powder used in protein supplements.

Once the curds have been formed, they can be treated to remove more whey. Many recipes call for cutting the cheese curds. This exposes more surface area, causing the curds to shrink and allowing more whey to leach out of the cheese. Cutting also allows for a more uniform heat distribution through the cheese curds. After cutting, some cheese curds may be heated again. This is called cooking the cheese. Cooking encourages the whey to evaporate and allows lactic acid to build up in the curds, giving them a more elastic texture. Heat treatments can also be used to eliminate undesirable bacteria. Once the cheese has been heated it is washed in cold water to yield a soft, moist product.

After the curds are removed from the whey, they are often placed on racks or in strainers to maximize drainage. As the cheese curds rest, they settle and knit together. During this process the texture changes from that of the individual curds to a more cohesive and familiar mass. The knitting process can be either passive or active, as with the kneading of provolone and mozzarella or the cheddaring process, where the cheese knits together and then is broken up again before being pressed into molds to create that characteristic crumbly texture.

Next the curds are salted and any additional seasonings are added. Cheeses range from 1 percent salt for a fresh cottage cheese to 5 percent for a Parmigiano or Roquefort. Once the curds are seasoned they are put into molds or other containers. The curds are naturally coated with a thin membrane of fat, which keeps them from sticking together. By packing them together and applying pressure, the curds split open, breaking the fat membrane and exposing their interiors, which then allows them to bond or mat together. This process is referred to as pressing. The cheese may be pressed simply by its own weight or by external pressure.

Finally, the cheeses are cured, or ripened. These two terms are used interchangeably and refer to the period where the cheese is kept at a specific temperature and humidity to achieve its characteristic flavor and texture. Needless to say, conditions vary widely and are tailored to each specific cheese. Fresh cheeses like mascarpone and fromage blanc skip this step. For aged cheeses, a secondary fermentation occurs, taking anywhere from two weeks to two years before the individual cheeses are considered ready to eat.

Once we understood how cheese is made, we started to experiment with making our own. As devoted cheese lovers and chefs, it's only natural that we would want to try it for ourselves. If nothing else, we knew the process would make us appreciate the wonderful cheeses that we are lucky enough to get from the cheesemonger. We decided to start with two of the easier cheeses, which just happened to be two of our favorites, ricotta and mozzarella. It quickly became clear that making cheese is fun and deeply satisfying. We could take the best characteristics from our favorite cheeses and bring them together to make something that we love. Isn't that what cooking is all about?

HOMEMADE MOZZARELLA

MAKES ¾ POUND

One of the benefits of making your own mozzarella is the ability to eat it fresh and warm. This is not an experience you can get from the store-bought product unless you happen to be there as they are making the cheese. If you're going to eat it right away, you can forgo the ice bath at the end of the recipe and serve it instead. It's an unforgettable experience and one that any cheese lovers worth their salt should try at least once.

¼ teaspoon/1.8 grams **strong lipase** (see Sources, page 309)

½ cup/112.5 grams **water**

1½ teaspoons/9 grams **citric acid** (see Sources, page 309)

1 cup plus 1 tablespoon/240 grams **water**

½ **rennet tablet** or ½ teaspoon **liquid rennet** (see Sources, page 309)

¼ cup/56.25 grams **water** (omit if using liquid rennet)

3 quarts plus 2½ cups/3,785 grams **whole milk** (not ultrapasteurized)

Fine sea salt

Dissolve the lipase in the water at least half an hour before making the cheese to allow its flavor to develop.

Mix the citric acid into the water until dissolved.

Mix the rennet tablet into the water until dissolved.

Pour the milk into a large pot set over medium heat. Heat the milk to 50°F (10°C), then stir in the citric acid and lipase mixtures. Continue heating the milk, stirring constantly, until it reaches 90°F (32°C). Remove the pot from the heat. Add the rennet, stirring slowly from top to bottom to fully incorporate it. Cover the pot and leave it undisturbed for 30 minutes.

After 30 minutes, check the curd. It will have come together into a uniform silky mass. With a long knife, cut the curd all the way through to the bottom, holding the knife at a 45-degree angle and cutting across the curds in both directions to form a uniform grid pattern. Place the pot over medium heat and heat the curds to 110°F (43°C). Use a slotted spoon to gently move the curds while they heat. Once the curds reach the desired temperature, remove the pot from the heat and stir anywhere from 2 to 5 minutes, shorter for a softer cheese and longer for a firmer one.

Place a colander in a bowl and drain the curds, reserving the whey.

Gently fold the curds a few times with a rubber spatula to release more whey. Weigh the whey and calculate 2 percent of its weight; this is the amount of salt you will need to add to the whey to make the cheese—roughly a very scant teaspoon of salt per cup of whey. Put the whey and salt back in a pot set over medium heat and heat to 185°F (85°C).

Meanwhile, divide the curds into three piles. When the whey reaches 185°F (85°C), use a slotted spoon to lower the curds one pile at a time into the whey. Dip the curds in and out of the hot whey until they warm up enough to be malleable and stretchable. Remove one pile of curds from the liquid and, with your hands, stretch and fold it until smooth and silky (in the same way you would fold bread dough). Do this quickly for a soft and delicate cheese. For fresh mozzarella we stretch and fold for a minute or less. When you are done stretching the cheese, form it into a ball and place it in an ice water bath if the cheese is to be stored (if serving the cheese right away, set aside on a plate). This will set the texture of the cheese. Once it is cold, remove it from the ice bath. Repeat the procedure with the rest of the curds. Store in the cooled whey or plain water in an airtight container in the refrigerator for up to 3 days.

HOMEMADE RICOTTA

MAKES 1½ TO 2 POUNDS

Homemade ricotta is nothing like the supermarket version. It is luxurious, with a sweet, rich flavor that will make you appreciate why this cheese is such an integral part of Italian cuisine. The addition of heavy cream gives it an amazing texture. This ricotta can easily hold center stage on a plate. We like to serve it alongside baked pastas, as a condiment of sorts, instead of inside them. Its sweet creamy flavor is a wonderful contrast to the intense flavors of lasagna or baked ziti. Sweetened with a touch of honey and spread on good toast, it is a wonderful pick-me-up for the midafternoon slump. In cheesecakes, it is revelatory. Even better, it's easy to make. A little bit of effort will net you something truly indulgent.

> 3 quarts plus 2½ cups/3,785 grams **whole milk** (not ultrapasteurized)
>
> 1¾ cups plus 1 tablespoon/475 grams **heavy cream**
>
> 1 teaspoon/6 grams **fine sea salt**
>
> ½ teaspoon/3 grams **citric acid** (see Sources, page 309; can be found in supermarkets, specialty baking stores, and online from cheese-making supply stores)

Place the milk, cream, salt, and citric acid in a pot set over medium heat and heat to 195°F (91°C). Stir the mixture as it heats so the milk and the forming curds do not scorch on the bottom of the pan. Alternatively, seal all the ingredients in a vacuum bag and cook in a circulating water bath set at 195°F (91°C) for 30 minutes. When the curds and whey separate, turn off the heat and let rest for 10 minutes.

Strain the curds through a cheesecloth-lined colander set inside a bowl. Let the cheese drain to a consistency you like, anywhere from 10 minutes to 2 hours. Remove from the strainer and let cool to room temperature. Transfer the ricotta to an airtight container. The cheese will keep in the refrigerator for up to 1 week. Reserve the whey for poaching meats and fish or making consommé.

CHEESE MELTING

We love melted cheese. There's nothing like that runny, chewy texture. The cheese itself seems saltier and more flavorful when it's cooked. Everything gets amplified. Admittedly, some cheeses are best eaten in their natural state. On the other hand, cheeses meant for melting can make for a special meal. In fact, fondue pots, baked brie, and flaming cheese have been known to turn dinner into a party all by themselves.

Several different factors affect the meltability of a cheese. Different cheeses have different reactions to heat. Mozzarella becomes stringy and chewy. Goat cheese softens and becomes creamy. Ricotta cheese forms crumbles. Cheddar has a tendency to break and release its fats. Knowing a bit about the factors that affect the ways that cheese melts will help you pick the right cheese for your recipe.

Cooked cheese is evaluated by two factors: melt and stretch. Melting is the change from a solid or crystalline state to a liquid one. Melt is often described as the flow or spread of a cheese. This is affected by several different factors, including the pH of the cheese as it was manufactured, heat treatments of the milk before and during the cheese-making process, cheese composition, and proteolysis, or the ability of the casein molecules to break down. Monterey Jack and provolone are good melting cheeses that remain creamy and smooth even as they spread.

The second factor in cooking cheese is the stretch. This is the ability of the casein network to maintain its integrity when pressure is applied. Imagine the melted mozzarella on a slice of pizza being pulled from the pie. If the cheese is warm enough you will probably have to cut the cheese with a knife or your finger before it will break on its own. This capability is what allows Swiss cheese to form holes around the gas pockets as it is aged. Stretch is indicative of various casein-casein interactions that break and re-form with ease throughout the manipulation of the cheese.

Acid-formed cheeses are considered nonmelting cheeses. These encompass most of the soft cheeses, like cottage cheese, ricotta, and fromage blanc. Because their protein structure remains intact when subjected to heat, they do not ever soften and flow. In fact, as water evaporates out of their structure, these cheeses tend to dry out and become crumbly when cooked.

During the cheese-making process, after rennet is added and the proteins have coagulated, the clot, or coagulated mass, is formed. This mass is made up of a series of interconnected casein groupings, or micelles. These micelles form aggregates, which are a network of casein molecules surrounding milk fats and serum, the watery portion of the milk, most of which is released when the curds are formed. When the clot is cut the groupings shrink, bringing the casein molecules closer together, and more serum escapes. The pH of the curd decreases, as the liquid drains off and the casein begins to be able to form and re-form bonds with other casein molecules. As this happens the calcium phosphate in the casein dissolves, is lost to the liquid, and is replaced by hydrogen. As the calcium is lost the melting ability of the cheese increases but only if the pH is not allowed to decrease too much.

Increasing the pH of the cheese increases the interactions between the casein and the calcium phosphate. When cheese is heated it goes through a softening stage before it actually melts. Once it reaches a critical temperature, known as the softening point, it melts and begins to flow. The greater the pH of the cheese the higher the softening temperature. Once the pH reaches 6.5, the resulting cheese will not melt or stretch, regardless of moisture content. At lower pH levels (below 5) cheese will still melt, but it loses the ability to stretch, and as the pH continues to drop the cheese is limited in its ability to stretch or melt.

The milk fat is surrounded by the casein network but is not affected by its structure. The fat globules are like the Styrofoam "peanuts" in a package. The peanuts are not part of what's inside the box but they can have a great impact on what happens when the box is opened. The more fat globules that are in the casein network, the more space there is between the aggregates. This weakens the casein network, resulting in a cheese that will melt and stretch at a lower temperature. This is one of the reasons why low-fat cheeses can be difficult to work with in melting capacities. They don't melt easily and just can't achieve the same textures as their high-fat counterparts when cooked.

Imagine the cheese as a fishing net of sorts, with casein strands holding the fat and water in suspension. Two important things happen when you apply heat to cheese. First, the casein proteins begin to denature, or break down. The relaxation of protein-protein bonds combined with thermal motion of the casein strands eventually leads to the collapse of the protein network holding together the structure of the cheese. While this is happening hydrophobic interactions within the casein network increase, pushing water out of the system. This leaves larger gaps for the fat to escape the system as it melts. This happens at 98.6°F (37°C), which corresponds to the body temperature of the cow. Although some of the triglycerides in the milk fat have higher melting points, they have been found to dissolve in the liquid fat. The immediate result is a softening of the cheese and the release of free oil, known as oiling out. This is why macaroni and cheese tends to break in the oven and the top of your slice of cheese pizza is oily. The amount of available free oil depends on the type of cheese. As the proteins continue to denature, there is a continuous tightening of the casein strands. When the casein system eventually fails, the cheese loses its structure and becomes a semisolid mass capable of flow. The relationship between how quickly and how much the casein structure tightens before it breaks determines how much free oil and water are released from the cheese.

Since the structure of cheese is dependent on the casein network, increased proteolysis will increase melt and decrease stretch. This is because a strong network is needed to maintain stretchability. Using less coagulant can slow proteolysis. Alternatively, you can increase the cooking temperatures during the cheese-making process, as with Swiss or mozzarella cheeses. Proteolysis increases casein solubility, causing fewer bonds to form within the casein network. Since proteolysis is abundant on the surface of mold-ripened cheeses, you will see that they tend to melt easily and have very little stretch.

Processed cheeses were first developed in Switzerland in 1912. Cheeses today are processed to eliminate any defects and create a more appetizing product for the consumer. In many ways fondue is considered the first processed cheese because it was originally made up of the odd ends of several cheeses melted down into a cohesive product that emphasized the best qualities of the cheese. Because melt is one of the most important qualities after flavor, processed cheeses today are always made with added melting salts. American cheese and Velveeta, with their smooth, creamy textures, are all about melt rather than stretch.

Melting or emulsifying salts have two main functions. They increase the pH of a system to bring it closer to the optimum range of 5.6 to 5.8. They also bind calcium ions to remove them from the casein. Once the calcium is isolated, the casein proteins and peptides are able to work together as natural emulsifiers, preventing the milk fats from coalescing as they melt. Citric acid was used as the first melting salt. Today sodium citrate and sodium phosphates are common melting salts in processed cheese. The technique of combining natural cheese and melting salts over high heat with constant stirring will create a smooth matrix of partially solubilized dairy proteins. This is how processed cheeses are made.

The best way to melt cheese is slowly. Shred or dice your cheese beforehand and use moderate heat to facilitate a smooth melt. Intense heat and thick pieces of cheese will increase the possibility of oiling out.

Fondue is actually a very thick cheese sauce. As cheese melts and the oil is released, it must be stirred to stay in suspension. The mechanical action allows the surfactants in the dairy to keep the oil droplets separate. As the oil melts out of the cheese, the remaining protein structure must be broken up in order to emulsify. The ease with which the protein structure breaks down and becomes soluble is indicative of how easily emulsification will occur. If the structure isn't broken down, the protein aggregates will separate out and sink to the bottom of the sauce. Fondue is generally made with wine because the acid helps break down the protein structure. Lemon juice can also be added to increase the cheese's ability to emulsify in the sauce. Traditional recipes often call for the addition of cornstarch to help stabilize the emulsion. Today we can easily purchase melting salts in the form of sodium citrate to stabilize the sauce. The amount of melting salts used depends on the amount of liquid; we add between 1 and 2 percent of the weight of the cheese sauce.

CHEESE FONDUE

SERVES 4 AS AN ENTRÉE

There's nothing better than melted cheese on a chilly winter evening. A wide range of dishes center around hot cheese, like Welsh rarebit, queso fundido, raclette, and the classic fondue. Fondue hinges upon a few ingredients handled well. Cooking temperature is very important—do not give in to the urge to increase the heat. Have a glass of sparkling water or wine while you're cooking and enjoy the process. A whisk helps bring everything together smoothly. Your fondue will start out thin and slowly thicken. At times the fat may threaten to break free, but have faith and keep whisking and everything will come together in the end. If you're the kind of person who likes added insurance, you can toss your grated cheese with a tablespoon (6 grams) of tapioca flour before adding it to the wine. It's not strictly necessary but will help compensate for a slightly distracted cook. We like to serve fondue with good bread, sliced apples, charcuterie, and occasionally a salad on the side.

> 2 cups/480 grams **dry white wine** (the more flavorful the wine, the better the fondue)
>
> 1 **garlic clove**, crushed
>
> 3 sprigs fresh **thyme**
>
> 2 teaspoons/12 grams **sodium citrate** (see Sources, page 309)
>
> 1½ pounds/680 grams **Gruyère**, **Comté**, or **Appenzeller cheese**, or a combination, grated

In a medium pan set over medium heat, bring the wine to a simmer. Turn off the heat, add the garlic and thyme, cover, and let the mixture steep for 20 minutes. Strain out the garlic and herbs, return the wine to the pot, and set over medium-low heat. Add the sodium citrate and stir to dissolve. Add the cheese in handfuls, whisking gently, waiting to add the next handful until the previous has melted. Keep adding cheese until all of it is incorporated. Do not let the mixture boil. Once the cheese is hot, smooth, and stringy, it is ready to serve.

MACARONI AND CHEESE

SERVES 4 AS AN ENTRÉE OR 8 AS A SIDE DISH

Yet another favorite of ours, this appears on our table in various guises every few weeks. The evaporated milk may seem like an odd choice but it serves a purpose, helping to stabilize the sauce. Evaporated milk is manufactured by exposing fresh milk to high heat in order to evaporate up to 60 percent of its water content. The resulting milk is concentrated in both flavor and nutrients. It usually has added stabilizers in the form of disodium phosphate and carrageenan. Although it is marketed as a substitute for fresh milk, it has a noticeably caramelized flavor that works nicely in sauces and soups. It produces an incredibly creamy sauce without the use of heavy cream or eggs. We'd like to say that we pair this mac and cheese with a salad or a vegetable, but truthfully, we tend to just savor the pasta with a glass of rich red wine or deep red berry juice depending on our age at the table.

1 pound/453 grams **dried elbow macaroni**

2½ quarts/2,250 grams **water**

8 tablespoons/113 grams **unsalted butter**, plus more for the baking dish

One 12-ounce/340-gram can **evaporated milk**

¾ teaspoon/4.5 grams **fine sea salt**

½ teaspoon/1 gram **cayenne pepper**

10 ounces/285 grams **Cheddar cheese** (we like extra sharp),
    grated

10 ounces/285 grams **pepper Jack cheese**, grated

⅔ cup/60 grams coarse fresh **bread crumbs**

½ cup/50 grams grated **Parmigiano cheese**

3 tablespoons/42 grams **unsalted butter**, melted

Put the macaroni in a large bowl and cover with the water. Let the pasta soak for an hour, stirring occasionally; then drain it and use as follows. It will finish cooking in the sauce.

Turn the broiler on low. Butter a 3-quart baking dish.

Put the butter, evaporated milk, salt, and cayenne in a 3-quart pot over medium heat. When the butter is melted and the milk is just steaming, slowly stir in the Cheddar and Jack cheeses, handful by handful, until they are both incorporated and evenly melted. When the sauce is made, stir in the soaked macaroni and cook over medium heat for 10 minutes. The pasta will absorb some sauce and the mixture will thicken slightly.

Pour the mixture into the prepared baking dish and spread it out evenly. In a small bowl, combine the bread crumbs and Parmigiano cheese; sprinkle them over the pasta. Drizzle with the melted butter. Put the pan on the middle oven rack, centered under the broiler, and broil the pasta for 5 minutes. When the topping is golden brown, remove the pasta from the oven and let rest for 5 minutes before serving.

CULTURED DAIRY PRODUCTS

There was a time when buttermilk, crème fraîche, and yogurt were always made from scratch at home. People had their own cows, and the raw milk easily fermented when left to its own devices. The natural acidity of soured dairy products protected them from harmful bacteria. With the advent of pasteurization, we needed a little help in the form of cultures to move things along. Although the vernacular hasn't changed, pasteurized milk actually spoils instead of souring. Fortunately, dairy cultures are readily available and easy to work with. They help us create gently soured dairy products using pasteurized milk and cream. Even premium butter has become a cultured product in order to mimic the tangy flavor of the past.

Butter is made from the cream that rises to the top of the milk. When we were kids many popular books evoked dreams of the American past. Images of little girls skimming cream from pans of milk and churning butter were abundant. Today's butter contains a minimum of 80 percent milk fat, no more than 16 percent water, and at least 4 percent milk solids. To make butter, you are changing the cream from an oil-in-water emulsion (milk) to a water-in-oil emulsion (butter). The excess liquid that separates out is known as the buttermilk. The cream that you start with should not be too hot or too cold; 55°F–60°F (12.8°C–15.6°C) works best. When you think of the texture of butter, this makes perfect sense, because at higher temperatures the fat particles disperse within the solution (melted butter) and at lower temperatures they will not clump together (cold butter).

You can easily try this at home using a food processor or an electric mixer. When we make butter by shaking, stirring, or centrifuging, the motion of the cream breaks the membranes around the fat globules. This allows the fats to escape from the cream's structure and congregate. Jersey cream is well known for having the largest fat globules. For this reason it churns into butter the most quickly. As this change occurs the cream separates into soft butter solids and butter-milk. The color of the butter granules depends on the cream used and ranges from white to deep yellow. This traditional buttermilk is a low-fat liquid with a smooth texture and a tangy flavor. Once the butter-milk is drained off, the butter solids are collected and rinsed in water until it runs clear. The mass of granules is then kneaded or churned at a slower speed until it forms a smooth, homogeneous paste. Any more water that is released is discarded. The butter can be salted at this point and then wrapped and refrigerated.

Butter is one of the most important ingredients in the kitchen. A little bit of cold butter swirled into a hot, flavored liquid makes an instant sauce. Butter melts in our mouths, a sensation we associate with pleasure and luxury. It is calorically dense and high in fat, which sets off pleasure centers in the brain. Lastly, butter contains naturally occurring glutamic acid and nucleotides, which boost umami flavors and add to butter's overall culinary appeal.

Traditionally the cream for butter was collected from a few differ-ent milkings. As it accumulated, some of the cream would naturally begin to ferment and the lactose would be converted into lactic acid. This introduced new flavor compounds and gave the cream a bit of a tang. French crème fraîche is made by using unpasteurized whole cream and allowing it to thicken naturally. It has a different texture and flavor than American sour cream. It thickens without breaking in warm sauces and has the ability to be whipped. You can make an approximation of crème fraîche at home by combining pasteurized heavy cream and buttermilk in a ratio of about a tablespoon (14.25 grams) of buttermilk per cup (260 grams) of cream, and allowing them to ferment at room temperature for twelve to twenty-four hours, until thickened. This process can be expedited by gently heating the cream to denature the proteins before adding the buttermilk. Alterna-tively, you can buy a dairy culture designed for crème fraîche and use it to produce your own. The benefit of using a culture is that you can control the fat content (by substituting nonfat milk, low-fat milk, light cream) and the tanginess of the finished product (by shortening or lengthening the fermentation period). From there it's one small step from crème fraîche to cultured butter.

Modern methods for producing cultured butter from pasteurized cream involve adding bacteria from the Bacilli order, usually *Lactobacillales*, to the cream. The cream is ripened to a pH of 5.5 at 70°F (21°C); then the temperature is dropped to 55°F (12.8°C) and the cream continues to ripen to a pH of 4.6. Maximum flavor development occurs in this pH range, especially when fermentation happens slowly at lower temperatures. Some supposedly "cultured" butters are created by adding lactic cultures directly to finished butter. The flavor develops during storage and saves manufacturers the expense of storing and fermenting the cream. Home cooks can make their own cultured cream for butter by heating cream to 86°F (30°C), adding lactic bacteria (easily procured from cheese-making supply companies), and letting the cream rest overnight at room temperature, 70°F (21°C). The flavor of cultured butter has been compared to that of cheese. It covers a wide range of nuances that depend on several different factors so that butter from different producers, or even from the same producer during different seasons, can have different flavors.

Traditionally buttermilk was simply the liquid left over from the butter-making process. That liquid was much thinner than the cultured buttermilk now available in supermarkets everywhere. Cultured buttermilk is normally made from skim or low-fat milk that has been pasteurized. The milk is then cooled to 72°F (22°C) and a bacterial culture that allows the milk to curdle and become tangy is introduced and allowed to ripen for twelve to twenty-four hours. Once the buttermilk has reached the desired texture and flavor, it is stirred to break up the curds and homogenize the mixture. Finally it is chilled to 45°F (7.2°C) to halt fermentation. This process can be replicated at home, with the same cultures used to make soft cheeses, to create your own version of buttermilk for both drinking and cooking. The live bacteria in buttermilk make it a popular beverage for digestive health.

Yogurt is another cultured dairy product touted for its ability to increase digestive and bodily health. It was probably discovered accidentally when milk fermented after being exposed to warm temperatures. Yogurt is found around the world; different countries prefer different textures in their fermented milk. Greek yogurt is famous for its thickness and rich mouthfeel. American yogurt is usually supplemented with a bit of gelatin to achieve the slightly firm, puddinglike consistency that is preferred here. On a trip to Mexico, we enjoyed small containers of yogurt with an appealing saucelike texture.

It is a testament to yogurt's recent popularity that yogurt makers are now a standard appliance in many kitchen and department stores. If you're planning to make yogurt on a regular basis, they are a relatively inexpensive and worthwhile investment. They usually come with starter cultures and regulate the temperature of your fermenting yogurt for the best results. Alternatively, you can purchase starter cultures from many health food stores or cheese-making supply companies. You can also use some of your favorite commercially produced plain yogurt to start your batch at home. Yogurt is made by heating milk to 180°F (82°C), letting it cool to 116°F (47°C), adding your starter culture, and letting the mixture set at 116°F (47°C) for at least six hours. The initial heating is to destroy any bacteria that will inhibit the action of your yogurt culture, denature your proteins, and increase your odds for successful yogurt making. Once the yogurt has thickened, it can be stored in the refrigerator for up to two weeks—if you can keep it around that long.

Cultured dairy products are a great way to get your feet wet if you're interested in trying your hand at cheese making. Actually, they are worth the effort in their own right. It's a lot of fun to play with the ingredients and you get the satisfaction of making your own butter, yogurt, or crème fraîche. We find that we get more creative with their uses when we've produced them ourselves. It's a lot harder to waste something that came from your own kitchen and that has led to many delicious new recipes.

CRÈME FRAÎCHE

MAKES 1 QUART

We love crème fraîche. Its slightly viscous, silky texture and sweet-and-sour flavor make it a staple in our kitchen. It probably goes without saying, but the better your cream, the better your crème fraîche.

1 quart/1,040 grams **heavy cream**
1 packet **crème fraîche cultures** (see Sources, page 309)

Put the cream in a medium pot set over medium heat. Heat to 86°F (30°C). Remove the pot from the heat and stir in the crème fraîche cultures.

Pour the cream into a glass bowl and cover with plastic wrap. Put the bowl in a warm spot (about 70°F/21°C) on the kitchen counter and let the crème fraîche develop for 12 hours. Taste it for flavor. If your kitchen is on the colder side the cream may need additional time to ripen to your taste.

After 12 hours, transfer the crème fraîche to an airtight container and refrigerate it for 6 hours to chill and thicken before using. It will keep for up to a week in the refrigerator.

BUTTER

MAKES ABOUT 1 POUND

Butter is the direct result of churning. You can use an electric mixer, a bowl and a whisk, or even a glass jar with a tight-fitting lid (shaken vigorously for ten to fifteen minutes) to make butter. Our tool of choice is the food processor. It works quickly, is easy to control, and is easy to clean—all good things in our kitchen. Use the best cream you can get your hands on because the better your cream tastes, the more delicious your butter will be.

> 3½ cups/900 grams **heavy cream** or **crème fraîche**
> ¾ teaspoon/4.5 grams **fine sea salt**

Leave the cream out at room temperature for 2 to 3 hours to come to the proper temperature. Pour the cream into the bowl of a food processor, making sure it is no more than half full. (Process in batches if necessary.) Process the cream. It will go through several changes, turning into whipped cream, then seizing and breaking into butter granules and buttermilk. This will take anywhere from 3 to 5 minutes. As the machine continues to process, the butter will collect around the blade and the liquid will pool in the bottom. Strain out the buttermilk, reserve it for baking or cooking, and add ½ cup (112.5 grams) cold water to the food processor. Process for 15 seconds, until the liquid becomes milky, then discard the water. Repeat 2 or 3 times until the water remains clear. Add the salt and process briefly to blend.

Remove the butter from the processor and pat dry. Wrap tightly and refrigerate; the butter will keep for up to 3 weeks.

YOGURT

MAKES 1 QUART

One of the benefits of finding a great container of yogurt is that you can save some of it to make more of your own batch. You can bump the action of natural yogurt cultures and increase the thickness of the finished product by adding powdered milk in the ratio of ⅓ cup (26.6 grams) powdered milk per quart (1,040 grams) of milk. Some cultured yogurt recipes call for the addition of gelatin, pectin, or carrageenan to thicken the finished yogurt. You can substitute powdered milk there as well, starting with 1 tablespoon (5 grams) per quart (1,040 grams) of milk and gradually increasing the ratio to reach a thickness you like. The yogurt will keep for up to two weeks in the refrigerator.

> 1 quart/1,040 grams **milk**, whole, low fat, or nonfat
>
> ½ cup/40 grams **nonfat dry milk**
>
> ½ cup/113 grams **whole-milk yogurt** with active live cultures
>   (we use Fage)

In a medium pot, combine the milk and milk powder. Set over medium heat until the milk reaches 180°F (82.2°C). Turn off the heat and let the milk cool to 110°F (43.3°C).

Put the yogurt in a bowl and stir one-third of the warm milk into the yogurt. Pour the yogurt-milk mixture into the pot with the rest of the milk and stir to combine. Transfer the mixture into yogurt-maker containers, put them in the yogurt maker, and let the yogurt develop for 9 hours.

Transfer the yogurt to the refrigerator and chill for at least 6 hours. It will keep for up to 2 weeks in the refrigerator. Reserve one container of yogurt to make the next batch. This can be repeated 2 or 3 times, at which point the yogurt cultures begin to mutate and a fresh starter should be introduced.

ICE CREAM

One of our earliest childhood pleasures was the chilly sweetness of ice cream melting across our tongues. When our daughter Amaya was teething, a few small spoonfuls were enough to distract her from the pain and bring a big smile to her face. That's the magic of ice cream; it makes people happy. There's a flavor for everyone, and it is luxury and comfort all rolled up into one delicious bite. You can make it out of almost anything if you balance all the elements carefully. On the other hand, it can be the easiest thing in the world as long as you have some heavy cream, sugar, and a freezer.

The simplest ice cream you can make is sweetened heavy cream, whipped to relatively firm peaks, spread in a pan, and placed in the freezer for a few hours. The air bubbles in the cream will keep it from becoming too hard and stiff. Of course, with so few ingredients, the quality of the cream makes all the difference. You can also vary the sugars: white, light, dark brown, maple, and so on. Add a splash of vanilla extract and you have vanilla ice cream. Swap out the sugar for condensed milk (yes, there is such a thing as organic condensed milk) and you have something with a little more richness and depth. Boil your can of condensed milk for a few hours first and you have dulce de leche ice cream.

Ice cream is actually pretty complex stuff. It is an emulsion that is whipped into foam. Air bubbles and ice crystals are dispersed through water-based liquid and destabilized fat globules. Milk fat makes up anywhere from 10 to 20 percent of commercially produced ice cream, and it has a large impact on the structure of the finished product. Milk fat is 98 percent triglycerides. There are many types of triglycerides within a milk fat globule. These globules are enclosed in a membrane, which is composed mainly of a combination of protein and phospholipids. The phospholipids are associated with the oxidation of milk. As milk stands, the fat globules collect and separate out of the liquid, the cream rising to the top. Creaming is a reversible clustering of the fat globules. A bit of shaking or stirring will return the milk to its previous condition. Creaming happens more quickly in cold temperatures because the fats are able to gather more rapidly. This starts a chain reaction. As the fat globules collect and their mass grows larger, their speed increases, and they clump together and rise to the surface of the liquid more quickly—kind of like a snowball rolling downhill, gathering more snow and momentum as it travels.

Homogenization decreases the size of the fat globules and forms a recombined membrane. This increases the surface area of each globule so that there is no longer enough of the original membrane to cover them. The new membrane is composed mainly of serum proteins and casein micelles (groups of casein molecules), which prevent the globules from consolidating and inhibit creaming. To create butter, whipped cream, and ice cream, a destabilization, or agglomeration, of the fat globules must occur so that they regain the ability to fully or partially combine. This agglomeration is a collection of fat globules held together by a combination of fat crystals and liquid fat; it is generally made possible by mechanical agitation or whipping. The agglomeration is a temperature-sensitive reaction because it is irreversible at cold temperatures but loses structure at warm temperatures when the fat crystals melt.

From the egg section we know that fats destabilize foam networks. Proteins are the foaming agents that form the network that holds the air bubbles in place. When cream is whipped it takes much longer than egg whites to create stable foam because the presence of the fat globules causes the larger air bubbles to collapse. Cream can only be whipped at cold temperatures because without the presence of solid fat, the air bubbles cannot survive. Agitation causes the fat globules to clump together. As this happens they begin to associate with air bubbles, gradually forming a network among the air bubbles, fat globules, and fat clumps. As beating continues, the fat clumps eventually get too large to enclose the air cells. When this happens the air bubbles merge and the foam begins to leak liquid, leading to the formation of butter and buttermilk.

The network of fat globules in ice cream is partially coalesced. Emulsifiers in ice cream destabilize the fat globules by replacing some of the surface proteins in the membrane surrounding them. The fat globules are then forced to form chains instead of clumping together; this structured network makes it easier to hold air bubbles in suspension. If there is too much protein in the mix, the fat is not able to partially coalesce and the resulting ice cream will be coarse and wet. If the fat becomes too unstable and too much of it clumps together, the fat globules become obvious in the finished ice cream. This is referred to as buttering. Egg yolks and the lecithin they contain were the original emulsifiers in ice cream—think custard style—but now many products are available for this purpose.

The structure of the ice cream also has an impact on the way it melts. Meltdown is a function of two reactions. The ice crystals melt back into water and the fat-stabilized foam structure collapses as the ice cream converts from a solid to a liquid. Ice crystals melt as the temperature increases and are affected mainly by the rate of heat transfer. Emulsifiers, such as mono- and diglycerides and polysorbate 80, can actually slow the collapse of the fat structure and delay the rate of meltdown. Frankly, these ingredients are controversial. Mono- and diglycerides have largely replaced trans fats for their ability to emulsify. They are made by modifying triglycerides, which are naturally occurring fats. Polysorbate 80 is an emulsifier used for foods and in vaccines. In studies it has been linked to infertility, although according to the U.S. Food and Drug Administration it is safe for use in various food products, vitamin formulations, and cosmetics.

Ice crystals are extremely important in determining the texture of the ice cream. Ice cream is almost never fully frozen. Although the freezing temperature of water is 32°F (0°C), the freezing point of an ice cream base is lower. As the water in an ice cream base (generally 55 to 60 percent of the total ingredients) freezes out, it concentrates the solvents, such as sugar and salt, in the base solution. As the solvents concentrate, they lower the freezing point of the remaining liquid. This is referred to as freeze concentration. At average temperatures of 5°F (−16°C), only about 72 percent of the water in ice cream is frozen solid. The rest of the water is held in a concentrated sugar solution that has a freezing point lower than the temperature at which it is being stored. This is what keeps the mixture smooth and scoopable.

The freezing point of the ice cream is relative to the amount of sugar and salt in the blend. Sweeteners generally make up about 15 percent of the recipe by weight. Different sugars will have varying impacts on the freezing point. Corn syrup is a popular sweetener in commercially produced ice cream because it is an economical source of sugar solids that adds shelf life by significantly lowering the freezing point and adds chewiness and body to the ice cream. Alcohol is sometimes added to balance a decreased sugar level. It will significantly decrease the freezing temperature of the ice cream base simply because the freezing point of the alcohol is well below the range of most home freezers.

Stabilizers in commercial ice cream are generally polysaccharides. Their role is to add viscosity to the unfrozen water in the ice cream base. This traps the free water and keeps it from migrating within the system. This is especially helpful during transport when commercial ice cream can be subject to heat shock as it is moved through different temperatures. Heat shock is what we commonly refer to as refrozen ice cream. There's nothing worse than taking a bite of ice cream and discovering that it is crunchy and studded with large ice crystals. By keeping the water in suspension, stabilizers reduce the formation of large ice crystals during melting and refreezing. Gelatin was the first stabilizer widely used by the ice cream industry, but it has largely been replaced by vegetarian alternatives such as carboxyl methylcellulose, locust bean gum, guar gum, carrageenan, sodium alginate, and, our favorite, gellan. These newer stabilizers are often used in combination with one another for optimum results. Stabilizers and emulsifiers together generally make up less than 1 percent of any commercial ice cream recipe.

Once an ice cream base is made, we recommend refrigerating it for a minimum of two hours after it has cooled down. This will allow the proteins and stabilizers time to fully hydrate and thicken. This resting period allows the fat to crystallize, partially coalesce, and interact with any emulsifiers present, enabling them to clump together in the ice cream maker. This agglomeration of the fat globules is necessary to protect the air cells that are formed during churning. The completed foam structure will give the ice cream texture and body on the palate. If the fat agglomerates poorly, resulting in weak air cells, the ice cream will be subject to shrinkage, its volume will decrease, and it will melt quickly.

The size of the ice crystals plays an important role in the texture of ice cream. By lowering the freezing point, we control the amount of ice crystals. How quickly the ice cream is frozen determines the size of the ice crystals. Smaller crystals translate into a smooth, creamy texture. The longer it takes for something to freeze, the larger the ice crystals that are formed. This is because at lower temperatures there are fewer nucleation sites, which are where the crystals begin to develop. The more nucleation sites there are for the ice crystals, the smaller the crystals will be. Liquid nitrogen, an extremely cold medium, can make incredibly smooth ice cream because its very cold temperature facilitates the formation of exceptionally small ice crystals.

Another way to control the size of the ice crystals is to stir the mixture while it freezes. This is the theory behind most commercial ice cream makers. They chill and churn at the same time. This does three things: it aerates, freezes, and beats the mixture.

Most ice cream makers consist of a cold chamber with a dasher, or paddle, fitted into the center. The chamber is cooled from the outside in, so as the dasher moves it scrapes the frozen ice cream from the outer wall and mixes it back into the warmer base in the center. As the ice crystals meet the warmer liquid, they melt, cooling the liquid until eventually all of the mixture is cold enough to form ice crystals and become ice cream. Each time the dasher passes along the wall, the mixture gets colder and more ice crystals are preserved. As the mixture cools down, viscosity increases, which allows the air bubbles in the mixture to remain stable. You can actually see the change occurring in your ice cream maker. Your base will change from a liquid into something resembling the texture of thick peanut butter. At this point you can either eat it immediately or put it in the freezer to harden further.

The amount of air whipped into the ice cream as it freezes is referred to as overrun. Premium ice creams have lower amounts of overrun than lower-quality brands. The variation can be seen if you compare the weight of individual pints and quarts of ice cream. That's the best way to know what you're getting. The volume may be the same, but the weight can vary significantly due to the level of overrun. We've seen differences of up to 4 ounces (113 grams) from brand to brand. Less air results in ice cream that melts more slowly and has vivid flavors that linger on the palate.

Once commercial ice cream has been churned, it must go through a period of hardening. This is because it is too soft to be scooped straight from the machine. Any mix-ins are added before the hardening period. The faster the ice cream is chilled at this stage, the smaller the ice crystals in the final product. Commercial manufacturers usually employ blast freezers for this step. They need to get the ice cream to much colder temperatures than homemade ice cream in order to counteract the temperature fluctuations during shipping and storage.

There are several different varieties of ice cream. Classic or "Philadelphia-style" ice cream is made without eggs. It can be made with heavy cream only, without using an ice cream machine, by whipping the cream into soft peaks and then freezing. We make a simple condensed milk ice cream by whipping a quart of cream to soft peaks with ¼ teaspoon (1.5 grams) salt, folding in one can of condensed milk, and letting it harden in the freezer for four hours. Old-time ice cream recipes are simply a combination of cream, sugar, and flavorings meant to be chilled, churned in an ice cream maker, and consumed almost immediately.

Although we describe ice creams made with only heavy cream at the beginning of this section, they are not practical for use in modern ice cream machines because the whipping action causes the cream to become grainy, and buttering occurs in the finished product. Custard-style ice creams contain eggs, which help stabilize the ice cream in the freezer. Sherbets contain less than 50 percent dairy in their liquid volume, and sorbets contain no dairy at all. There are no regulations involving gelato in the United States so there are no solid parameters by which we can define it here. Generally speaking, gelato is milk based and contains less butterfat, has less overrun, and is held and served at slightly warmer temperatures than ice cream. The warmer temperature means that it melts more quickly in your mouth, giving the gelato a chance to release its flavors more rapidly, which helps account for its increasing popularity here in the States.

When we make ice cream ourselves, the blend depends on our mood. We're not afraid to go savory on occasion and we can calibrate the textures to suit our fancy. Best of all, we can create our own flavor combinations and make things we've never found in the supermarket or at the local ice cream parlor.

BROWN BUTTER ICE CREAM

MAKES ABOUT 1 QUART

Brown butter refers to butter that is heated quickly in a sauté pan until the milk solids just turn golden brown; it is then used immediately for cooking. It is a delicate operation because if heated a few seconds too long, the butter solids turn black and an unpleasant bitter taste is all you have to work with. Brown butter has developed a cultlike following and is now made specifically to be used as a flavoring agent in nontraditional recipes from sweet to savory.

While we were working on ideas for increasing our output of brown butter, Michael Laiskonis, pastry chef at Le Bernardin, blogged about his experiments with brown butter. He shared a technique of reducing heavy cream until it separated into clarified butter and milk solids. This led to a discussion in the blog comments about the best way to extract the most milk solids from dairy and how to get the best yield of brown butter solids to play with. The discussion culminated with a tip from Cory Barrett, the pastry chef at Cleveland's Lola Bistro. He suggested using nonfat dry milk to increase the yield of caramelized milk solids, and recommended letting them brown slowly in butter, then steeping them overnight to increase the butter flavor.

This is why we love the Internet. It brings like-minded people together. Thanks to Michael and Cory, we now have access to a new approach, which yields a bounty of brown butter solids to be integrated into innumerable dishes. For our brown butter solids, we melted 2 sticks (224 grams) of unsalted butter and added 1 cup (80 grams) of nonfat milk powder. One of our favorite uses for brown butter is this ice cream. Just wait until you taste it.

> 1¾ cups/455 grams **half-and-half**
>
> 7 tablespoons plus 1 teaspoon/200 grams **liquid glucose** (see Sources, page 309)
>
> ¾ cup/200 grams **Brown Butter Puree** (recipe follows)
>
> ½ cup/120 grams **agave nectar**
>
> ½ teaspoon/3 grams **fine sea salt**

Combine the half-and-half, glucose, brown butter puree, agave nectar, and salt in a heavy-bottomed pot set over medium heat and bring to a simmer. Turn off the heat, cover the pot, and let the flavors marry for 20 minutes.

Pour the mixture into a blender and puree until smooth. Strain the base through a fine-mesh conical strainer into a metal bowl set in an ice bath and let cool. Transfer the base to an airtight container and refrigerate. Let the base rest overnight to let the flavors mature.

The next day, churn the base in an ice cream maker according to the manufacturer's instructions.

BROWN BUTTER PUREE

MAKES ABOUT 1½ CUPS

Once you've tasted this puree we're sure you will want to use it for more than just ice cream. It has a lightly sweet, deep caramel flavor. The leftover puree or the brown butter solids themselves can be incorporated into bread and cookie doughs, ravioli fillings, cake batter, frosting, vegetable purees—the list goes on and on. The reserved butter definitely won't go to waste in your kitchen. It can be treated like ghee and used for sautéing proteins and vegetables or substituted for vegetable oil in cake batters with wonderful results.

16 tablespoons/224 grams **unsalted butter**
1¼ cups/100 grams **nonfat dry milk**
½ teaspoon/3 grams **fine sea salt**
3 tablespoons/45 grams **agave nectar**
½ cup/112.5 grams **water**

Melt the butter in a medium saucepan set over low heat. Add the milk powder and salt. Cook, stirring occasionally, until the solids turn a rich caramel brown. Remove the pan from the heat and let the mixture cool. Let it infuse in a lidded container in the refrigerator overnight. Reheat the butter until it is just liquid and strain the solids from the mixture, reserving the fat separately to use for cooking like bacon fat.

Measure out 1 cup (200 grams) of the brown butter solids and combine them with the agave nectar and water in a blender. Puree until smooth. Strain and reserve the puree. It can be stored in an airtight container in the refrigerator for up to a week.

PARSNIP ICE CREAM

MAKES ABOUT 1 QUART

*This is an unusual use for an underutilized vegetable. Parsnips are
naturally sweet and flavorful, with a delicate earthy flavor. This ice
cream was originally developed as part of a caviar dish with sake-cured
steelhead trout roe, nasturtium leaves, and fruit leather made from tart
cherries. Its creamy color makes people think of vanilla or sweet cream,
but once they taste it they are caught, intrigued by the unusual flavor,
and they often make a game out of guessing what flavor it is. The caviar
dish was a great success, and since then we've paired the ice cream with
strawberry pie, chocolate tarts, and rhubarb crumble. It goes almost
anywhere vanilla ice cream does and adds an extra layer of flavor and
an element of surprise.*

12 ounces/340 grams **parsnips**, peeled and sliced

¾ teaspoon/4.5 grams **fine sea salt**

6 tablespoons/80 grams **agave nectar**

4 tablespoons plus 1 teaspoon/120 grams **liquid glucose**
    (see Sources, page 309)

1¾ cups/455 grams **half-and-half**

Combine the parsnips, salt, agave nectar, glucose, and half-and-half in
a heavy-bottomed pot set over medium heat. Bring the mixture to a
simmer and cook until the parsnips are tender, about 30 minutes.

Pour the mixture into a blender and puree until smooth. Strain the
base through a fine-mesh conical strainer into a metal bowl set in an
ice bath and let cool. Transfer the base to an airtight container and
refrigerate. Let the base rest overnight to let the flavors mature.

The next day, churn the base in an ice cream maker according to
the manufacturer's instructions.

MEYER LEMON CURD ICE CREAM

Meyer lemons are believed to be a cross between the Mandarin orange and the common lemon. They are available seasonally and have a delicate floral aroma and less acidic juice than common Eureka lemons. Here we make a traditional lemon curd and then thin it to make the ice cream base. If you want to use just the curd, simply eliminate the milk. We use it to balance the richness of the curd and produce a smooth, creamy ice cream that is not overly heavy on the palate. The bright Meyer lemon flavor really makes this a standout.

4 large **eggs**

1 cup/200 grams **sugar**

Zest and juice of 4 **Meyer lemons**

     (approximately ½ cup/110 grams juice)

1 teaspoon/6 grams **fine sea salt**

¼ teaspoon/0.5 gram **cayenne pepper**

8 tablespoons/113 grams **unsalted butter**, cut into small pieces

1¾ cups/455 grams **whole milk**, at room temperature

Heat a circulating water bath or a pot of water on the stove to 167°F (75°C).

Combine the eggs, sugar, lemon zest and juice, salt, and cayenne in a blender. Puree the mixture until it is smooth and pale yellow, about 3 minutes. Pour the mixture into a vacuum bag or zip-top plastic bag and seal, removing as much air as possible. Place the bag in the water bath and cook for 30 minutes.

Pour the egg mixture into a blender. Turn the blender on low and slowly add the butter, allowing each piece to be fully absorbed before adding the next. When all the butter is incorporated, pour the milk into the blender and increase the speed to high for 10 seconds just to combine everything. Strain the base through a fine-mesh conical strainer into a metal bowl set in an ice bath and let cool. Transfer the base to an airtight container and refrigerate for at least 4 hours or overnight to let the flavors mature.

The next day, churn the base in an ice cream maker according to the manufacturer's instructions.

WHITE CHOCOLATE FROZEN YOGURT

MAKES ABOUT 1 QUART

Adding homemade nonfat Greek yogurt is one of our favorite ways to add the richness of dairy to recipes without making them heavy. It has a wonderful creamy texture and tang that balance the sweetness of white chocolate. It's important to use a good-quality white chocolate because it makes a real difference in the flavor of the ice cream. We like Valrhona, although several premium brands are available in supermarkets and gourmet stores. You can deepen the flavor by caramelizing the chopped white chocolate in a 250°F (120°C) oven for 45 to 60 minutes, stirring occasionally. Depending on the season, this frozen yogurt is wonderful with fresh berries or macerated citrus slices.

8 ounces/225 grams **white chocolate**

1 cup plus 2 tablespoons/250 grams **half-and-half**

¾ teaspoon/4.5 grams **fine sea salt**

1 cup plus 3 tablespoons/300 grams **nonfat Greek yogurt**

Chop the white chocolate into small pieces and place it in a blender.

Put the half-and-half in a pot set over medium heat and bring to a simmer. Stir in the salt, then pour the hot mixture over the chocolate in the blender. Turn the blender on low and gradually increase the speed to medium high. Blend for 1 minute to emulsify the chocolate into the hot liquid. When the chocolate is completely melted and blended into the dairy, add the yogurt. Blend until smooth. Pour the yogurt base into a metal bowl set in an ice bath and let cool. Transfer the base to an airtight container and let it rest overnight in the refrigerator.

The next day, churn the base in an ice cream maker according to the manufacturer's instructions.

GRILLED POTATO ICE CREAM

MAKES ABOUT 1 QUART

We created this ice cream on a whim one day. We were debating what to do with a batch of grilled potatoes that were striking for their sweet, smoky flavor. Aki tasted and joked that they would make an amazing ice cream, and Alex took the idea and ran with it. We were both surprised by how good the resulting ice cream tasted, and it has since become a staple in our repertoire. Ice creams with a savory slant are becoming more common, especially in warm weather. We like to serve this with caviar, steak tartare, and as a garnish for chilled potato leek soup.

2 large **russet potatoes**, parcooked, quartered lengthwise, and trimmed so only 1 inch (2.5 centimeters) of flesh remains on the skin

2 cups plus 1 tablespoon/540 grams **skim milk**

5 tablespoons/75 grams **agave nectar**

¾ teaspoon/4.5 grams **fine sea salt**

1⅔ cups/370 grams **plain whole-milk yogurt**

Heat a grill to high. Grill the potato quarters on high until charred on all sides, about 20 minutes. Cut them into chunks and put them in a pot set over medium heat. Add the milk, agave nectar, and salt. Bring the mixture to a simmer and cook until the potatoes are falling apart, about 20 minutes.

Turn off the heat and fold in the yogurt. Pour the mixture into a blender and puree until smooth. Strain the base through a conical strainer into a metal bowl set in an ice bath and let cool. Transfer the base to an airtight container and refrigerate for at least 4 hours or overnight to let the flavors mature.

The next day, churn the base in an ice cream maker according to the manufacturer's instructions.

FRUITS *and* VEGETABLES

BLANCHING AND POACHING

Restaurant kitchens are busy places. Long before the customers begin showing up for meals, the cooks are hard at work in the kitchen. A lot of prep needs to be done so that guests in the dining room receive beautifully cooked food in a timely fashion. One of the biggest projects in any given day is that of prepping the vegetables. They need to be cleaned, cut, and blanched or cooked so they can be finished quickly in the heat of the moment. On any given day there are several large pots boiling on the range with large bowls of ice water standing nearby to blanch vegetables for that evening's service. Certain vegetables, like artichokes, are a big draw to restaurant diners because they don't want to deal with the work of prepping them at home. Streamlining the process makes vegetable cookery less onerous in all kitchens.

Vegetables are blanched for a variety of reasons. The brief cooking in boiling water followed by a dip in ice water to halt the cooking process is used to brighten and lock in colors and to tenderize the vegetables. The exception to the general rule is root vegetables, which may be started in cold water with salt and occasionally sugar, and then brought to a boil. The common rule taught in most kitchens is to briefly blanch vegetables in copious amounts of boiling salted water. Large quantities of water are stressed so the added veggies don't lower the temperature too far and extend the cooking period. The longer the vegetables stay in the pot, the more likely they will be overcooked. Blanching denatures many of the surface enzymes that can lead to browning, making this technique equally useful for vegetables that are going to be frozen for later use.

The enzymatic browning of fruits and vegetables is a common issue in the kitchen. There's nothing worse than watching your peeled and shredded potatoes turn brown on the counter. This occurs because fruits and vegetables contain polyphenols, a broad category of chemicals that act as antioxidants. When combined with polyphenoloxidase they are responsible for the enzymatic browning of food. Polyphenols are important because they encompass flavonoids as well as nonflavonoid components. Flavonoids are aromatic compounds and water-soluble antioxidants that are considered beneficial for our health. Anthocyanins, a subcategory of flavonoids, supply the natural pigments in food. The aromatic amino acids phenylalanine and tyrosine are nonflavonoid components that contribute to taste and flavor. Basically, polyphenols are greatly responsible for the way many ingredients look and taste.

Enzymatic browning occurs when polyphenoloxidase enzymes react with oxygen, which begins the process of transforming polyphenolics to quinones (aromatic compounds), which then change into dark, insoluble polymers known as melanins. The term *melanin* is familiar to most people, generally referring to tanning (and melanoma), so it is an easy one to remember. Melanin in plant tissue acts as a protective layer, with antimicrobial properties that prevent the spread of bruising or infection. In reality, very few phenolics in fruits and vegetables act as platforms for enzymatic browning. The process requires oxygen and is reliant on pH. The optimum window for enzymatic browning is at pH levels from 5 to 7.

In healthy plant tissue the polyphenols and polyphenoloxidase are separate. Once we cut into the fruit or vegetable, they are exposed to one another. The speed of their reaction depends on the amount of available polyphenoloxidase, the amount of polyphenols, the level of oxygen, the temperature, and the pH. Because there are several different varieties of phenolic compounds, there are different ways to slow the process of enzymatic browning. In fact, techniques that work for one vegetable, like sprinkling lemon juice on cut apples, may not work for another; potatoes, for instance, require soaking in water once they are peeled.

The most common method for actively slowing enzymatic browning is the application of heat to deactivate the surface enzymes. Most enzymes are deactivated by temperatures of 212°F (100°C), although a few require temperatures up to 275°F (135°C). Blanching time is determined by the fruit or vegetable being cooked. Extended blanching or cooling in an ice water bath can result in a loss of flavor, texture, and water-soluble nutrients. Because this process will not cancel out all of the possible enzymes, eventually browning will occur.

Chilling can also be used to control enzymatic breakdown. For some vegetables, such as broccoli, berries, and spinach, refrigeration can significantly slow browning. Lower temperatures decrease the kinetic activity in the molecules. It's important to keep perishable fruits and vegetables above their critical temperatures, as some tropical fruits may be harmed by storage conditions that are too cold.

Freezing will also temporarily inhibit the process, although enzymatic activity resumes upon thawing. The process of freezing fruits and vegetables causes damage to cell walls that actually increases the interactions of the polyphenoloxidase upon thawing. This leads to a shorter window of time to use the vegetables once they are defrosted.

Polyphenoloxidase needs water for the browning reaction to take place. This makes dehydration an effective inhibitor of enzymatic browning. This is why freeze-dried fruits and vegetables have such brilliant color when you buy them. However, you have to use them quickly once you rehydrate because the enzymes are only temporarily inhibited and will resume activity once rehydration occurs.

Now that we understand the enzymatic browning that occurs in all fruits and vegetables, let's talk about green vegetables specifically. They are subject to another kind of browning that occurs on a cellular level. All plants have chlorophyll; divided into two types, a and b, which differ slightly in chemical composition, it is the molecule that allows them to absorb sunlight and then use its energy to transform carbon dioxide and water into sugar and oxygen. This process is known as photosynthesis. The first pigment change occurs when the gases between the cell walls expand, collapsing the cell walls and allowing the chlorophyll pigment to become more clearly visible. This accounts for the bright color that occurs when green vegetables are dropped into an environment of intense heat or cold or are subjected to the controlled bruising of a vacuum chamber.

The second change occurs because chlorophyll contains an atom of magnesium at its center. When the vegetables are heated for longer periods of time or exposed to acid, the magnesium is removed from the center of the molecule and replaced with an atom of hydrogen, which in turn changes the chlorophyll a and chlorophyll b into pheophytin a and pheophytin b. This transformation changes the pigment from a bright green to more of a grayish-green color, a hue that is not appetizing or desirable.

In restaurant kitchens we walk a fine line between efficiency and productivity. We need things to be done properly and as quickly as possible. Now that we're cooking at home instead of in a professional kitchen, the quantities of food may be smaller, but then again so is the number of cooks. Blanching vegetables at home can be equally time consuming. It is a process that is easily shortchanged due to lack of time and space.

For years we were taught that blanching needed to be done in large pots of boiling water. *Sous vide* is the French term for "under vacuum." In kitchens it refers to a cooking technique where food is vacuum sealed in plastic and cooked in these hermetically sealed packages. (You may remember this technique from several earlier recipes, such as Twice-Cooked Scallops on page 25.) Many people wonder about the safety of cooking in plastic bags. According to the FDA, food-grade plastic, including sous vide bags and plastic wrap, can only be made with polypropylene and polyethylene. They never contain plasticizers that can leak into your food. To be safe you may want to look for zip-top bags designed specifically for steaming or microwave cooking.

There are several good books on sous vide, and they all state that green vegetables should not be cooked in this manner because they will darken and turn a sad army green tinged with brown undertones. For a long time we believed they were right. Finally one day, curiosity got the better of us, and we decided to find out what exactly would happen if we tried it.

We took four stalks of celery from the same bunch. The first two were cooked in ample amounts of boiling salted water for four minutes, shocked in an ice bath, and patted dry. The second two pieces of celery were seasoned lightly with salt, sealed in a bag using a chamber vacuum machine, dropped into boiling water and cooked for four minutes, and then shocked in an ice bath. Once the celery was cool we simply opened the bags and removed the cooked vegetable for a side-by-side comparison.

The results were striking. Both versions retained a bright vibrant green color, although the sous vide celery seemed a shade brighter. The blanched celery stalks were tender, supple, and toothsome. Their sous vide counterparts, which cooked for an equal amount of time, were similar in texture, although they definitely had a bit more snap and crunch, similar to al dente pasta. This would be due to the insulating characteristics of the vacuum bag. The traditionally blanched stalks were lightly seasoned and had a sweet celery flavor. On the other hand, the stalks cooked sous vide definitely had a much more intense flavor. Although the results involving texture and color were similar, in the taste category there was simply no comparison. The sous vide vegetable was head and shoulders above the blanched version.

In vegetables cooked for short periods of time, the chlorophyll is preserved. In fact, cooking green vegetables for fewer than five minutes produces the most vibrant retention of chlorophyll. The shift from magnesium to hydrogen, facilitated by the vegetable's acids, takes place over an extended cooking period and produces the color transformation to olive gray. To cook green vegetables quickly and maintain a temperature high enough to destroy the chlorophyllase enzyme, large amounts of boiling water are needed. However, in this method, flavor transfers from the vegetables to the cooking water. In addition, bringing multiple large pots of water to the boil is extremely inefficient in terms of both time and energy. You cannot reuse the same water to blanch multiple vegetables, because it will affect the flavor of each subsequent vegetable cooked in the same liquid.

It seems clear that cooking your green vegetables sous vide for short periods of time in boiling water is a much more efficient cooking method than blanching. When cooking sous vide, the pot can remain covered to avoid evaporation and retain the temperature of the water, which can be reused, and the minerals, nutrients, and flavor are preserved in the bag. It even makes cleanup easier. We are actually improving the consistency of our vegetable cookery while increasing the flavor in a functional way.

POACHED ARTICHOKES

SERVES 8 AS A SIDE DISH

We like these artichokes both cold and hot. The green olive brine adds a wonderful flavor. Even better, it comes free in your jar of olives. Alternatively, olive brine is now sold as its own ingredient for mixing cocktails. The artichokes are great with potato gnocchi or on top of pizza. They can be sautéed in butter or lightly breaded and deep-fried. They are delicious wrapped in pieces of prosciutto or served as a salad with sliced tomatoes and a simple lemon vinaigrette. If you don't want the flavor of lemon in your artichokes, you can add citric acid at a ratio of 0.5 per- cent to your water instead to prevent oxidation.

3 **lemons**

8 medium **artichokes**

⅞ cup/200 grams **green olive brine** (see headnote)

Fill a large bowl with water. Cut the lemons in half and squeeze the juice into the water. The lemon water will slow the oxidation of the artichokes as they are prepared for cooking.

Bring a large pot of water to a boil. Set up an ice bath; set aside.

Discard the first two layers of leaves from each artichoke. Trim the tops of the leaves toward the heart so that 1½ inches (3.75 centimeters) of leaves are still attached to the artichoke heart and stem. Use a veg- etable peeler to trim around the base of the artichoke until the tender heart flesh is just exposed. Remove more layers of the leaves if they interfere with the peeling of the artichoke heart. Use the peeler to remove the outer dark green skin of the heart and stem. Start at the edge of the heart and peel upward toward the stem end. Peel in long uniform strokes, rotating the artichoke so it is peeled evenly. When the coarse exterior skin is removed and the white interior flesh is free of fibers, trim the tip of the stem. Peel off the tender interior leaves to expose the heart of the artichoke, which is full of the inedible fibers known as the choke. Use a medium melon baller or a spoon to gently remove these fibers. Cut the artichoke into 8 wedges and drop them into the lemon water. If an artichoke starts discoloring as it is being cleaned, dip it briefly in the lemon water and continue trimming.

Remove the artichokes from the water and divide them between 4 vacuum-seal or zip-top bags. Add equal parts of olive brine to each bag and quickly turn the artichoke slices in the bag to coat them with the brine. Vacuum seal the bags, or close the zip-top bags while squeezing out as much air as possible. Depending on the size of the pot, drop anywhere from 1 to 4 bags into the boiling water and cook for 20 minutes. To see if the artichokes are done, remove a bag and gently squeeze a piece of artichoke. It should be firm but feel tender. When the artichokes are done, place the bags in the ice bath to cool quickly. When the artichokes are cold, place the bags in the refrigerator and let rest for a few hours before serving to allow the artichoke flavor to develop.

GREEN BEANS AMANDINE

SERVES 8 AS A SIDE DISH

Green beans and almonds are a classic combination. Here we've given it our own interpretation by pairing the blanched green beans with an almond-yogurt dressing. We like French feta for this because it tends to be sweeter and less salty than Greek or Bulgarian feta. This is a wonderful cold dish that travels well for picnics or meals on the go.

4½ cups/1,012.5 grams **water**

5 teaspoons/30 grams **fine sea salt**

2 pounds/900 grams **green beans**, trimmed

2¼ cups/320 grams **blanched almonds**

1¾ cups/200 grams **French feta**

½ cup/112.5 grams **water**

5 tablespoons plus 1 teaspoon/75 grams **plain whole-milk yogurt**

Set up an ice bath; set aside.

Put the water in a large pot and bring to a boil. Dissolve the salt in the water and turn off the heat. Pour the brine into a metal bowl set over the ice bath to cool.

Place the beans in the cooled brine and let them soak for 10 minutes.

While the beans are soaking, bring a large pot of water to a boil over high heat and set up another ice bath. Remove the beans and arrange them in vacuum-seal or zip-top bags. Make sure the beans are not more than two layers thick. Vacuum seal the bags, or close the zip-top bags while squeezing out as much air as possible, and then cook them in the boiling water for 2½ minutes. Transfer the bags to the ice water bath and let the beans cool completely. They can be stored in an airtight container for up to 3 days.

Combine the almonds, feta, water, and yogurt in a blender and puree until smooth. Strain the mixture to make sure any coarse particles are removed. Place the beans in a serving bowl, pour in the dressing, and toss to coat evenly.

CONTROLLED BRUISING

The FoodSaver may be responsible for allowing the sous vide movement to really take off. This is because it makes vacuum sealing easy and affordable for the home cook. Commercial vacuum sealers have come down in price and size over the years, though they still represent a major investment. They've become common in well-equipped restaurant kitchens only recently and they were practically unheard of in home kitchens. We were forced to wait and wonder what could be possible in our kitchen until 2003, when we found a FoodSaver at Costco for around $100. We've never looked back.

Vacuum packing became popular with the commercial food industry because it slows the deterioration process in food. It removes oxygen from the package, which dramatically slows the process of oxidation, the single greatest cause of food spoilage. Vacuum-sealed foods stay fresh for three to five times longer than foods wrapped in foil or plastic. Nuts, seeds, grains, and other highly perishable dry goods benefit greatly from vacuum sealing. Charcuterie, proteins, and cooked fruits and vegetables will all keep longer vacuum-sealed in refrigeration. Frozen foods are protected from freezer burn because the moisture in the food is trapped inside the hermetically sealed packaging. If you look around your pantry and freezer you will see vacuum packaging almost everywhere. This same packaging helps keep all of the nutrients and moisture in the food when it is cooked sous vide.

Vacuum sealers work by using a pump to remove oxygen from the chamber containing the food, creating a low-pressure environment through the use of suction. This low-pressure environment allows cell walls to expand without atmospheric constraints. Once a sensor indicates that the air has been removed from the chamber, the bag is sealed. Then the oxygen is returned to the chamber and the bag collapses around its contents, uniformly squeezing them flat. This oxygen-reduced environment allows food to stay fresh for a longer period of time.

As chefs, we were intrigued by the changes in the food. The uniform pressure damages the structure of the cells, softening the texture of the fruits and vegetables and causing their pigmentation to look brighter, their color more saturated. In most instances this results in food that looks and tastes better. We call this technique controlled bruising, and we use it to highlight the almost meaty texture of fresh fruits and vegetables like melon and asparagus. It works to our benefit when we are cooking vegetables sous vide because tenderization is one of the goals of the cooking process. Food cooks more evenly in the vacuum packaging because there is no oxygen to slow the transfer of heat. We use the controlled bruising effect to our advantage when serving raw produce, highlighting the almost meaty texture that appears in melons and pineapples and the grassy snap of bruised green asparagus.

The process responsible for controlled bruising in fruits and vegetables also allows for hydration and flavor absorption. This is because the void created in the cells by removing the oxygen creates a corresponding suction effect when the environment returns to equilibrium. In marinating and infusing fruits, vegetables, and even fish and meat, the food absorbs liquid seasonings that are sealed into the bag with it. The same process allows the flour in various doughs to hydrate quickly and efficiently. Controlled bruising allows us to preserve a fresh, vibrant color and flavor while also making the fruits and vegetables more delicious. It is especially useful when dealing with highly perishable and seasonal fruits and vegetables that can use a bit of an accent and are best showcased in their raw state.

Another place that controlled bruising is helpful is in peeling some fruits and vegetables. We have found that controlled bruising makes it easier to slip the skins off of peas and fava beans without having to blanch them first. When the bags are sealed, the skin stretches around the vegetable. When the bag is cut open, the rush of oxygen seems to help separate the softened and stretched skins from the legumes. They slide off as easily as ones that have been blanched. After we've peeled the beans we find that they cook better, retaining brighter colors and firmer textures than when they are blanched, peeled, and cooked again.

One potential problem with vacuum sealing is botulism. It thrives in an anaerobic environment. This is why storing raw fruits and vegetables in vacuum-sealed packaging is not recommended. When we apply controlled bruising to uncooked produce, we are careful to remove the fruits and vegetables from their bags on the same day to avoid any potential bacterial issues. This is not a hardship by any means, because most fresh fruits and vegetables clamor to be eaten immediately. There is little to gain by refrigerating them for long periods of time. We believe in prompt indulgence whenever possible.

ROSEMARY PINEAPPLE

SERVES 8

The aroma of rosemary is reminiscent of a pine forest. We thought it would be fun to pair this herbal aromatic note with the juicy, sweet-tart flesh of the pineapple. The effect of the controlled bruising brightens and tenderizes the pineapple while preserving its bright flavor. This pairs nicely with a variety of sweet and savory preparations. We like it with white, meaty fish like snapper and flounder or with shrimp or calamari. The pineapple is also pretty darned good with a scoop of vanilla ice cream.

1 ripe **pineapple**, approximately 2 pounds/900 grams

2 teaspoons/12 grams **Beef Seasoning** (page 18)

8 sprigs fresh **rosemary**

Cut the top and bottom off the pineapple. Stand it on one end and carefully remove the coarse exterior skin, cutting from top to bottom. Cut the pineapple into quarters vertically. Lay each quarter on a cutting board, core facing up, and carefully cut out the core. This will form 4 pineapple planks.

Lightly season the pineapple with the beef seasoning and then put the 4 planks into a vacuum bag. Arrange a stem of rosemary on top and underneath each plank. Vacuum seal the pineapple on high pressure. Place the pineapple in the refrigerator for a few hours to let the flavors blend. Alternatively, you may place the pineapple and rosemary in a zip-top bag, squeezing out excess air, in the freezer for 8 to 12 hours and then thaw them in the refrigerator in the bag to mimic the results of the vacuum sealing. Cut open the bag and remove the pineapple. Discard the rosemary. The pineapple may now be sliced and served, or it can be diced for a quick relish or pan roasted to add a caramelized note to the fruit.

STRAWBERRIES AND SYRUP

SERVES 4

This preparation takes fresh strawberries to another level. Paired with whipped or sweet cream, these berries are pure indulgence. They can be served over pancakes, waffles, or French toast for brunch, spooned over pound cake, or paired with biscuits for shortcake. They can even make a relatively healthy dessert spooned over nonfat Greek yogurt with a grating of fresh cinnamon or nutmeg to liven things up.

> 1 pound/454 grams **strawberries**
> 2 tablespoons/35 grams **Grade B maple syrup**
> 2 tablespoons/24 grams **Grand Marnier**
> ½ teaspoon/3 grams **fine sea salt**

Rinse the strawberries and pat dry. Remove the stems.

Put the syrup, Grand Marnier, and salt in a bowl. Stir to combine. Add the strawberries and toss to coat. Put the strawberries and the juices in a medium vacuum bag. Vacuum seal using an extended run time if possible so the machine works to pull air out of the strawberries' cells. The color of the fruit will transform from bright red to dark red.

Refrigerate the strawberries in the bag for 30 minutes. Cut open the bag, pouring the juices into a bowl, and put the strawberries on a cutting board. Cut the strawberries into quarters and put them in the bowl with the juices. Toss the strawberries to coat evenly.

MICRO STOCKS

The creation of a soup is often a benchmark for judging skill in the kitchen. Ingredients are brought together in stages, flavors are layered, and elements are incorporated to pique palates and soothe tummies. Soup tends to elicit a visceral reaction because it is often perceived as pure comfort food.

The backbone of every soup is the broth, or base. Traditional stocks call for the long simmering of bones, fortified with vegetables and herbs, skimmed often, strained, and degreased. It is a long process that can yield amazing results. Although there is definitely a place for chicken stock and beef broths, more often than not, these days that place is not in our kitchen.

Years of cooking professionally made us realize why so many soups taste similar to one another. It is because many of them are built on a basic chicken, beef, or vegetable stock. The resulting soups may be delicious but they are never a clear expression of a single ingredient. A natural evolution began when we started replacing the stockpots in our batterie de cuisine with the pressure cooker. Its rapid cooking process allows us to make intensely flavored liquids in a minimal time period. This, in turn, gives us the ability to make soups that taste of their main ingredient, perhaps accented with a supporting flavor. These micro stocks, which are focused on bringing out the flavor of a single ingredient, allow us to build soups from the ground up rather than relying on a universal base.

Vegetable stocks have a much shorter cooking time than meat or seafood stocks. Cooks often assume that this is because it takes longer to extract flavor from bones than from vegetables. In reality, the longer cooking times are to break down the collagen and extract the gelatin from the bones in order to give body to the finished stock. The aroma and flavor compounds that are going to dissolve usually have done so at the end of an hour. Any perceived flavor increase comes from reduction and concentration. This means that if you don't require the additional gelatin in your recipe, you can make strongly flavored protein broths in about an hour on the stovetop. (On the other hand, if you are looking to extract body from your bones, you may want to think about using your pressure cooker. It will do the job in a fraction of the time.)

The mantra that fat is flavor, which was so popular ten years ago, no longer applies to our approach to cooking. It's true that many flavor compounds are fat soluble, which makes fat a good vehicle for them. But in excess, fat can actually mute flavor by coating the tongue with richness that masks nuance and quickly exhausts the palate. Nowadays we believe that plain water can be used to great effect in the creation of a savory soup. That splash of water in a glass of single-malt Scotch dilutes its intensity just enough to allow you to appreciate its many layers of flavor. This approach is quite effective with any strong flavor. The trick is finding the balance of just enough water to amplify without diluting the overall experience.

The pressure cooker and its ability to bring ingredients together has given us the opportunity to fine-tune the ubiquitous mushroom soup. Now we start it with a mushroom stock made from button mushrooms, onions, garlic, soy sauce, water, and sherry, and infused with basil. The resulting soup has an intense mushroom flavor.

Infusions are another wonderful flavor tool. Hot water is poured over aromatics, which are then covered and left to steep until cool. The phenolic compounds for flavor and aroma dissolve into the mixture, and you are left with an intensely flavored liquid that can be used in many culinary preparations. Alcohol infusions are even more effective because ethanol has the ability to dissolve fats. The essential oils, which give plants their flavors and aromas, dissolve in the alcohol more efficiently than in water. In baking, flavorings are added via either extracts with an alcohol base or oils, because they are the most efficient mediums for absorbing and transferring flavor. It's easy to make homemade infusions by steeping aromatics in alcohol or oil in a cool, dark spot for several weeks.

One thing is always true: the first step in building a dish is often the most important one. We like to use micro stocks because they build a solid foundation of flavor that can support and enhance everything that comes after them.

TOMATO STOCK

MAKES ABOUT 4½ CUPS

This micro stock makes a great base for tomato soup, either hot or cold. It can also be used for soaking or finishing pasta, poaching fish or vegetables, or making Bloody Marys. The hoisin and hibiscus flowers (available from tea companies and gourmet supermarkets in the specialty tea section) round out the natural flavors of the tomatoes and give the stock that little something extra that makes the difference between good and great.

One 28.2-ounce/800-gram can **San Marzano tomatoes**

2¼ cups/506.25 grams **water**

½ cup/140 grams **hoisin sauce**

⅓ cup/15 grams **dried hibiscus flowers**

Combine the tomatoes, water, hoisin sauce, and hibiscus flowers in a 6-quart pressure cooker. Cook on high pressure for 20 minutes. Let the pressure dissipate naturally. Alternatively, combine the ingredients in a heavy-bottomed pot and bring to a simmer over medium-high heat. Simmer gently, skimming any foam off the surface as needed, for 1 hour. Remove from heat, cover, and let steep for 30 minutes.

Strain the finished stock through a fine-mesh strainer lined with damp cheesecloth. Use immediately, or chill and reserve (or freeze) for future use.

MUSHROOM STOCK

Mushrooms are well known for their meaty flavor. They are rich in natural umami elements and we enhance that here with the addition of soy sauce and sherry. The finished stock has a rich flavor that can be used for vegetarian soups and sauces or to enhance meat dishes. You can easily turn this into a rich mushroom soup with the addition of some sautéed mushrooms and a touch of cream.

4½ cups/1,012.5 grams **water**

18 ounces/500 grams **button mushrooms**, cleaned and cut into quarters

1 medium **onion**, sliced

½ cup plus 2 tablespoons/140 grams **oloroso sherry**

6 tablespoons/120 grams **soy sauce**

1 **head garlic**, peeled and separated into cloves

Put the water, mushrooms, onion, sherry, soy sauce, and garlic in a 6-quart pressure cooker and cook on high pressure for 15 minutes. Let the pressure dissipate naturally. Alternatively, combine the ingredients in a heavy-bottomed pot and bring to a simmer over medium-high heat. Simmer gently, skimming any foam off the surface as needed, for 1 hour. Remove from heat, cover, and let steep for 30 minutes.

Strain the finished stock through a fine-mesh strainer lined with damp cheesecloth. Use immediately, or chill and reserve (or freeze) for future use.

MEAT *and* SEAFOOD

ROASTING

Holiday meals bring to mind images of golden roast turkey and standing rib roasts. Large gatherings are the perfect time to roast large pieces of meat for a festive and delicious meal. Smaller roasts of lamb or pork appear throughout the year, and roast chicken graces our table on a regular basis. It looks easy to put a large piece of meat in the oven and leave it alone, but because every animal is made of different muscles that all have to be done to perfection, it's actually not as straightforward as it seems.

Muscles are made up of protein fibers and the connective tissue that binds them to each other and attaches them to the bones. If you've ever eaten pieces of meat or steak, you've seen evidence of both the protein bundles and the connective tissue. Each muscle is made up of a different arrangement of muscle fibers, and this affects the way we need to cook them. In many cases butchering animals is a simple matter of following the natural lines of the muscles. If you look at a T-bone steak, whether beef, pork, or lamb, you can clearly see the different muscles separated by bone, fat, and connective tissue. As you eat the chop, you experience different textures and flavors—clearly illustrating that the muscles are different.

Each muscle is made up of bundles of muscle fibers. When you cut into cooked meat, you can actually see these strands of muscle fiber as the "grain" of the meat. They resemble the fibers in a piece of cloth. The muscle fibers are made up of several different proteins. Actin and myosin make up approximately 65 percent of the proteins in muscles. These two proteins slide against one another as the muscle contracts to generate movement. When we talk about cutting meat against the grain to increase tenderness, we are literally cutting across the bundles of muscle fiber. The proteins in the muscle fiber denature when heated above 104°F (40°C). When this happens they coil up, causing the fibers to contract; the muscle shrinks and tightens in the same way your bicep does when you flex your arm. As more heat is absorbed by a muscle, it continues to contract, becoming tougher as the temperature increases.

The other two main components of meat are fat and connective tissue. The connective tissue is composed of collagen, reticulin, and elastin. Elastin is associated with blood vessels and the nervous system and is present in very minimal amounts in meat. Reticulin was originally thought to be a separate protein but is now considered a special type of collagen. Collagen is by far the main component of the connective tissue we deal with in the kitchen. Imagine collagen as a braid. Each molecule is made up of three polypeptide strands. The collagen is woven throughout the muscle to hold the muscle fibers and fat in place. The strength and elasticity that allow it to do this often translate into toughness in cooked meat. For this reason cuts high in collagen are not usually roasted but braised. Generally speaking, we whole roast only smaller animals that have less and softer connective tissue running through the muscles; when dealing with larger animals we usually roast tender pieces from the center of the animal.

Fat collects in the bodies of animals below the skin, around internal organs, and in the connective tissue of muscles. *Marbling* refers to the distribution of fat in the connective tissue throughout the muscle. Marbling is something that we look for in our meat products; it is one of the standards by which the USDA grades beef. The presence of fat minimizes drying and moisture loss during cooking. As it melts, it migrates along the bands of connective tissue in the meat. This helps limit shrinking of the muscles and helps the meat stay juicy. The fat located just underneath the skin of an animal is especially helpful when roasting because it acts as a moisture barrier to minimize the evaporation of water from the muscles.

Muscle fibers vary in number and size from muscle to muscle. Muscle texture is defined by the coarseness of the muscle. Coarseness increases with the animal's age, a fact that is more apparent in large muscles than in smaller ones. The muscle fibers and bundles in large male animals are much larger than those found in young females. Equally important is the amount of connective tissue that is woven through and around the muscles. Pork is more tender than beef because pigs are smaller animals with finer muscles and less connective tissue than cattle. When you compare stew meat from lamb with that of beef, the difference in the size of the muscle fibers is striking.

Roasting is a dry-heat cooking method characterized by the slow browning of ingredients in a hot oven, a reaction known as the Maillard effect. It begins at approximately 250°F (121°C) and occurs when almost any food is heated. Amino acids and sugars react with one another to create unstable Amadori compounds. These compounds can form a variety of chemical structures that react in different ways as they break down, affecting changes in color and flavor. Once the Amadori compounds are formed, they immediately begin to degrade. As this happens, dehydration begins at the outer layer directly in contact with the heat. Think of that crunchy exterior that develops on pan-roasted meat and fish. The surface amino acids break down into brown pigment and flavor compounds known as melanoidins, giving the food its caramelized color and complex flavors and aromas. Interestingly, the Maillard reaction is sensitive to pH. Baking soda can be added to a food in small amounts to speed up the effect. Conversely, if your meat or vegetables are burning in the pan, a judicious splash of vinegar can slow down the reaction.

The extreme Maillard effect is what makes direct-heat cooking methods like roasting, grilling, and broiling stand out. The changes in texture and flavor wrought by exposure to intense heat are delicious. Although roasting at high temperatures dries out the surface of the meat or fish, the resulting crunchy, caramelized texture more than makes up for this. When roasting vegetables, the moisture loss concentrates and intensifies their inherent flavors while the Maillard reaction gives their exterior a complex sweet flavor touched with bitterness.

The trick with high-heat roasting is not to overcook your food; the insides should remain moist and juicy to balance out a crackling exterior. A long, hot rest is the key. First, it gives the heat from the cooking process time to carry over and finish cooking the meat. Then as the meat cools, the muscle fibers relax and the meat becomes more tender. Poke a hot steak with your finger straight from the grill, then let it rest in a warm spot for at least five minutes. When you touch it again you will be able to feel the difference in the texture of the meat. The fibers will have loosened and the steak will be more pliable. As the muscle fibers relax they are less apt to squeeze water out of the structure, something we will explore further in the next chapter. This means that meat that has rested will retain more of its juices than meat that is cut as soon as it is removed from heat. If the surface of the meat still feels tight, then you should probably let it rest a little bit longer.

ROAST CHICKEN

SERVES 4 WITH LEFTOVERS

This is one of our favorite meals. The hardest part is waiting for the chicken to finish resting before we dig in. We love the slightly bitter sweetness of broccoli rabe, although if you prefer you could substitute broccoli or cauliflower. And really, the best part of this preparation is the amount of crispy chicken skin; because the bird is roasted flat, all the skin renders and crisps, which makes for an all-around better chicken.

2 bunches **broccoli rabe**

1 medium **onion**, thinly sliced

2 teaspoons/4 grams **crushed red pepper flakes**

2½ teaspoons/15 grams **fine sea salt**

6¾-pound/3-kilogram **roasting chicken**

1 **lemon**, preferably Meyer

Preheat the oven to 425°F (220°C) or 400°F (205°C) with convection. Line a roasting pan with aluminum foil.

Trim the bottom third from the rabe, then wash and dry it. Put the broccoli rabe in a large bowl and add the onion, red pepper, and 1 teaspoon (6 grams) salt. Toss the ingredients together to season evenly.

Put the chicken on the cutting board with its legs in the air and the tail and back facing you. Use a serrated knife to cut to the right of the tail and straight down along the backbone to open up the chicken. Spread the chicken open flat. Use the remaining 1½ teaspoons (9 grams) salt to season the skin side and then the inside cavity.

Mound the broccoli rabe mixture in the center of the prepared pan. Lay the chicken on top of the broccoli rabe, skin side up. It will look like the chicken is lying on a nest, with some rabe exposed at the edges. Roast for 45 minutes. With a heatproof pastry brush, baste the bird with the fat that has collected in the bottom of the pan. Rotate the pan and continue to roast for another 30 minutes. Then turn off the oven without opening it, and leave the chicken in the oven for 20 minutes. Remove the chicken from the oven and let it rest in the pan for 10 more minutes.

Transfer the chicken to a clean cutting board. Carve the chicken and arrange the meat on a platter. Squeeze lemon juice over the vegetables in the pan and gently toss them with the pan juices, scraping up any brown bits stuck on the bottom. Put the dressed broccoli rabe and any juices in a bowl and serve with the chicken.

OLIVE-ROASTED MONKFISH

SERVES 4

In this recipe we use the olive sauce both to glaze the fish during roasting and to serve alongside it. It has an elusive sweet, savory flavor that will have your dinner guests smiling. It's also a good use of leftover coffee. Leftover sauce is wonderful with grilled steaks and tossed over roasted potatoes.

1 cup/150 grams **salt-cured olives**, pits removed

¼ cup/65 grams **buckwheat honey**

¼ cup/62.5 grams fresh **brewed coffee**

2⅛ pounds/900 grams **monkfish tails**, bone-in, cleaned

2 **scallions**, thinly sliced

Put the olives, honey, and coffee in a blender and puree until smooth. Strain through a fine-mesh strainer. Divide the puree into two parts, one for brushing the fish and the other for sauce.

Line a baking sheet with aluminum foil and set a roasting rack on top. Put the monkfish tails on the rack. Using a pastry brush, evenly coat the monkfish with half of the olive mixture designated for coating the fish. Refrigerate for 20 minutes so the puree will adhere to the fish. After 20 minutes, brush the monkfish tails with the puree again and return them to the refrigerator for another 20 minutes.

Meanwhile, preheat the oven to 450°F (230°C).

Remove the fish from the refrigerator and brush again with the olive puree. Roast the fish for 10 minutes. Rotate the pan and roast for 10 more minutes. Turn off the oven without opening the door and let the fish rest for 10 minutes. Remove the fish from the oven and let it rest for 5 more minutes.

While the fish is resting, heat the reserved half of the olive puree in a small pot over medium-low heat. Stir frequently so it does not stick to the pot.

Working with one tail at a time, cut the meat off either side of the central bone. Slice each monkfish loin into medallions.

To serve, put a pool of sauce on each of 4 plates and arrange the monkfish slices on top. Sprinkle with the scallions.

GINGER SALT-ROASTED BEETS

SERVES 4 AS A SIDE DISH

We like roasting in salt because it transfers heat and flavor beautifully. Here we've combined the salt with ginger and egg whites to form a crust around the whole beets. The roasting process sweetens and intensifies the flavor of the vegetables. The roasted beets peel easily and have a gentle, tender texture. Their surface layer will be well seasoned and the flavor of the ginger will have permeated their interior. Remember, almost any aromatics can be blended with the salt: lemongrass, cumin, star anise—the pantry is your palette.

1 large piece of **ginger**, approximately 11 ounces/310 grams

2 large **egg whites**

2¼ pounds/1,000 grams **kosher salt**

2 large **red beets**, washed and stems removed

Preheat the oven to 350°F (175°C).

Wash the ginger and cut it into small pieces. Puree the ginger in a food processor until it becomes a rough paste. Add the egg whites and puree to combine. Add the salt and puree again to combine. The mixture will resemble wet sand.

Spread one-quarter of the mixture over the bottom of a 5 × 9-inch loaf pan. Nestle the beets, stem side down, into the salt. Cover the beets with the rest of the ginger salt, packing it around the beets and making sure they are covered. (The bottom tips of the beets may be the only part exposed.) Roast for 1 hour. Remove the pan from the oven and place on a wire rack. Using a metal cake tester, poke the beets. They are done when the beet feels firm but tender as the tester goes through it; it will feel like testing a baked potato. Let the beets rest in the hot salt for 30 minutes.

Use the back of a spoon to crack the salt crust, then scoop the salt away from the beets. Remove the beets and, using paper towels, wipe off the salt and peel the skin. Put the beets on a cutting board and cut each one into 8 wedges. Serve the beets warm or let them cool to use in a salad or other cold preparation.

BRAISING

Braised beef is a bone of contention between the two of us. Aki loves beef stew and its myriad variations. Alex, not so much. He complains that braised beef is usually dry and chewy, and asserts that the flavor is in the liquid and not the meat. He truly enjoys the sauce made from the braising liquid but would prefer to leave the meat aside and feed it to the cats and the dog or to the garbage pail. In his mind there are only a few exceptions to this rule. In his opinion beef short ribs, oxtail, pork belly, lamb necks, and the cheeks of almost any animal can be cooked to a point that is tender and still juicy and flavorful under the right circumstances.

All meat cookery is a true balancing act because we want a combination of juiciness and tenderness in cooked meat. Juiciness is a result of the amount of water in the meat. People often refer to rare meat as being "bloody." In fact, the juices released when meat is cooked are a blend of water, proteins, and other water-soluble compounds. Tenderness is usually measured as the ease at which the meat fibers break apart under our teeth. Meat that is tough to chew tends to be more work than pleasure.

As meat cooks, different reactions take place at different temperatures. The two basic types of meat cookery are fast and slow. Quick cooking methods keep the meat temperature below 140°F (60°C) in order to preserve texture and juiciness. This type of cooking works best for tender cuts, although a quick sear is integral to most braising recipes, whether it is advocated at the beginning of cooking, as in classical recipes, or at the end, as with many sous vide techniques. Meat is seared before braising for various reasons. The practical motivation is to destroy bacteria on the surface of the meat. The real reasons are to add flavor and to improve the appearance of the finished dish. Either way, for slow cooking methods, the meat is cooked for long periods of time at a low temperature to tenderize the muscle fibers while retaining moisture.

Meat is typically aged after slaughter in order to increase tenderness, a process known as ripening or conditioning. It can be dry aged or wet aged. Wet-aged meat is stored under vacuum for a minimum of one week after slaughter. Dry-aged meat is hung in refrigeration for at least two weeks, without wrapping, so it is subject to air circulation and slight dehydration. Dry aging is a more time-consuming process and produces a significantly lower yield after trimming, but it is widely believed to produce much more flavorful meat. During both types of aging, natural enzymes in the meat, known as calpains, break down the proteins in the muscle fibers. This results in a fragmentation of the myofibrils (the small threads that make up muscle fibers) that is perceived as increased tenderness on the palate. According to Harold McGee, if you slow down the initial heating process during a braise, taking up to two hours for the meat to reach an internal temperature of 250°F (121°C), you will allow these same enzymes to have a tenderizing effect on the meat during cooking. Theoretically this reduces the cooking time at higher temperatures and allows the meat to retain more of its myoglobin pigment so that it retains a pinkish hue. This color is often seen in meats that are cooked sous vide.

As the meat heats up to 120°F (49°C), the molecules of myosin, a protein in the muscle fibers, begin to denature and coagulate. As this happens they begin to bond with one another, pushing away the water molecules that separate them. Water collects around these protein bonds, and if the meat is cut, it will leak out as juice. As the meat continues to increase in temperature, the proteins harden, the meat starts to firm up, and the color begins to change from red to pink. Around 132°F (56°C) the collagen begins to shrink, a process that continues until the meat reaches 144°F (62°C). This weakens the collagen fibers, increases their solubility, and exerts pressure on the cells. This pressure, combined with the protein hardening, squeezes out significant amounts of loose water in the meat. The meat starts to become tough and dry out. Think of the differences between a medium-rare and a well-done steak. Then at 140°F (60°C) the color begins to change from pink to brown. By 158°F (70°C) the color is fading into a grayish brown and the meat is stiff and dry.

At 158°F (70°C) the collagen begins to melt into gelatin. Moist cooking environments, like simmering or braising, are necessary for proper collagen hydrolysis, its transformation into gelatin. Collagen from younger animals is more soluble than collagen from older ones because the collagen molecules form covalent cross bonds with each other over time. This is why veal bones are preferred for stock—they yield much higher levels of gelatin than beef bones. Hydrolysis speeds up as the temperature rises from 158°F to 176°F (70°C–80°C). As the meat continues to cook and the collagen breaks down, the muscle fibers begin to fall apart.

Connective tissue is made up of collagen, elastin, and reticulin. Collagen is referred to as white connective tissue and elastin as yellow connective tissue. Elastin does not break down during cooking and must be removed during the butchering process. As its name implies, it is tough and elastic in texture. Reticulin is now considered a type of collagen. Slow-braised meat dishes are usually made from cuts that are rich in collagenous connective tissue. These tend to be the muscles that the animal used the most, usually found at the front and hind of the animal. The active muscles are tough and not as high in moisture as the ones used for quick cooking methods. They depend on a slow, moist cooking environment to break down the collagen. The challenge is to keep the internal temperature from rising above 176°F (80°C) so that the meat does not become completely tough and dry before the collagen has melted enough to tenderize it. Modern chefs recommend braising at temperatures ranging from 140°F to 175°F (60°C–80°C). The higher the temperature, the more quickly the collagen converts into gelatin. On the other hand, lower temperatures are recommended to minimize the drying out of the muscle fibers.

Once the collagen has denatured enough to loosen the muscle fibers, perceived as fork tenderness, the meat should be removed from heat. For best results, let the meat cool in its liquid before serving. The gelatin will allow the meat to hang on to some of its remaining water, and the muscle fibers will absorb some of the surrounding braising liquid or sauce as it cools. Gelatin makes the sauce sticky, allowing it to cling to the meat, which contributes to the sensation of juiciness and tenderness that we enjoy with braised meat.

Although many experts state that collagen only begins to break down into gelatin at 158°F (70°C), our own experiences have proven that this is not the case. Collagen will break down at lower temperatures, beginning at around 140°F (60°C); it just takes significantly longer for hydrolysis to occur. We cook our short ribs sous vide at 149°F (65°C) for twenty-four hours. For us, this temperature provides a meaty, tender rib that requires only a butter knife as opposed to a steak knife. It is unctuous on the palate because a good portion of the collagen has converted to gelatin, and the meat is not dry or overly chewy. We cook all pork and lamb braises at 152°F (67°C) because they are softer, more tender meats that can take the higher temperature while still remaining juicy and flavorful. Beef cheeks are cooked at the highest temperature because they have the largest amount of connective tissue. We cook our cheeks at 158°F (70°C) for twenty-four hours for a meltingly tender bite that still has some texture and chew. You don't need a vacuum sealer to achieve these results. You can seal your braises in a zip-top bag, removing as much air as possible to maximize heat transfer, and cook them in a circulating water bath or a large pot on the stove at these temperatures.

Perfect tenderness is subjective. Every chef we know has slightly different times and temperatures for their braises. Some prefer the classic oven method, perhaps setting the temperatures a bit lower than traditional wisdom dictates and keeping a close eye on the internal temperature of the meat, while others prefer the controlled cooking of a circulating water bath or CVap steamer where they can set a timer and walk away. The key to formulating your own recipes is understanding what is happening to the meat so you can make the necessary adjustments to find your perfect braise.

You must be careful not to boil braised meat when you reheat it. This will undo all of the work that went into cooking it in the first place because the high temperature will cause the meat to dry out and become tough. Reheat gently until just hot enough to enjoy. We like to serve braised meats with crusty bread and use a few spoonfuls of the juices to dress an accompanying salad. Nothing more than a glass of smooth, silky red wine is needed for a cozy evening of good food and conversation.

ROOT BEER–BRAISED SHORT RIBS

SERVES 4

These short ribs are everything you want braised meat to be. They are tender and juicy with a rich beefy flavor that is nicely balanced by the sweetness of the carrots. The root beer and birch bark draw on familiar aromatics and tastes but we use them in a slightly different manner. Come to think of it, these short ribs are not too far off from a traditional cola-glazed ham.

4 pounds/1.8 kilograms **boneless short ribs**

6½ cups/1,462.5 grams **water**

1 tablespoon/15 grams **birch bark** (see Sources, page 309)

⅓ cup/71 grams packed **light brown sugar**

2½ tablespoons/45 grams **fine sea salt**

2½ teaspoons/10 grams **vanilla extract**

3⅓ cups/750 grams **water**

3¼ cups/740 grams **root beer**

1 medium **onion**, sliced

1 cup/240 grams **red wine**

¾ cup plus 1 tablespoon/235 grams **ketchup**

1 **head garlic**, peeled and separated into cloves

1 pound/455 grams **carrots**, trimmed and peeled

Trim the short ribs of any fat, sinew, and connective tissue. While cleaning the meat, reserve all the trimmings in one pile (for the sauce) and the cleaned ribs in another. Lay the short ribs together, arranging them in two stacks, each in a double layer. Use butcher's twine to tie the pieces together, starting at one end and placing each tie about 1½ inches (3.75 centimeters) from the previous one.

Set up an ice bath.

In a small pot set over high heat, bring 2 cups (450 grams) of the water to a simmer. Add the birch bark, turn off the heat, and cover the pot for 15 minutes. Strain the birch bark from the water and pour into a medium-sized metal bowl. Combine with the remaining 4½ cups (1,012.5 grams) water, the sugar, salt, and vanilla. Chill the brine in the ice bath.

Place the short ribs in 2 separate zip-top bags and cover them with the cooled brine. Seal the ribs in the bags with the brine and refrigerate them for 24 hours.

Measure out approximately 1½ pounds (670 grams) of the reserved short rib trim. Put the trimmings, 3⅓ cups (787.5 grams) water, the root beer, onion, wine, ketchup, and garlic in a pressure cooker and cook on high pressure for 1 hour. Let the pressure dissipate naturally. Strain the sauce, discarding the solids, let it cool to room temperature, and refrigerate for at least 2 hours.

Preheat a circulating water bath or a large pot of water on the stove to 149°F (65°C).

Skim off the layer of fat that has solidified on top of the sauce and discard.

Remove the short ribs from the brine. Pat them dry and place them in 2 vacuum-seal bags. Add equal amounts of the root beer sauce to each bag and seal shut. Alternatively, you can seal them in zip-top bags, removing as much air as possible. (You may want to use a double layer of bags to avoid any leaks.) Place the bags in the water bath and cook for 24 hours (using a large pot over low heat to maintain the temperature). Set up an ice water bath and transfer the bags to it so they can cool off quickly.

When the ribs are cool, remove them from the bag and strain the cooking liquid.

Divide the cooking liquid in half. Pour half into a pressure cooker and add the carrots. Reserve the other half for sauce. Cook on high pressure for 3 minutes. Let the pressure dissipate naturally. Let the carrots cool in the liquid. Alternatively, simmer the carrots in the liquid until tender and let them cool down naturally. When the carrots are cool, cut them into oblique shapes and reserve them in the cooking liquid.

To serve, preheat a circulating water bath or a large pot of water on the stove to 140°F (60°C). Put the short ribs and reserved liquid in either vacuum bags or zip-top bags, making sure to remove any excess air, and cook for 10 to 15 minutes until heated through.

While the short ribs warm up, heat the carrots and their reserved liquid in a separate pot set over medium heat.

Place a large cast-iron or other heavy-bottomed skillet over medium-high heat. When the ribs are warm, remove them from the bag, straining the liquid into a small pot, and brown them briefly on each side in the skillet. Keep the sauce warm on low heat. Transfer the ribs to a cutting board. Slice the ribs and divide among 4 plates. Add the carrots and pour the root beer sauce over all.

BRAISED VEAL BREAST

SERVES 4

Veal breast is a flavorful and economical alternative to the traditional veal shanks used to make osso buco. In fact, it produces a better yield and makes portioning a heck of a lot easier. We've braised the breast in apple cider and added some horseradish for a bit of heat and spice. We like to serve this with Sourdough Spaetzle (page 87), but it's equally delicious with buttered egg noodles, risotto, or a stew of salt-roasted root vegetables. Alternatively, season the veal with nutmeg, lemon zest, ground fennel, and black peppercorns to change up what is soon to become a staple in your kitchen.

6½ cups/1,625 grams **apple cider**

1 cup/250 grams **prepared horseradish**

3½ teaspoons/21 grams **fine sea salt**

6 pounds/2.7 kilograms bone-in **veal breast**

Preheat the oven to 180°F (80°C).

Mix the cider with the horseradish and salt.

Wrap the veal breast in a single layer of cheesecloth. Put the veal, bone side up, in a pan large enough to hold the meat and the cider mixture. Pour the cider mixture over the veal and cover the pan with foil. Place in the oven and cook for 19 hours. When the breast is fork-tender, remove the pan from the oven, remove the foil, and allow the veal to cool in the liquid for 1 hour.

Put on a pair of disposable rubber gloves. Lift the veal out of the liquid and unwrap it. The meat will still be warm and pliable. Remove any bones and cartilage from the meat. Unfold the veal and carefully clean up the meat, pulling out the rubbery connective tissue. Put the cleaned meat back into a rectangle shape and wrap it in plastic. Refrigerate the meat until you're ready to use it.

Preheat the oven to 180°F (80°C).

Strain the veal braising liquid into a small saucepan and discard the fat. Warm the liquid over medium-low heat.

Cut the breast into slices. Arrange the sliced veal in an ovenproof serving dish and pour the warm braising liquid over it. Place the veal in the oven for 15 to 20 minutes, basting the veal occasionally with the sauce, until it is warmed through. Serve immediately.

BRAISED GROUPER

SERVES 4

This dish was inspired by an incredible meal at Rasika in Washington, D.C. The chef, Vikram Sunderam, used Cheddar cheese in a tomato-based marinade for his black cod that was utterly delicious. If you didn't know that the cheese was there, you wouldn't have identified it as what gave the sauce its unusual depth of flavor. Here we've borrowed that technique for our braising sauce. Because we use canned tomatoes, the recipe makes two quarts of sauce, so we recommend that you freeze half for another time or double the amount of fish for a dinner party. Either way, this spicy yet delicate dish will transport you.

1 **onion**, roughly chopped

1 **jalapeño**, sliced

1 tablespoon/7 grams **garam masala**

1 teaspoon/6 grams **fine sea salt**

One 35-ounce/992-gram can peeled **plum tomatoes**

2 cups/456 grams **buttermilk**

¼ cup/80 grams **soy sauce**

7 ounces/200 grams sharp **white Cheddar cheese**, grated

Four 6-ounce/170-gram **grouper fillets**, brined in salt water
(see page 25)

The day before you plan to serve this dish, put the onion, jalapeño, garam masala, and salt in a food processor. Pulse until the vegetables are finely minced. Add the canned tomatoes and their juices and pulse to combine and chop the tomatoes.

Pour the tomato mixture into a large pot over medium heat and bring to a simmer. Add the buttermilk and soy sauce, and stir to combine. Cook until the mixture is reduced by half, about 45 minutes. Stir in the cheese until it is melted. Let the mixture simmer for another

20 minutes. The cheese will break down and be absorbed by the sauce. Cool the sauce to room temperature and refrigerate overnight.

Preheat the oven to 350°F (175°C).

Heat half of the sauce in a high-sided ovenproof skillet over medium heat. Freeze the other half for another time. When the sauce is steaming hot, add the fillets and, using a spoon, cover them with sauce. Transfer the skillet to the oven and cook for 15 minutes. Remove the pan from the oven and let the grouper rest in the hot sauce for 5 minutes. Spoon the grouper and lots of sauce into 4 bowls. Serve immediately.

CONFIT

Confit is thought to be one of the oldest cooking methods. Before the development of pottery people used to boil meat in the animal's skin over a fire. As the water boiled out, the meat would cook in the fat that had rendered, creating the earliest version of confit. The cooking method gradually progressed into a two-step process that consisted of curing meat and then gently cooking it in its own fat. This usually occurred in the fall when animals were slaughtered and butchered and was followed by a period of aging or ripening, where the meat was covered completely in the fat it was cooked in and stored for several months, to be eaten in the wintertime. Anyone who is interested in experiencing traditional confit would be well served to try the recipe in either Madeleine Kamman's book *The New Making of a Cook*, or Paula Wolfert's *The Cooking of Southwest France*.

The curing of the meat was a technique to draw out the juices, which would speed the rate of spoilage if left in the cooked meat. The salt also denatured the proteins and helped disable harmful microorganisms, both of which helped to extend the life of the confit. Covering the meat in fat protected it from oxygen, slowing the natural oxidation process. What began as a practical measure became a technique revered for its flavor. Nowadays people prepare confit because they love the taste. Confits are less highly seasoned than they were traditionally and the preparations are usually consumed within a few days instead of being stored for months.

When you cure the meat you are rubbing it with a mixture of seasonings, sugar, and salt. The cure draws water from the meat and hydrates along the surface, forming a concentrated solution. The process of osmosis works by pulling water out of the cells because there is more water in the meat than there is in the flavored solution clinging to its surface. Once again, diffusion also comes into play to pull the salt, sugar, and seasonings into the cells and flavor the meat, even as water is being removed. (See "Brining," page 22.) As with brining, the salt denatures the proteins in the meat. It dissolves some of the muscle fibers, making the meat more tender, and increases the water-holding capacity of the meat so that it remains more juicy after cooking. Finally, and perhaps most importantly, it allows the meat to be seasoned throughout and not just on the surface layer.

The key is the long, slow cooking process. Making confit is very similar to braising except that here the liquid is made entirely of fat. Because of this, collagen hydrolysis is slowed significantly, leading to longer cooking times, often at higher heats. There is enough water in meat to allow the collagen to eventually break down into gelatin; it simply takes more time for the reaction to take place. As with braising, this slow cooking period is meant to create a rich, succulent dish where the meat is tender without being dry. The fat creates a uniform cooking medium to help regulate temperature fluctuations during the cooking process. It also absorbs the flavors of the meat and the cure. The flavored fat is a beneficial by-product of the cooking process and can be used to cook legumes and vegetables to serve alongside the confit or to lightly sear the pieces of meat to create a textural contrast in the finished dish.

As always, we like to think of different ways to layer flavors. For confit, it makes sense to infuse the cooking oil with other seasonings. The main ingredients absorb the flavor of the cure, and some chefs will also add herbs and garlic to the cooking fat. Alternatively, you can infuse flavor into the oil before cooking with it. The use of food-grade essential oils is becoming more popular; they can be added to the cooking fat to add a variety of flavors to the finished dish.

We have played around with sous vide versions in order to cut down on the amount of fat needed to cook the confit and found that the technique not only works beautifully but also saves us the expense of several pounds of duck fat or lard. We still get the benefit of the flavored fat, just in usable quantities. This allows us to confit pig belly in rendered bacon fat left over from cooking breakfast or confit chicken parts in fat rendered from the cavities of whole roasting chickens. One of our favorite techniques is using smoked beef fat to confit beef cheeks and black cod. The smoky, meaty aroma of the fat penetrates both the cheeks and the cod, generating delicious, unctuous results.

CHICKEN LEG CONFIT

SERVES 4

This chicken confit utilizes our favorite piece, the thigh. You can of course substitute your favorite part of the bird when making this deeply flavored chicken dish at home. We like to keep any extra seasoned fat in the refrigerator—we use it like bacon fat, sautéing vegetables, potatoes, fish, and anything else we happen to be cooking. The thighs pair nicely with Green Beans Amandine (page 203) for a lighter meal, as a replacement for the duck in a classic confit salad, or with roasted potatoes and bitter greens for a hearty winter supper. It's a versatile preparation whose do-ahead nature makes it easy to put together a great meal in a hurry.

1 medium **onion**, roughly chopped

1 bunch **parsley**, roughly chopped

2 tablespoons/30 grams **Lime Pickles** (see page 40)

1 teaspoon/6 grams **fine sea salt**

3 pounds/1.4 kilograms **chicken thighs**

¾ cup/170 grams **bacon fat**

¾ cup/170 grams **duck fat**

Put the onion, parsley, lime pickles, and salt in a blender. Puree until completely pulverized. Pour the mixture into a bowl and add the chicken thighs. Mix the chicken in the paste and then put everything in a zip-top bag. Marinate in the refrigerator for 48 hours.

Preheat a circulating water bath or a large pot of water to 150°F (65.5°C).

Remove the thighs from the refrigerator and place them, along with any paste that sticks to them, in a vacuum-seal bag. Add the bacon and duck fat to the bag and seal it shut. Alternatively, put the thighs in a zip-top bag, removing any excess air. (You may wish to double the bag to prevent any leaking.) Cook the chicken in the water bath for 2 hours. Set up an ice bath and transfer the bags to the bath to cool quickly. Refrigerate when completely cool. The chicken will keep for 3 days in the refrigerator.

Preheat a circulating water bath or a large pot of water to 150°F (65°C).

Put the bag of chicken in the water bath and warm for 15 to 20 minutes. Open the bag and remove the chicken, wiping off any residual herb paste sticking to the meat. Strain the fat left in the bag through a fine-mesh conical strainer and set aside.

Heat a large cast-iron or other heavy-bottomed skillet over medium heat and pour a thin layer of the flavored fat into the pan. Add the chicken, skin side down, and cook for about 5 minutes until the skin becomes crisp. Serve immediately.

OCTOPUS CONFIT

Octopus is an acquired taste. People who enjoy it really love the meaty texture and slightly sweet taste. Here we've cooked it in oil flavored with garlic and smoked ham hocks. We like the gentle nutty flavor of rice bran oil, but you can substitute the vegetable oil or fat of your choice. The slow, gentle cooking leaves you with incredibly tender and flavorful meat.

4 cups/900 grams **olive oil**

2 **ham hocks**

1 **head garlic**, cut in half

3 pounds/1.36 kilograms **octopus** (4 small whole octopi)

1½ teaspoons/9 grams **fine sea salt**

¼ teaspoon/0.5 gram **cayenne pepper**

Put the oil, ham hocks, and garlic in a medium heavy-bottomed pot over medium heat. Bring the oil to 212°F (100°C), then turn the heat down to low; the garlic and the ham will bubble gently. Cook for 2 hours, until the garlic is dark golden brown. If the garlic begins to get too dark, remove it and let the hocks continue cooking. After 2 hours, turn off the heat and remove the garlic.

While the oil is infusing, rinse the octopi and cut off their heads. Remove the beak, which is at the union of the eight legs. Put the octopi in a medium bowl and season with the salt and cayenne. Toss to coat evenly, then refrigerate for 2 hours.

Remove the octopi from the refrigerator and rinse off the salt mixture. Dry with paper towels. Put the octopi into the pot of oil with the ham hocks. Put the pot over medium heat and bring the oil to 181.4°F (83°C). This takes about 30 minutes. Turn the heat down to medium-low to maintain this temperature and cook for another 90 minutes. Remove from the heat and let the octopi cool in the oil.

When the octopi are cool, use a fork to gently remove them from the oil and place in a storage container. Strain the oil over the octopi, discarding the ham hocks and any sediment from the pot. Refrigerate overnight.

The octopi can be served at room temperature as part of a salad or quickly grilled to warm them. The infused oil can be decanted and frozen for another use. Make sure to discard any octopus liquid.

CELERY ROOT CONFIT

SERVES 4 AS A SIDE DISH

This is a fun and unusual way to serve celery root.

½ cup/45 grams **coffee beans**

½ cup/106.5 grams packed **light brown sugar**

2 teaspoons/12 grams **fine sea salt**

1 large **celery root** (2 pounds/900 grams)

2 cups plus 7 tablespoons/550 grams **rice bran oil**

Use a coffee grinder or a blender to grind the coffee beans. Put the ground coffee in a bowl large enough to hold the celery root, add the sugar and salt, and stir with a rubber spatula to combine.

Wash the celery root under warm water to remove any dirt. Put it on a cutting board and slice off the top and bottom. Set the celery root on a cut end so it lies flat. Use a knife to cut off the skin, following the shape of the vegetable from top to bottom. Set the cleaned celery root aside.

Put all of the celery root peelings into the bowl with the coffee mixture and stir to coat the pieces evenly. Remove the peelings from the coffee mixture, put them in a medium pot, and cover with the rice bran oil. Reserve the remainder of the coffee mixture. Bring the oil to a simmer over medium heat, and cook the peelings at 210°F (99°C) for 10 minutes. Turn off the heat and cover the pot. Let the peelings infuse in the oil for 30 minutes. Strain the oil into a clean pot and reserve.

Meanwhile, cut the cleaned celery root into 32 pieces. (Cut the celery root in half, cut each half into 8 wedges, then cut the wedges in half so they roughly resemble quarter moons.) Put these pieces into the reserved coffee mixture and mix to coat evenly. Cover the bowl with plastic wrap and refrigerate for 2 hours.

Remove the celery root from the coffee mixture and place it in the pot with the infused oil, set over medium heat, and bring the oil to 210°F (99°C). The oil will bubble around the vegetables. Turn the heat down to low and cook for 15 minutes. Use a cake tester to poke the celery root. It should be tender with a bit of firmness in the center.

When the celery root is cooked, serve immediately or pour the entire mixture into a shallow brownie or cake pan to cool. The celery root will be in an even layer just covered with oil. Warm the celery root in its oil either on top of the stove or in a low oven (200°F/93°C) to serve.

IDEAS
for
PROFESSIONALS

There's a whole lot of information in this section and we hope that you will take it into your kitchen and make it your own. Great food is all about execution. The more you know, the better you can cook. That's what *Ideas in Food* is all about. We can find a way to achieve almost anything in the kitchen if we try hard enough. When we ask ourselves what is possible, we open new doors and allow creativity to blossom in a positive environment. In doing so we are not discounting traditional methods or procedures, we are simply trying new things to see if the evolution of technology and the supply chain have given us the tools to do things in a better way. The answer is sometimes yes and sometimes no. But we never know for sure until we actually try to find out.

Here we explain how some seemingly esoteric ingredients can work for you in your kitchen. A lot of them are fun to play with once you get past that first leap. They allow chefs and curious home cooks to create what was never possible before, like making your own snack foods in the form of fried vegetable cracklings, clarifying liquids quickly and efficiently with agar, or using liquid nitrogen to make popcorn gelato that actually looks and tastes like popcorn. Transglutaminase can improve yields and presentations when working with fish and meat and creates new possibilities when working with dairy. Xanthan gum can make sauces that are glossy and cling to your food without sacrificing flavor.

We do a lot of experimenting in the kitchen. Perhaps the most valuable thing we offer other chefs is our understanding of how things go awry. We get a lot of emails that begin with, "I'm not exactly sure what went wrong but . . ." Very often people just need a level of familiarity to efficiently work with new ideas and ingredients. There are some expensive textbooks that cover hydrocolloids and transglutaminase, but we haven't found any to be approachable and comprehensive for the modern chef who wants to understand how these ingredients work without needing a chemistry degree to use them. This section is about giving you the tools to take advantage of some not-so-common pantry items and make magic in your kitchen. So turn the page and see what is possible.

Note: For all of the recipes in this section, ingredients—liquids included—must be weighed in grams. As precision is required when working with these ingredients, we do not provide weights or volumes in ounces.

HYDROCOLLOIDS

Hydrocolloids are a hot button in culinary discussions. They were the harbinger of molecular gastronomy, a term that almost everyone agrees is inaccurate and makes little sense to the consumer. Simply put, a hydrocolloid is a substance that forms a gel in the presence of water. For culinary purposes they are important because at very small concentrations they act as thickeners and stabilizers, which can positively affect the textures, flavor, and presentation of food. These characteristics are what make hydrocolloids popular in the ready-made food sector. Understanding their traditional uses can help us see what they can do in our kitchens.

In commercial food production their primary role is to help stabilize the food products for long periods of time while retaining texture and flavor almost indefinitely. Hydrocolloids are especially useful in low-fat products to enhance mouthfeel and to fool the brain into thinking that lower-fat products are similar to the original high-fat formulations. Despite the unfamiliar name, the average home kitchen contains several hydrocolloids, ranging from flour to gelatin, that have been part of our culinary lexicon for generations. It's unfortunate that some of the less familiar ones have long been used to make substandard food products. When used in minute quantities and combined with great ingredients, hydrocolloids can help make mouth-wateringly tasty dishes.

Our main goal when using hydrocolloids is to control water and create specific textures in food. The amount of hydrocolloid needed to thicken a liquid or form a gel is calculated as a percentage of the total weight of a recipe and normally added in quantities of less than 1 percent of the whole. Here are three keys to working successfully with hydrocolloids:

Dispersion: Adding a hydrocolloid to the main ingredient and diffusing it equally throughout the volume of the product are essential to successful results. Shearing, or grinding, the hydrocolloid into the product is often a necessary step in this process. This is achieved with a standing blender. The strength of the finished gel structure depends on proper dispersion.

Hydration: Once the hydrocolloid has been dispersed, the particles must absorb water and swell to be able to activate the gel structure. Some hydration will occur as soon as the hydrocolloid is exposed to liquid, but many of them must then be brought to a specific temperature to reach the full hydration necessary to produce a strong gel structure. This step is what allows the hydrocolloid to create the invisible web that will hold the liquid in suspension. The purity of your water can have a profound effect on the finished gel. For example, high calcium levels can cause a premature reaction in many products. If you are unsure about the composition of your tap water, it pays to use highly filtered or distilled water when working with these products.

Thickening or Gelation: Once the hydrocolloid has reached full hydration, its colloidal or gelling properties can be activated. This may be a one-time metamorphosis that is stable once it's complete (nonreversible), or it may be a temperature-sensitive (thermo-reversible) reaction that holds only within a certain range of temperatures. Think of Jell-O and its firm, wobbly texture that slowly melts back into a liquid as temperatures rise. The finished sols (thickened liquids) or gels can cover a range of viscosities and opacities depending on which hydrocolloid is used.

All three steps must be completed for the full impact of the hydrocolloid to take effect.

Following is an overview of several commonly used hydrocolloids, beginning with the most familiar and easy to find and ending with ones that are a little more challenging (and expensive) to procure. All of them are available through online retailers. We have provided several recipes to help you get a feel for the different ingredients and their capabilities.

XANTHAN GUM

One of our most popular classes is our introduction to hydrocolloids. This class always begins with xanthan gum, which we call "my first hydrocolloid" because of its functionality and ease of use. Xanthan gum is one of the most commonly used hydrocolloids. It is produced through a fermentation of glucose or sucrose by *Xanthomonas campestris* bacterium. Here in the United States xanthan gum is commonly fermented from corn sugars. It thickens liquids but cannot form a gel by itself.

The first rule of working with hydrocolloids is that if you can taste them or feel them on your palate, then you've used too much. We begin the class with a simple glass of water. Everyone tastes it. We ask them to roll it around on their tongues and experience the texture and flavor. Then we add some xanthan gum, 0.1 percent to be exact, to the water.

The xanthan gum is added using a standing blender. We pour the water into the blender and turn it on. Once a vortex is formed, we sprinkle in the xanthan gum. Once the powder is absorbed, the change is almost instantaneous. The texture of the water thickens and becomes more visibly fluid—in that you can see its texture more clearly—while remaining transparent. We pour a little for everyone to taste. Again we ask that they roll the liquid around on their tongues to evaluate the texture and talk about the changes. It clings to the glass in larger droplets and forms clear legs on the glass. It is a subtle yet clearly discernible change. Then again, fine cooking is all about subtleties.

We add more xanthan gum to the water, taking the mixture to 0.2 percent. The changes are a bit more evident this time. The water is still glossy and clear, but there is an underlying stickiness to the texture. Straight from the blender it looks slightly whitish from the tiny bubbles that have gathered. These will dissipate over time or they can be sucked out with a chamber vacuum machine. The pseudoplasticity, or ability to thin with agitation, becomes more visible as water spooned onto a plate slowly thickens and begins to hold its surface tension without running or spreading.

The final addition brings the xanthan gum concentration to 0.4 percent. This time the mixture is clearly viscous. The texture is sticky and mucouslike and receives mixed reviews among the group, usually weighted heavily toward the negative. This is a good illustration of why concentrations are important and how too much of a good thing can become unpleasant. It's a great jumping-off point because now the students are observing closely, tasting, and opening their minds to new possibilities.

Xanthan gum is very easy to use. It is cold-water soluble and thermally irreversible. Once you've added it to something, you can't take it out again, although you can dilute it. Xanthan gum is a quick and easy stabilizer for mixtures that tend to fall out of suspension. It is often used as an emulsifier to prevent syneresis, or the weeping of fluids from an emulsion or puree. Xanthan gum is stable across a wide range of pH levels, from 2.5 to 11, which gives it great flexibility in the kitchen. It is thixotropic, which means that its viscosity will thin out when shaken and then thicken again once it sits. These qualities are all especially useful in working with sauces and vinaigrettes. The thixotropic ability allows a cook to coat the main ingredient with a light layer of sauce, which will thicken as it travels from the kitchen to the dining room. Meanwhile, the viscosity allows the sauce to cling to the food and the emulsifying properties keep everything in suspension to avoid any separation of flavor.

One of our favorite extrapolations with xanthan gum is the "oil-free" vinaigrette. Classically, a vinaigrette is made with three parts fat to one part flavored acid. Because of the quantity of fat needed in traditional vinaigrettes, more expensive oils are usually stretched with less expensive neutral oils. We like oil-free vinaigrettes because they allow us to work with balanced, brightly flavored liquids instead of straight vinegars or citrus juice. With the help of a little xanthan gum (0.15 percent), our blends gain mouthfeel and pseudoplasticity. Then, if we like, we can finish with a few drops of premium oil that are separate from yet complementary to the vinaigrette, so that the flavors can work together to create something special and delicious.

Additionally, xanthan gum is known to inhibit the formation of ice crystals. Its strength is actually improved by the freeze-thaw cycle. It is often used in frozen preparations to ensure a smooth texture and mouthfeel. Xanthan gum also holds its properties after being microwaved. This makes it well suited to applications that are cooked, frozen, and reheated in addition to traditional ice creams and sorbets.

Xanthan gum also has the ability to create a structure that is capable of trapping air bubbles. This ability is very useful in providing stabilization for foams, especially when combined with other hydrocolloids like methylcellulose and hydrolyzed soy proteins. Xanthan gum is used in gluten-free baking to provide viscosity to doughs and batters. Combined with its ability to trap air bubbles, this viscosity allows the dough to rise without the benefit of a gluten structure. Xanthan gum is hydrophilic and can help retain moisture in finished recipes, yet another useful benefit in baked and frozen goods.

Xanthan gum is used in low-fat preparations to replace egg yolks as a thickener and to mimic the texture of fat on the palate. It can be used to thicken alcoholic beverages. It cannot be hydrated directly in pure alcohol, but it can be added to the alcohol in a prehydrated form in a water-based solution. Finally, it is resistant to enzymatic degradation, making it a useful stabilizer for foods with a high level of active enzymes. So if you were making a bellini you could add xanthan gum (0.1 percent) to the peach puree; then when you add the puree to your champagne, it would blend evenly into the wine instead of separating into layers. We've made mojitos with an intensely flavored mint infusion thickened with xanthan gum (0.3 percent) and added to a rum base, resulting in brilliant color and great mouthfeel.

One of the more practical aspects of xanthan gum is that it can be used in very small quantities. This means that there is very little dilution of the flavor of the main preparation. For most culinary purposes it is used at quantities of less than 0.4 percent. This allows chefs to have the benefits of xanthan gum's more functional qualities while avoiding the slimy texture that can occur at higher concentrations. It is usually clear and does not affect the color or flavor of the food.

CRABAPPLE SAUCE

MAKES 1 QUART

Applesauce is a classic example of a delicious and down-home recipe that sometimes suffers from syneresis, or separation of liquid from the gel. In this recipe, we use crabapples for a slight twist on the original. We like them for their tartness and color; they make a beautiful pink sauce. You'll find that crabapple sauce will make a striking counterpoint for a variety of dishes, both sweet and savory. The little bit of xanthan gum added at a ratio of 0.1 percent of the total weight of the other ingredients makes it almost perfect.

> 675 grams **crabapples**
> 225 grams **apple cider**
> 50 grams **sugar**
> 3 grams **fine sea salt**
> 0.61 gram **xanthan gum** (see Sources, page 309)

Wash the crabapples in cool water and remove their stems. Put the crabapples, cider, sugar, and salt in a large pot set over high heat. Bring the mixture to a simmer, then turn the heat down to medium. Cook the apples until soft and falling apart, about 10 minutes. As the apples cook, use a ladle to skim off any foam from the surface. Turn off the heat and let the mixture rest for 20 minutes.

Put the apple mixture through a food mill to remove any seeds and coarse fibers.

Pour the apple mixture into a blender and set on low speed. Increase the speed until a vortex forms in the center of the applesauce. Sprinkle the xanthan gum into the vortex and increase the speed to fully disperse the powder. Let the blender run for 30 seconds. Strain the applesauce through a fine-mesh sieve. Serve immediately, or cool to room temperature and refrigerate in an airtight container for up to 3 days.

WHIPPED CHERRY JUICE

MAKES ABOUT 9 OUNCES

This recipe demonstrates the way that xanthan gum and Versawhip combine to form elegant and flavorful foams. Versawhip is an enzymatically treated soy protein that creates stable foam structures that can tolerate small amounts of acid but no fat. The whipped cherry juice is great over lime seltzer for a play on a lime rickey. It also works well sprinkled with chopped marcona almonds on top of marinated fish. The light, ethereal texture adds volume to dishes and the intense cherry melts on the palate, lingering so as to present more cherry than is actually there. The ratio of 0.15 percent xanthan gum and 1.5 percent Versawhip may be applied to many other liquid mediums.

> 250 grams **cherry juice**
> 1.25 grams **salt**
> 3.75 grams **Versawhip 600** (see Sources, page 309)
> 0.375 gram **xanthan gum** (see Sources, page 309)

Pour the cherry juice into a blender. Set the speed on medium and allow a vortex to form. Sprinkle the salt, Versawhip, and xanthan gum into the vortex. Increase the speed to high and blend for a few seconds to fully disperse and hydrate the powders. Turn the blender off and pour the cherry base into the bowl of a stand mixer. Using the whisk attachment, whip the mixture until it forms soft peaks that hold their shape. If you aren't using the whipped cherry right away, store it in the refrigerator for up to 3 days and whip to stiff peaks again just before serving. The cherry mixture can be rewhipped multiple times without any problems.

STARCH

Some of the most commonly found household hydrocolloids are food starches. It is rare to find a kitchen that does not have at least flour and cornstarch gracing the shelves. Food starches are carbohydrates that are derived primarily from plants, such as wheat, corn, rice, potatoes, and tapioca. They tend to share basic properties, including a lack of sweetness, insolubility in cold water, and an ability to form pastes and gels in hot water. They appear naturally as starch granules, which can be distributed throughout a suspension and when heated will absorb liquid, swell, and gelatinize. This process increases viscosity and creates a paste. Upon cooling, the paste can become a gel. The pastes are most often used to thicken sauces. The gels can be affected by acid and sugar and are often used in desserts. The thickening properties of starch are relatively stable, although the pastes and gels can be broken down through freezing or aging.

All starch is manufactured into the form you find on supermarket shelves. Modern starch processing can be chemical, biochemical, or physical. These treatments are designed to stabilize the thickening process and improve the shelf life of the thickened product. They can also vary the viscosity and gel strength of the thickener. Chemically treated starches are labeled as modified starch. Heat treatments can strengthen the starch granules and slow the thickening action. Precooking or pregelatinization gives the modified starch cold-water solubility. Designer starches are manufactured to achieve specific culinary purposes with maximum efficiency.

Starches are often used as fat replacements in ready-made foods. They are found in low-fat dairy products, baked goods, condiments, and processed meats. The gelatinized starches can produce soft, stable, thermo-reversible gels that mimic the fat traditionally found in these food products. Resistant starches, which are resistant to digestion, are often used as a source of fiber in convenience foods to satisfy the current fashion for high-fiber food. In addition, they increase the ability to retain moisture and can be used to replace higher-calorie ingredients.

Three factors to consider when choosing starches are how much acid, sugar, and fat are in a recipe. As starches gelatinize, hydrogen bonds are formed that trap water in the structure. Acid disrupts hydrogen bonding, which can lead to a weaker gel. Sugar competes with the starch for water, which leads to a higher gelatinization temperature. Since starches need to be cooked to achieve the intended results, it can be beneficial in high-sugar recipes to add a percentage of the sweetener after the starch has gelatinized. Fats have a tendency to coat the starch granules and block hydration. When using starch in a high-fat recipe it is best to use one that has been pregelatinized, like Wondra flour, to avoid clumping and ensure a smooth emulsion.

RED CABBAGE KIMCHI CRACKLINGS

MAKES A LARGE BOWL OF CRACKLINGS

We originally developed this recipe with homemade ramp kimchi. Then we tried it with the Red Cabbage Kimchi. You could substitute any other pickle of your choice. To make these spicy, crunchy snacks, first we puree the kimchi with tapioca flour to form a dough. We chose tapioca because it has a very bland flavor, allowing the taste of the added ingredients and seasonings to stand front and center. We rolled the dough into thin sheets and steamed it for fifteen minutes to gelatinize the starch. We then dehydrated the steamed dough in a low (180°F/80°C) oven, flipping it over every so often until the sheets of dough were dry and brittle. Using this method we needed the dough to dry out to a level of 4 percent moisture for optimum puffing to occur. Since we were unable to effectively evaluate the exact percentage of moisture, we decided that completely dry was the best way to maximize our results. Then we broke the dehydrated dough into pieces and fried them in 400°F (205°C) oil. The kimchi cracklings puffed beautifully, tripling in size and creating gorgeous, crispy pieces that resembled traditional cracklings or fried pork rinds. A quick sprinkling of salt and we were happily crunching away.

200 grams **tapioca flour**
220 grams **Red Cabbage Kimchi** (page 38)
20 grams **kimchi pickling liquid**
Rice bran oil or **canola oil**, for frying
Fine sea salt

Puree the tapioca flour, kimchi, and pickling liquid in a food processor until a smooth dough is formed. Divide the dough in half and roll one portion into a thin cylinder about ¾ inch (2 centimeters) in diameter. Place the cylinder on a sheet of plastic wrap and cover with another sheet. With a rolling pin, roll the cylinder into a flat, thin sheet approximately ⅛ inch (3 millimeters) thick. The dough should be nearly translucent. Repeat with the other cylinder.

Prepare a steamer. We use a deep hotel pan filled with steaming water with a shallower perforated hotel pan inserted above the water line to make a long steamer. This way both sheets of dough fit lengthwise on top of each other. If you have a smaller steamer, you'll need to cut the sheets into pieces that fit in your steamer and stack them or cook them in batches.

Steam the dough sheets, still wrapped in plastic, for 15 minutes.

Meanwhile, preheat the oven to 180°F (80°C). Line a wire rack with parchment paper and set it over a large sheet pan. (This will allow for even airflow.)

Unwrap the steamed dough and lay it on the parchment. Place the pan in the oven and bake for 60 minutes or until the dough has dried. Flip the dough sheets occasionally to allow for even drying. When the sheets are completely dry and brittle, remove them from the oven and allow them to cool to room temperature.

Once the dough is completely cool to the touch, break or cut it into bite-size pieces.

In a large pot set over high heat, add enough oil to fill the pot halfway and heat it to 400°F (205°C). Line a wire rack with paper towels. Fry the crisps in batches. They will puff quickly and triple in size. Remove the crisps from the hot oil with a slotted spoon and put on the rack to drain. Season lightly with salt and serve.

GELATIN

Gelatin is probably one of the most familiar hydrocolloids, since Jell-O is one of those ubiquitous childhood foods. It is still considered one of the best for producing a soft, appetizing texture with sharp edges and good flavor release. The downside is its low melting point. Gelatin is a protein derived from collagen. It contains no fat, cholesterol, or carbohydrates, and is preservative free. In an aqueous solution it is hydrophilic, which means it is attracted to water. It is odorless, almost tasteless, and brittle in its solid form and usually pale yellow in color. It is assessed by gel strength, viscosity, color, and clarity.

Edible gelatins are traditionally derived from pig and beef skin through the process of hydrolysis. In these modern times of dietary restraint, the practice of producing gelatin from fish sources is becoming more popular. In addition to making gelatin-based desserts and confections, you can use gelatin as a stabilizer, a thickener, an emulsifier, or a texturizer and to clarify beverages such as apple juice or wine.

Gelatin is vulnerable to the papain and bromelain found in tropical fruits and figs. Papain and bromelain are proteases, or protein-digesting enzymes that break the bonds needed to form the gel structure. The enzyme is neutralized at 158°F (70°C), so cooking these fruits before adding them to gelatin can neutralize the problem.

Gelatin is typically found either as a powder, as granules, or as sheets. Three different types of gelatin are commonly available: Knox, which is powdered, with a bloom of 225; silver, which comes in sheets, with a bloom of 160; and gold, also in sheets, with a bloom of 200. The higher the bloom number, the stronger the gelatin. It's usually best to use the manufacturer's guidelines if you're not sure what kind of gelatin you're using and then extrapolate from there if you don't like the results.

PECTIN

Pectin is found in a wide variety of fruits. A traditional gelling agent in jams and jellies, it can also be used for thickening, binding water, and stabilizing. Commercially manufactured pectins are most commonly derived from citrus peel and apple pomace, both of which are by-products of juice production. Once produced, pectin is then divided into two categories, high-methoxyl gelation and low-methoxyl gelation. The type of pectin is usually clearly stated on the packaging. If not, just remember that pectins designed for low- or no-sugar applications are low methoxyl and those meant for traditional jams and jellies are high methoxyl. Pectin has a synergistic relationship with dairy products, utilizing them for their calcium while enhancing their creamy mouthfeel. It is often seen in low-fat cheese applications because it improves the texture on the palate, making the low-fat version much more comparable to the original.

High-methoxyl (HM) pectins require the presence of sugars at 60 to 65 percent of the finished gel. The sugar is thought to help bind water so it remains stable in the gel. It also is contained in the gel at high enough levels to effectively kill off microorganisms. HM pectin also needs sufficiently low pH levels in a range of 2.8 to 3.6, with 3.3

considered optimal. If there is not enough acid, the gel will not set; if there is too much, the pectin will form a loose, weak gel and syneresis, or weeping of liquid from the gel, will occur. Setting times for HM pectin are normally categorized as rapid, medium, or slow set. More methoxyl groups removed during the processing of the pectin will result in slower setting times.

Low-methoxyl (LM) pectins are set with calcium. These gels are formed with ionic bonds, and the calcium cross-links with the carboxyl groups on the LM pectins. Because LM pectins do not need sugar, the gels they form tend to be much lower in calories than those created using HM pectins. They also have the distinction of being heat stable. LM pectins have slower setting times than HM pectins, and can gel at pH levels ranging from 2.8 to 6.5, with 10 to 80 percent soluble solids in the presence of calcium. Amidated pectins, which are low-methoxyl pectins that have been treated with ammonia, need less calcium than standard low-methoxyl pectins and are more tolerant of calcium fluctuations. Amidated pectins are thermo-reversible and allow for the ability of the gel to reset after shearing.

TWO-MELON TERRINE

MAKES 4 TERRINES

We pursued the idea of using low-methoxyl pectin to create a fruit and vegetable adhesive that would allow us to create entirely edible terrines that were held together with an almost invisible but flavorful glue. This technique was the result of that exploration. First, we make fruit-flavored solutions with 0.5 percent calcium lactate or calcium gluconate. The choice of one over the other is based on taste. Calcium lactate is derived from lactose and has a slightly acidic taste. Calcium gluconate is derived from glucose and tastes slightly sweet. Calcium lactate has slightly more available calcium than calcium gluconate, although not enough to make a difference in most applications. You will sometimes find blended calcium under the label calcium lactate-gluconate. Then we impregnate the fruit with the calcium by vacuum sealing them together. It takes about five minutes for the calcium to be absorbed by the fruit, after which time we open the vacuum bag and pat the fruit dry.

Next we dissolve 3 percent pectin in water at 203°F (95°C) to hydrate it, then let it cool. Once the pectin is cool, we brush it on one piece of the calcium-infused fruit and lay another piece on top. Then we vacuum seal the fruit to compress it together and let it rest in the refrigerator overnight. The following morning when we cut open the bag, we will find that the fruit has been sealed together with a pectin gel. The pectin gel is soft and seamless in the preparation.

The resulting presentation is as beautiful as it is delicious. We enjoy the terrine sliced and served with seared scallops and crumbled blue cheese on hot days, and served warm with crispy soft-shell crabs on cool evenings. Even slicing and topping it with thinly shaved prosciutto is an elegant preparation.

250 grams **water**

7.5 grams **low-methoxyl pectin** (we use 18CG from Le Sanctuaire; see Sources, page 309)

1 **cantaloupe**

1 **honeydew melon**

2 grams **fine sea salt**

Calcium lactate (see Sources, page 309)

Put the water in a small pot over high heat and bring to a boil. Pour the hot water into a blender and carefully turn the blender on low. Increase the speed until a vortex forms; then slowly sprinkle the pectin into the water. Make sure the lid is secure and increase the speed. Blend for 5 minutes. Pour into a small bowl and reserve until needed. Skim off and discard any foam that may collect on the surface.

Cut the top and bottom off of each melon. Stand them on end and carefully cut away the exterior skin and rind from top to bottom. Cut into quarters and scrape the seeds and juices into a small bowl. Trim each melon quarter into as thick a plank as possible with flat sides. Place all the melon trimmings in the bowl with the seeds; set the bowl aside. Season the planks lightly with salt. Put each melon plank into separate vacuum-seal bags and seal on high pressure. This process will weaken the cell walls and allow for the calcium to penetrate the fruit.

Put the melon seeds, juices, and trimmings in a blender and turn on low to begin breaking up the flesh. Increase the speed to medium so that the juices are released and the seeds remain intact. Strain the mixture through a fine-mesh strainer, pushing on the solids to extract the juice. Weigh this liquid and calculate 0.5 percent of its weight. Weigh out that amount of calcium lactate. Put the juices into a clean blender and add the calcium. Turn the blender on medium speed and blend for 2 minutes to disperse and dissolve the calcium. Turn off the blender and reserve the juice.

Cut open the vacuum bags and divide the melon between two new vacuum bags. Add the calcium-enriched melon juice and vacuum seal the bags. You may not need all the juice. Let the melon infuse for 5 minutes.

Cut open the bags and remove the melon planks. Pat them dry and lay them out in a row. Use a pastry brush to apply the pectin to the honeydew planks and then place a cantaloupe plank on top of each. Place the stacked melon planks in vacuum bags and seal on high pressure. The vacuum sealing will apply a uniform pressure on the melons and keep them together so they will glue tightly. Place the bags in the refrigerator for several hours or ideally overnight.

Once the melon has had time to set, cut open the bags, remove the melon, and trim the planks to make clean, sharp edges. At this point you will have four rectangles of two-melon terrine. The terrine may be diced or sliced and even gently warmed in the oven or on a grill before serving.

AGAR-AGAR

Agar is the gelling agent used in many Japanese confections. It often produces a crumbly textured gel resembling firm Jell-O Jigglers, which are very popular across the ocean. Agar produces vegetarian gels that are stable at room temperature and even when slightly warmed. Agar, also known as *kanten*, is a phycocolloid, a gelling agent derived from marine algae. The family includes agar, alginates, and carrageenan. Agar is a strong gelling agent that results in a firm, brittle gel that has a very short texture on the palate. Eating a straight agar gel is like sinking your teeth into a soft pencil eraser that breaks apart under pressure. It must gently simmer for a full five minutes in order to hydrate properly. Gelling occurs as the agar cools to temperatures between 90°F and 109°F (32°C–43°C). It is a thermo-reversible gel and can be reheated back into a liquid form at temperatures of 185°F (85°C) and above. It can be melted and regelled with no loss of strength.

Agar can be utilized at pH levels ranging from 5 to 8 to create unflavored gels. It easily adopts the flavor of whatever is blended into it and acts as a fragrance fixer, so that aromas remain present for longer periods of time. Agar can be used to make transparent or brightly colored gels for attractive presentations. Sugar, glucose, and glycerin can be used to increase sheen in the finished gel. Agar is traditionally used in Japan to create confections that are flavorful, visually appealing, aromatic, and can be served at room temperature.

Agar has a synergistic relationship with locust bean gum (see page 260) at a ratio of 9:1; this combination is added at less than 1 percent of the total base. They work well together and when the two are combined, the resulting texture becomes less rigid and more elastic, creating a gel much more palatable than a straight agar gel. Agar does not work well with acid, so any acidic ingredients in agar formulations should be added after the agar is hydrated in a neutral pH environment.

BACON CONSOMMÉ

MAKES ABOUT 2 QUARTS

Chefs have chased the perfect consommé for as long as there has been cuisine. Traditionally clarified using a raft of egg whites, meat, and aromatics, it was inevitable that chefs would start looking for modern alternatives. The first solution was introduced by Professor Gerd Klöck in 2004 and popularized by Heston Blumenthal of The Fat Duck. Ice clarification is a method of freezing gelatin-rich stocks and then slowly defrosting them through layers of cheesecloth and a fine sieve to create a perfectly clear liquid. As the gel is frozen, the water trapped in the gelatin crystallizes. This causes the sharp edges to damage the cell walls. As the frozen gel warms up, the water and all of the water-soluble components melt before the gelatin or the fats and leak out of the damaged cell structure, leaving everything else behind.

The next innovation was using agar instead of gelatin to speed up the freeze-thaw process. Agar works more quickly because it has a much higher melting point. If there is no fat in the preparation, it can actually be defrosted into a filter at room temperature, which greatly reduces the filtration time. From there we made the leap of eliminating the time spent in the freezer when using agar. Syneresis is the process by which the liquid leaks out of the gel structure. Agar naturally creates a hard, brittle gel that is prone to syneresis. It seemed reasonable to us that we could easily make an agar gel and break it up in the vacuum sealer, causing the clear liquids to leak out while the impurities were trapped in the gel. Once we poured the broken gel into a cheesecloth-lined filter, we would have a clear liquid almost immediately. It worked beautifully and was a huge breakthrough for us. As we worked through the process, we realized that brisk stirring of the agar-thickened liquid was enough to break it apart and create syneresis, effectively giving us a low-tech clarification process that could be easily accomplished at home. We use a ratio of 0.25 percent agar to clarify most of our liquids. Occasionally in liquids with more dissolved impurities we increase this to 0.3 percent.

> 1 kilogram sliced **bacon**, cut into ½-inch (1.25-centimeter) pieces
>
> 2 small or 1 large **onion**, peeled and diced
>
> 1 **head garlic**, peeled and separated into cloves
>
> 2 grams **crushed red pepper flakes**
>
> 170 grams **red wine**
>
> 170 grams **smoked soy sauce** (see page 62)
>
> 2,500 grams **water**
>
> 6.25 grams **agar** (see Sources, page 309)

Put the bacon in a large skillet set over medium heat. Cook the bacon slowly to render the fat, about 30 minutes. As the fat renders, pour it into a metal bowl or other heatproof container and reserve for another use. When the bacon is evenly browned, add the onions, garlic, and red pepper. Cook until the onions are tender and lightly browned. Transfer the mixture to a strainer set over a bowl and drain any excess bacon fat.

Return the pan to medium heat, add the wine and soy sauce, and deglaze the pan, scraping up any browned bits on the bottom. Pour the pan drippings into a pressure cooker and add the bacon and onion mixture. Add the water and cook on high pressure for 1 hour. Let the pressure naturally dissipate. Strain the stock through a fine-mesh sieve, pushing on the solids to extrude any juices. Let the stock cool and transfer to the refrigerator. Refrigerate for at least 4 hours or until thoroughly chilled. Any bacon fat left in the stock will solidify on the surface. Remove and discard this fat and strain the stock one more time. You need 2,500 grams of bacon stock.

Pour the bacon stock into a stockpot set over medium heat. Whisk the agar into the stock. Bring the stock to a simmer, stirring to prevent the agar from settling to the bottom of the pan. Cook the stock for

5 minutes to fully hydrate the agar. Pour the mixture into another pan to cool, then refrigerate.

When the bacon stock is cold and gelled, use a whisk to finely break apart the gel structure. Return the stock to the refrigerator for several hours to rest. Once the broken gel has rested, it releases its liquid more easily.

Line a strainer with four layers of cheesecloth and set over a container large enough to hold the strainer and the liquid. Place the straining setup in the refrigerator and let the broken gel strain for a few hours. Merely breaking the gel and squeezing it in batches through the cheesecloth can speed up this process. While this produces consommé quickly, the final yield is less.

LOCUST BEAN GUM

Locust bean gum is rarely used by itself; rather, it is a supporting character that helps bring out the best effects in other food gums. Locust bean gum is extracted from the seeds of the locust bean or carob tree. Hydrocolloids derived from food seed pods are known as galactomannans. They must be hydrated in hot water and sheared into mixtures with a standing blender. Locust bean gum forms nonreversible weak gels that do not freeze well and begin to degrade at temperatures above 176°F (80°C). It has synergistic relationships with agar, kappa carrageenan (see page 262), and xanthan gum, giving elasticity and strength to gels that are otherwise crumbly or nonexistent. Locust bean gum can be combined with any of these to form an elastic gel. It is often used as a starch replacement in foods to maintain thickness while reducing calories. It adds fiber and decreases the fat content in prepared foods. It is used in ice creams to help prevent the formation of ice crystals and to improve texture.

WHITE CHOCOLATE SHEET

MAKES ENOUGH TO GARNISH 8 DESSERTS

*These white chocolate sheets are a wonderful example of the synergy
between agar and locust bean gum. They are delicate and flexible, with
a rich flavor. They can be draped across fruits, cheeses, or desserts. If
you prefer, you can also let the chocolate set in one piece and slice
it for serving as custard, or puree it for something softer and more
puddinglike. The sheets are best served cold, although they will hold
their shape at room temperature.*

> Nonstick cooking spray
>
> 3 grams **fine sea salt**
>
> 3 grams **ground cumin**
>
> 1 gram **grated nutmeg**
>
> 750 grams **whole milk**
>
> 4.5 grams **agar** (see Sources, page 309)
>
> 0.5 gram **locust bean gum** (see Sources, page 309)
>
> 500 gram **white chocolate**, chopped

Spray two 12 × 16-inch metal baking pans with nonstick cooking
spray. Prepare an ice bath.

Place the salt, cumin, nutmeg, and milk in a small pot set over
medium heat. Bring to a simmer, cover, and turn off the heat. Allow
the milk to infuse for 20 minutes. Transfer the mixture to a metal
bowl set in the ice bath and let cool.

Strain the infused milk into a blender, discarding the spices. Turn
the blender on low and slowly increase the speed until a vortex forms
in the center. Sprinkle the agar and locust bean gum powders into the
vortex. Blend at medium-high speed for 30 seconds.

Pour the milk into a clean pot set over medium-high heat and
bring to a simmer. Cook for 5 minutes to fully hydrate the agar. Pour
the milk back into the blender. Turn the blender on low and slowly add

the white chocolate. Once all the chocolate is incorporated, increase the speed to medium for 30 seconds to make sure the chocolate and milk are emulsified. Turn off the blender and carefully pour the mixture onto the prepared pans. The sheet should be as thin and even as you can make it, approximately ⅛ inch (3 millimeters) thick. It will set within 5 to 10 minutes and will benefit from resting in refrigeration for 1 hour. Then the sheets can be cut into shapes and used as desired.

GUAR GUM

Guar gum is manufactured from the seeds of the common cluster bean, a vegetable plant native to India. It is a less expensive alternative to locust bean gum and has greater thickening powers. It is soluble in hot or cold water. Guar gum is notable for its film-forming abilities, high viscosity, and water-binding capability. It functions well at low temperatures and is often used as a stabilizer in ice cream formulations because it retards ice crystal formation and improves stability in the freeze-thaw cycle. It is high in soluble fiber, has intense thickening powers, and is stable in a pH range of 5 to 7. Guar gum has a slow hydration time when used with cold liquids, taking up to two hours to fully hydrate, and when used in higher percentages can add a discernible raw dried bean flavor to the finished product.

CARRAGEENAN

Carrageenan is well known for its affinity for dairy products. In fact, one of its earliest uses in Europe was to make puddings by boiling harvested seaweed in milk. The family of carrageenans is derived from red seaweed and covers a wide range of colloidal behavior, from a thickener to varying thermo-reversible gels ranging in texture from soft and elastic to firm and brittle. The three main types of carrageenan are kappa, lambda, and iota. During manufacturing the different types of seaweed are sorted and then treated with a different range of alkali during the extraction process in order to develop the desired characteristics.

Kappa creates firm, brittle gels. It is most often utilized for its ability to increase the strength of an emulsion, to hold things in suspension, and to create body and texture in the finished gel. Kappa carrageenan needs potassium to form a gel. Once it has been frozen it should not be thawed, because the gel structure will be weak and begin to leak fluid. Kappa carrageenan is unique in its ability to hold cocoa particles in suspension in dairy systems at very low percentages. It has a synergistic relationship with locust bean gum at ratios of 4:6 and 6:4. This combination can create elastic, cohesive gels with properties similar to gelatin. We have found that a slightly amended ratio of 62.5 percent kappa to 37.5 percent locust bean gum produces results that best suit our palates, and its clarity is unsurpassed.

Iota forms soft, elastic gels and can happily be frozen and thawed while still holding its structure. Iota requires calcium ions to form a gel. It is notable for its ability to re-form the gel structure. Iota can be combined with kappa to achieve a variety of gel consistencies that have the ability to withstand a moderate range of temperatures.

Lambda does not gel; instead it creates sols, or thickened liquids. It is often used in conjunction with dairy products, and is valued for its ability to create a creamy texture as it thickens.

All carrageenans are soluble in hot water. Once the carrageenan has been dispersed, it hydrates at about 175°F–185°F (79°C–85°C). It is sensitive to acidity and will begin to lose its gel strength below pH levels of about 4.3. When using acidic ingredients with carrageenan, add them last; you should also expect longer setting times. Carrageenan gels are thermally reversible. The actual setting and melting temperatures tend to fall into a range rather than being exact. Most carrageenans will set between 104°F and 140°F (40°C–60°C) and melt at 41°F to 68°F (5°C–20°C) above the gelling temperature.

Carrageenans have a synergistic relationship with dairy due to their unique ability to interact with kappa-casein proteins. This ability can increase the gel capability of the carrageenan up to ten times its normal strength. Kappa is often used as a stabilizer in items like processed cheese, ice cream, and evaporated milk. Lambda can be combined with kappa in dairy systems to create a creamy gel. This combination or that of kappa and iota is often found in fluid dairy products such as skim milk or soy milks to stabilize the suspensions and improve mouthfeel. Carrageenan can be combined with low levels of starch to create body and viscosity in desserts like puddings and flans.

PEANUT BUTTER CUSTARD

MAKES 8 SERVINGS

This custard shows off the way that you can combine different types of carrageenans to create a custardlike dessert with a soft, tender texture that holds its shape beautifully. It gives you the gentle, set texture of a baked egg custard but it can be cooked on top of the stove. Beyond that, if you love peanut butter, you are going to be in hog heaven. It's that good.

> 200 grams **maple syrup**
>
> 1,010 grams **whole milk**
>
> 7.1 grams (0.5%) **iota carrageenan** (see Sources, page 309)
>
> 1.4 grams (0.1%) **kappa carrageenan** (see Sources, page 309)
>
> 200 grams **creamy peanut butter**
>
> 4 grams **fine sea salt**

Put the maple syrup in a blender with 112.5 grams of the milk. Turn the blender on low and slowly increase the speed until a vortex forms. Sprinkle in the carrageenans and blend for 30 seconds to disperse them. Add the remaining milk to the blender and pulse to combine.

Pour the mixture into a pot set over medium heat. Slowly heat to 185°F (85°C) to hydrate the carrageenans.

In a small bowl, microwave the peanut butter for 1 to 2 minutes to warm it through. When the milk reaches the desired temperature, add the peanut butter and salt and stir together. Pour the mixture into a clean blender and puree to fully combine the ingredients.

Pour the custard base into eight 6-ounce molds and refrigerate for at least 3 hours. When the custards are completely cool, unmold and serve. Once the custards are completely cool they can be covered and kept in the refrigerator for up to 3 days.

METHOCEL OR METHYLCELLULOSE

The most common place that consumers find methylcellulose is in a bottle of Metamucil. It is often used as a fiber supplement in foods. Methylcellulose is derived from cellulose pulp, which is a complex carbohydrate found in the cell walls of plants. It is used as a food gum, which is neutral in flavor, odorless, colorless, and clear when in solution. It forms a gel at warmer temperatures and reverts to liquid form as it cools. Methylcellulose in powdered or granular form will absorb water from the air and should always be kept in an airtight container.

Methocel, produced by the Dow Chemical Company, is a commercial brand name for readily available methylcellulose products. Methocel is cold-water soluble and is easily dispersed in 194°F (90°C) water or other water-based liquid, which is then sheared into the base ingredients using a standing blender to combine. The mixture is then cooled to hydrate the Methocel. It must be cooled to below 50°F (10°C) for at least half an hour to fully hydrate. Chilling and holding the mixture in refrigeration gives this time to happen. Once hydrated, it forms thermo-reversible gels of varying strengths at different temperatures, depending upon which variety of Methocel you use, which will revert back into a liquid state at lower temperatures. This can provide a gel stability at higher temperatures that is impossible to obtain with many other hydrocolloids.

This reversible thermal gelation and the cohesive nature of Methocel at lower temperatures allow you to use it as a binding agent. You can mix your product at cooler temperatures and, once heated, the mixture will gel and bind itself together. This action is useful in the creation of fried foods because it helps to seal the main ingredient inside a batter or coating and prevents any liquids from leaking out.

Low-viscosity varieties of Methocel (A, E, F, J, K) lower the surface tension of water. They can be used to trap air bubbles and help stabilize whipped toppings and mousselike creations without the use of cream. Methocel works especially well for this purpose when combined with xanthan gum (we use 1 percent Methocel F50 and 0.15 percent xanthan gum in our whipped applications).

Methocel is useful in creating stability during the freeze-thaw cycle. It can help prevent crystallization and syneresis as the product moves through temperature cycles. Many preparations will separate after they've been frozen and thawed. Some vegetable purees develop an unpleasantly rubbery texture after they've been frozen. The addition of a small amount of Methocel is helpful because it means that you can prepare recipes in advance, freeze them, and cook them directly from frozen, and they will still look and taste great.

Methocel products are useful in preparing edible films and crisps. The Methocel adds viscosity, which makes the base mixture more spreadable and easier to work with. In the formation of crisps, this allows the cook to make thin, even layers of the mixture that dry evenly in a low oven or a dehydrator. For the formation of edible films, these same mixtures will form a gel when heated. This allows cooks to lift the film and drape it over other foods or place it on a serving plate.

When using Methocel in an emulsion, its ability to reduce surface tension allows thicker ingredients to be broken up into smaller droplets that blend together more easily. In fat-based applications, Methocel forms elastic films around oil droplets, which then help keep them from coalescing. When the oil droplets remain separate, the mixtures will stay emulsified for longer periods of time.

Methocel may be used over a wide range of pH levels (3–11) because the products are nonionic. This means that they have no ionic charge and will not react with metallic salts or other charged compounds. This slows the separation of insoluble materials, which would normally settle at the bottom of the solution. Its ability to work with both basic and acidic ingredients makes Methocel very functional in the kitchen for both sweet and savory purposes.

The one drawback we've found when working with Methocel products is their inability to play nicely with sugar. When Methocel is mixed with high-sugar solutions, it produces an unpleasant odor and flavor reminiscent of corked wine. We originally worked around this by adding sugar components after the Methocel had hydrated. Thanks to Harold McGee, we've extrapolated a better solution. He advocated a simple trick of using a piece of plastic wrap to absorb the corked flavor of wine. This works because the molecule in infected corks that produces the unpleasant odor and flavor (2,4,6-trichloroanisole) resembles polyethylene on a molecular level and sticks to the plastic wrap. Since the aromas were identical, we tested his theory by submerging a piece of plastic wrap in a corky Methocel mixture and it was successful in removing both the unpleasant odor and flavor. It is a simple solution to an exasperating issue.

METHOCEL PRODUCTS:

A4C: medium viscosity with firm gels forming between 122°F and 131°F
(50°C–55°C)

F50: low viscosity with semifirm gels forming between 143°F and 154°F
(62°C–68°C)

While many more types of Methocel are available, we have stream-lined our pantry down to these two. We find that too many options can make things confusing, and we have been able to achieve all of our goals with these types of Methocel.

YUZU MERINGUE

MAKES JUST OVER 1 QUART

This makes a gorgeous whipped topping that is fabulous on margaritas or strawberry lemonade. We've also been known to use it for garnishing fresh berries and various dessert preparations. It's a nice introduction to using Methocel and xanthan gum together to create foaming action. Unlike whipped toppings made with other products, such as Versawhip, these preparations can tolerate heat and moderate amounts of fat in the mixture simply because Methocel is such a good emulsifier. In this recipe we are able to shear the Methocel directly into the base because we are working with an entirely liquid medium. For this recipe we use 1 percent Methocel F50 and 0.15 percent xantham gum.

458 grams **water**

84 grams **yuzu juice** (see Sources, page 309)

40 grams **sugar**

3 grams **fine sea salt**

5.84 grams **Methocel F50** (see Sources, page 309)

0.876 gram **xanthan gum** (see Sources, page 309)

Put the water, yuzu juice, sugar, and salt in a blender. Turn the speed to medium and blend until the sugar is dissolved, about 2 minutes. Turn the speed down to low, then increase the speed until a vortex forms. Sprinkle the Methocel and the xanthan gum into the vortex. Increase the speed to medium-high and blend for 1 minute.

Prepare an ice bath. Line the inside of a bowl with plastic wrap. Pour the yuzu mixture into the bowl. Place the bowl in the ice bath and stir until the temperature reaches 50°F (10°C). Let the mixture stand at that temperature for 60 minutes, stirring occasionally. The mixture should smell clean and fresh. If there is any lingering aroma of corked wine, continue to stir the mixture in the bowl and let it rest for another hour.

These bubbles may be whipped hot or cold. Pour the base into either the bowl of a stand mixer or a double boiler. Discard the plastic wrap. If a cold meringue is desired, use the stand mixer. If a warm meringue is desired, use the whisk attachment to a stick blender to aerate the base as it warms in the double boiler. A warm gentle heat is best to facilitate the aeration and gelation of the bubbles.

MOZZARELLA CHAWAN MUSHI

SERVES 4

This recipe demonstrates Methocel's ability to form a warm gel. This custard mimics the texture of the classic chawan mushi, hence the recipe's name. We add Methocel at a ratio of 1 percent of the total weight of the other ingredients. The flavor of the cheese gives it an unusual twist. We've served this with marinated baby tomatoes, fresh cherries with tarragon, or a little crab salad garnished with fresh lovage. Any garnishes should be room temperature or slightly warm because as the custard cools the texture will soften, although the individual ramekins help preserve their heat.

560 grams **buffalo mozzarella**, at room temperature

70 grams **mozzarella water** (the water in which the mozzarella was stored)

15 grams **olive oil**

2 grams **fine sea salt**

161.75 grams **mozzarella water** (25% of the combined weight of the first 4 ingredients)

8.08 grams **Methocel A4C** (see Sources, page 309)

Cut the mozzarella into small pieces. Put the mozzarella, 70 grams of mozzarella water, olive oil, and salt in a blender and puree until smooth. Set aside.

Prepare an ice bath.

Put the 161.75 grams of mozzarella water in a small pot set over medium heat and bring it to a simmer. Sprinkle the Methocel into the water and thoroughly disperse it using a small whisk. Pour the water into the blender and shear it into the mozzarella mixture at medium speed, slowly increasing the speed to high until the cheese becomes smooth and homogeneous, with a slight sheen. Using a rubber spatula, scrape the cheese mixture into a metal bowl set in an ice bath and let cool until the temperature is below 50°F (10°C). Cover with plastic wrap and let rest in the refrigerator for at least 20 minutes or up to 2 days before using.

Preheat the oven to 250°F (120°C).

Spoon the mozzarella mixture into four 3-ounce ramekins and place them on a baking sheet. Cover the ramekins with plastic wrap and bake them in the oven until the mozzarella is just firm and soft to the touch, 10 to 15 minutes. Serve immediately.

REHEATABLE BROWN BUTTER HOLLANDAISE

SERVES 4

Classic hollandaise sauce cannot be chilled or reheated without losing the wonderful silky texture that it is known for. Here we've used Methocel at a ratio of 1 percent of the total weight of the other ingredients to make a hollandaise that can be made ahead of time while retaining its semifluid consistency. Even better, it has a spreadable texture when cold that makes it wonderful for sandwiches.

> 370 grams **Brown Butter Hollandaise** (page 147)
>
> 92.5 grams **water**
>
> 2 grams **fine sea salt**
>
> 4.64 grams **Methocel F50** (see Sources, page 309)

While the hollandaise sauce is still warm, bring the water to a boil in a small pot set over medium-high heat. Sprinkle the salt and Methocel over the hot water and whisk to dissolve.

Pour the hollandaise sauce into a blender and turn it on low speed. Gradually drizzle the water into the sauce. Slowly increase the speed to medium and blend until the mixture looks well blended with a slight sheen, about 30 seconds.

Set up an ice bath. Pour the mixture into a metal bowl set in the ice bath and let the mixture chill, stirring occasionally, until it reaches 50°F (10°C). Then let it rest in the refrigerator for at least 20 minutes. The sauce will keep for up to 2 days in an airtight container in the refrigerator.

Reheat the sauce in a small pot set over low heat, stirring occasionally. Do not let the sauce boil. Serve immediately.

GELLAN

Gellan gum is a bacterial polysaccharide produced by the fermentation of *Sphingomonas elodea* bacteria. It is used both as a gelling agent and to create fluid gels. Fluid gels are thick homogeneous liquids that have been gelled and then pureed, usually in a blender. They can also be formed by whisking a base as it sets. Fluid gels are characterized by the fact that they look like a liquid but are actually a gel. They are strong enough to hold other ingredients in suspension.

Gellan is insoluble in cold water. The easiest way to disperse gellan gum is in a liquid in a running blender. Sprinkle the gellan in the vortex until it is completely dispersed. Alternatively, gellan can be mixed with sugar, glycerol, alcohol, or oil before being added to a liquid medium in order to facilitate dispersion. Gellan is easily dispersible in dairy liquids.

Gellan gum comes in two forms, high acyl and low acyl. The high-acyl gellan forms soft, elastic gels, while the low-acyl forms stiff, brittle gels. The two products can be used together to create a variety of gel textures, from fluid to extremely firm. Gellan gums are comparable to gelatin in their flavor release and the clarity of their gel. In fact, gellan is often used in conjunction with gelatin to improve stability and to raise the setting temperature. Gellan gums are activated by calcium. Because the two types of gellan are typically blended together and all of their particular quirks come into play when combined in a recipe, it's important to understand the characteristics of both types.

Hydration temperatures vary depending on the type of gellan and the ion concentration of the mixture being gelled. Low-acyl gellan will not hydrate at pH levels below 3.9, but we can use sodium citrate to adjust pH levels in gellan recipes. With low-acyl gellan, high ion concentrations, particularly calcium, will inhibit hydration and affect the hydration temperature. For this reason sequestrants, like sodium citrate and sodium hexametaphosphate, are used for their ability to bind free calcium ions and keep them from interacting with the gum. Depending on the amount of available calcium in an ingredient, we vary the amount of sequestrant from 0.05 to 0.3 percent of the total weight of the solution to allow for hydration in a temperature range of 194°F–203°F (90°C–95°C). When working with high percentages of sugar and salt, they should be added after the gellan has hydrated.

A good starting point when working with gellan is to add it to a recipe with low-acyl gellan at 0.1 percent and high-acyl gellan at 0.3 percent of the total weight of the base mixture to create a firm, flexible gel. Gellan sets quickly as its temperature cools; high-acyl gels at 176°F (80°C) and low-acyl gels at about 158°F (70°C). For best results, you should warm your molds. Low-acyl gellan is thermally irreversible but high-acyl will melt at temperatures ranging from 158°F to 176°F (70°C–80°C). After it has set, this type of gel is very elastic and can be manipulated into knots or other shapes. It can also be gently heated up to 158°F (70°C) or pureed to form a fluid gel.

Low-acyl gellan works well as an ice cream and sorbet stabilizer. It encourages the formation of very small ice crystals and acts as an emulsifier. We like to add it to recipes at a ratio of 1 percent of the weight of the other ingredients.

As a first step we separate out the milk in a recipe and heat it to 194°F (90°C) before shearing in the gellan and hydrating it. This avoids the clumping that normally occurs between 104°F and 122°F (40°C–50°C) as we hydrate the gellan. The calcium in milk is naturally sequestered until we heat it. As the milk cools it sets in a firm block. We chop up the gelled milk and add it to the blender when we puree the other ingredients. It will take about five minutes to completely break down, and then we simply finish the base as we normally would.

CELERY ROOT ENCAPSULATION

MAKES AT LEAST 48 BITE-SIZE ENCAPSULATIONS

These small orbs have big celery flavor from both the celery root centers and the celery stock that encapsulates them. The cream cheese gives the celery root a little extra body and tang. The gellan in the water bath reacts with the calcium in the celery root, forming a delicate gel around each orb. They may be heated in the celery stock and served warm like miniature raviolis, topped with brown butter, or hidden in a soup or stew as pockets of exploding flavor. You can also serve the orbs as single bites topped with shaved country ham and chopped celery leaves.

> 1,000 grams **water**
>
> 235 grams **celery**
>
> 7 grams **fine sea salt**
>
> 500 grams **celery root**, peeled and cut into chunks
>
> 220 grams **cream cheese**
>
> 1,000 grams **water**
>
> 5 grams **low-acyl gellan** (0.5%) (see Sources, page 309)
>
> 0.5 gram **sodium hexametaphosphate** (0.05%) (see Sources, page 309)

Put the water, celery, and salt in a pressure cooker. Cook on high pressure for 5 minutes, then let the pressure dissipate naturally. Alternatively, put the ingredients in a medium pot over high heat. Bring the mixture to a boil, reduce the heat to low, and simmer for 1 hour. Strain the stock, weigh out 500 grams for cooking the celery root, and reserve the remaining stock in the refrigerator.

Put the 500 grams of celery stock and the celery root in a pressure cooker. Cook on high pressure for 10 minutes, then let the pressure dissipate naturally. Strain the celery root, add the liquid to the reserved celery stock, and puree the celery root in a blender. Add the cream cheese and puree until smooth. Strain the mixture through a fine-mesh sieve and refrigerate for 4 hours or until completely cold.

Put the water in a blender. Turn the blender on low and increase the speed until a vortex forms in the center of the water. Sprinkle the gellan and the sodium hexametaphosphate into the water. Increase the speed to high and blend for 30 seconds. Pour the mixture into a bowl, and let rest for 30 minutes at room temperature.

Use a tablespoon measure to drop spoonfuls of the celery root puree into the gellan bath. Use a clean spoon to ladle the bath over the spoonfuls of puree, making sure they are fully encapsulated. Leave each orb in the bath for 2 minutes. Use a slotted spoon to transfer the orbs to a bowl of clean water and rinse off any excess gellan. Transfer them to the reserved refrigerated celery stock. While the orbs are stored in the stock, the stock will infuse the membrane with the flavor of celery.

To serve, warm enough celery stock from the storage container to cover the number of orbs you are heating in a pot set over low heat. Slide the orbs into the stock and just heat through. Serve immediately.

CHEDDAR TOFU

MAKES ABOUT 1⅓ POUNDS

We call this Cheddar tofu because of the texture. Imagine soft tofu, silky against your tongue, infused with a rich Cheddar flavor. It's pretty awesome stuff. You can use it in exactly the same way that you would real tofu. It happily sits center stage as the main component in a salad or soup, or it can be diced and incorporated into a dish much like gnocchi or small dumplings. We use both the high- and low-acyl gellans at a ratio of 0.2 percent of the weight of the other ingredients. The gellan makes it relatively heat stable, and it holds its shape beautifully when cut or molded.

    500 grams **whole milk**

    250 grams **aged Cheddar cheese**

    260 grams **firm tofu**

    1.5 grams **fine sea salt**

    1.3 grams **high-acyl gellan** (0.2%) (see Sources, page 309)

    1.3 grams **low-acyl gellan** (0.2%) (see Sources, page 309)

Preheat the oven to 200°F (95°C). Set a 9-inch square Pyrex baking dish in the oven to warm. (Warming the dish will prevent the hot Cheddar mixture from seizing when it is poured into the dish.)

Put the milk and the cheese in a heavy-bottomed pot set over medium heat. Bring the mixture to a simmer and cook for 5 minutes, until the cheese is melted. Turn off the heat, cover the pot, and let steep for 20 minutes. Strain the mixture through a cheesecloth-lined strainer, pressing gently on the solids to extract the milk from the solids. Discard the solids. Weigh out 385 grams of Cheddar milk. Discard any extra.

Put the Cheddar milk, tofu, and salt in a blender. Puree the mixture until it is silky-smooth. While the blender is running, sprinkle both gellans into the vortex to evenly disperse the hydrocolloids. This will take about 30 seconds.

Pour the gellan mixture into a heavy-bottomed pot set over medium heat, stirring to prevent the mixture from sticking to the bottom of the pot. Continue to cook the mixture, stirring constantly, until it reaches 194°F (90°C). At this temperature the gellan will be fully hydrated.

Quickly pour the mixture into the warmed baking dish. Pour the liquid as quickly as you can without splashing, keeping the flow as smooth and even as possible because the gellan sets rapidly once removed from the heat. Set the baking dish on the counter and let the Cheddar tofu cool in the dish.

When the tofu is cold, remove it from the dish and trim off any rounded edges. Cut it into ½-inch (1.25-centimeter) cubes and reserve on a baking sheet in the refrigerator until ready to use. It can be kept, covered, in the refrigerator for up to 3 days.

SODIUM ALGINATE

Sodium alginate has become very popular in restaurant kitchens as a stabilizer and an emulsifier. It is derived from brown algae, which is naturally abundant. Alginates form gels with acids and with calcium. At pH levels above 3.5, alginates can be used to effectively thicken and stabilize. Liquid solutions thickened with sodium alginates are notable for their pseudoplasticity, or the ability to thin out when briskly stirred or shaken and rethicken as they sit. They are popular because they are characterized by cold-water solubility, an unusual trait in a gelling agent. The gels can set at room temperatures and once formed, they are heat stable to a large degree. The temperature at which the gels set can affect the properties of the final gel. The fact that temperature does not control their gelling action can make alginates a bit tricky to work with. Calcium and/or acid are used to trigger the gel structure. They combine with alginates to form thermo-irreversible gels.

Sodium alginate is often used for diffusion setting. This process is used to create restructured foods, like the pimiento cube found in the middle of a green olive. An alginate gel is characterized by a rapid setting process that moves from the outside in and by the fact that the final product can accommodate an unequal distribution of alginate, with a higher concentration at the surface. This gradually decreases toward the center of the gel, allowing for the creation of a liquid encased in a gel structure. Popular restaurant offerings using sodium alginates are Ferran Adrià's liquid-filled olives and fruit-based caviars.

TRANSGLUTAMINASE

Many years ago Alex and I were having dinner at WD-50. At the time we were living in Colorado and were back in town for our yearly vacation to visit friends and family and eat our way through New York City. Alex and the chef, Wylie Dufresne, had been introduced by a mutual friend and were slowly getting to know each other. At the end of the meal Alex disappeared into the kitchen to thank Wylie and chat for a bit. Having already said hello earlier, I finished my tea and waited, and waited, and waited. Eventually I flagged down our server and politely asked her to let Alex know that I was leaving. He came racing out the front door of the restaurant just as I was getting into a taxicab.

The reason for the long delay? They were talking hydrocolloids and meat glue. It was the beginning of a new era in our kitchen, one that I embraced rather half-heartedly. Methocel and Activa fascinated Alex. At the time the Methocel left me cold, although I could definitely see the possibilities of "meat glue." Meat cookery has always been a favorite of mine and the idea of butchering without strings was seductive.

Activa is the proprietary name of a family of products that contain transglutaminase. Transglutaminase is classified as GRAS ("generally regarded as safe") by the FDA. It is a naturally occurring enzyme, a protein that acts as a catalyst. The most widely available transglutaminases are produced through the fermentation of *Streptomyces mobaraensis.*

Transglutaminase used for culinary preparations works by cross-linking food proteins such as casein, glutens, egg proteins, soybean globulins, myosins, and whey proteins. The transglutaminase catalyzes a covalent bond between glutamine and lysine. These bonds are considered stable, insoluble, and irreversible. Because of this bond, transglutaminase is an effective protein adhesive (hence the name "meat glue"). This means that you can trim off all the fat, sinew, and silverskin from a piece of meat, even if it means dividing it into smaller pieces, and "glue" everything back together. In the end there will be no strings or fillers, just a beautiful piece of meat.

Transglutaminase also works as a texturizer. This, in combination with its ability to bond proteins, makes it very popular in manufacturing charcuterie and prepared foods. Transglutaminase's effectiveness is directly related to the amount of lysine available in the protein being used. For this reason transglutaminase reacts very well with egg albumen, soy, and casein products and only moderately well with gluten and egg yolk proteins. Efficiency can be improved with the addition of gelatin, caseinate, potassium chloride, and fiber, and these ingredients are sometimes added to transglutaminase blends to facilitate the bonding process. Salt and phosphates also increase the effectiveness of transglutaminase by increasing the availability of salt-soluble proteins.

Transglutaminase works within a pH range of 5.5 to 8, with optimal levels between 6 and 7. It works within a temperature range of 32°F–149°F (0°C–65°C), with optimal results at 122°F–131°F (50°C–55°C). It is stable at lower temperatures, although the enzyme loses stability rapidly once temperatures rise above 140°F (60°C), and the enzyme is completely denatured and ineffective by 167°F (75°C). The formation of bonds is dictated by the combination of time and temperature, with faster reactions occurring in the optimum temperature zone. Once a package of transglutaminase is opened, the live enzyme is subject to oxidation and any remainder should be vacuum sealed and kept in the refrigerator or freezer for maximum shelf life. We can't tell you how often we've heard from cooks and chefs who complained that their transglutaminase lost effectiveness too quickly— but who had not bothered to reseal the bag, had transferred the enzyme into plastic deli containers, had left it sitting out at room temperature, or all of the above. Proper storage is critical.

Charcuterie often relies on fat emulsification by salt-soluble proteins. This is why you've probably never eaten an unsalted sausage. Transglutaminase can be added to a chopped or minced meat mixture to strengthen the protein network that keeps the fat emulsified through a range of temperatures, resulting in more snap and texture in the finished product. It is an effective ingredient in lower-salt meat or fish charcuterie products to preserve texture and stability. On the other hand, too much transglutaminase can result in dry, tough textures, so it's important to calculate the right ratios for these applications. Start experimenting with a small amount of your base material and once you've arrived at the right texture, you can simply apply the ratio to whatever quantities you need to make.

When bonding with transglutaminase it is important to know that it has less strength when interacting with collagen, and even less with actin. Transglutaminases manufactured for bonding purposes generally contain additional protein in the form of gelatin or sodium caseinate acting as a protein bridge in order to form gels more quickly and efficiently. Transglutaminase for bonding can be applied in its powdered form or as liquid slurry. When using powder, you should know that the enzyme is activated as soon as it becomes wet. The transglutaminase is blended with an inert powder, like maltodextrin, to prevent clumping and make dusting easier. We like the powdered enzyme when working with large muscles and bonding fewer pieces together. The liquid slurry contains a combination of transglutaminase, gelatin, and phosphate designed so that the enzymes do not activate until they are brushed on a protein source, which then pushes the pH level into the necessary range to activate bonding. When using either wet or dry enzymes, the proteins need to be pressed together, generally by vacuum sealing, within fifteen to thirty minutes of application for maximum effectiveness. Once the enzyme has been activated, it should be left to rest in refrigeration for six to eighteen hours to give the transglutaminase time to complete its work.

Different proteins require different amounts of transglutaminase to work effectively. The reaction depends on several factors, including protein makeup, available amino acids, and protein source. In general, pork, beef, and dark meat chicken require less transglutaminase and shorter setting times than shrimp, scallops, and white meat chicken.

Transglutaminase can be used in conjunction with seasoning and marinades. Marinades can be added at levels from 5 to 30 percent as long as the protein source easily absorbs them. The surface of the protein after marination should be just tacky to the touch before applying the enzyme. Tenderizing enzymes, like papain and bromelain (found in papaya, pineapple, and off-the-shelf meat tenderizers), can negate the effects of transglutaminase. If they are part of a recipe they should be added after the transglutaminase (see page 252).

Transglutaminase is also making inroads in industries other than meat and seafood. It is used in dairy products for its ability to interact with whey proteins and caseins. Transglutaminase will increase water-holding capabilities in a dairy-based gel system like yogurt or sour cream. This results in increased viscosity and improved texture, especially in low-fat preparations. It also helps stabilize the gel so that liquid does not seep out. Imagine the water that sometimes appears on top of your yogurt. Transglutaminase is used in the processed cheese industry for its ability to help improve the texture of the cheese, for its emulsifying capabilities, and to increase elasticity when the cheese is melted. The ability to cross-link gluten proteins has led to its use as a dough strengthener for wheat breads. There is some controversy over its use in gluten-free products because it is unclear whether or not its interaction may make gluten more accessible to absorption by the human body and trigger celiac reactions.

In our kitchen transglutaminase is a tool for efficiency and creativity. When butchering meat and fish, we can eliminate sinew and silverskin while still being able to fabricate large steaks and roasts for cooking. It allows us to create various terrines without the use of fillers, and it gives us the ability to work with dairy and soy products in a way that was unimaginable just a few years ago.

ACTIVA QUICK USAGE GUIDE

Activa is the proprietary name for the most commonly available source of transglutaminase in the United States.

Activa Y-G: 100 parts per gram transglutaminase
Ingredients: maltodextrin, lactose, yeast extract, safflower oil, transglutaminase

This product is designed specifically for use with dairy, and because of this it does not have an added protein bridge in the formulation. The blend of ingredients lets it be more active in milk systems. Y-G can be dry mixed, pureed, or blended with a smaller amount of non-chlorinated water or milk and added to a base mixture. Once the Y-G is blended with dairy proteins, it must rest in the refrigerator for at least twelve hours for the enzyme to take effect.

The lactose in Y-G helps the enzyme blend with milk. The yeast extract is an enzyme inhibitor, which allows the Y-G to work with raw milk products. Y-G was designed to improve texture and mouthfeel, and to reduce syneresis in dairy products. It is normally utilized in small amounts—for example, in yogurt, 0.008 to 0.033 percent; in cheese, 0.0025 to 0.35 percent.

Activa TI: 100 parts per gram transglutaminase
Ingredients: maltodextrin, transglutaminase

Activa TI must be used with ingredients containing readily available proteins for it to be effective. It can be mixed with dry ingredients for easier dispersion and added to the base mixture or it can be pureed into the base. TI works best if the finished products are vacuum sealed and allowed to rest for at least six hours under refrigeration.

Activa TI does not work well with raw milk. Y-G is recommended instead. Activa TI is very effective with tofu and can be used to make flavored and restructured products, like tofu noodles, when added at 0.5 percent. It is also used in emulsified food preparations such as bologna or sausages to bond the proteins together.

General usage amounts are 0.1 to 0.3 percent by weight.

Activa RM: 50 parts per gram transglutaminase
Ingredients: sodium caseinate, maltodextrin, transglutaminase

Activa RM can be either sprinkled directly onto proteins, which are then vacuum sealed, or pureed into a mixture. Another option is to blend it in a 4:1 ratio to water by weight and brush it onto proteins, which are then pressed together for adhesion. The slurry method has a very short working time (twenty to thirty minutes) and so is not recommended for high-volume applications. GS is recommended for large amounts of butchering. The sodium caseinate in this formulation acts as a protein bridge for bonding pieces of meat or fish by facilitating the formation of protein bonds.

We use Activa RM in amounts of 1 percent or less of the total weight of the other ingredients in a recipe. For example: crabmeat tater tots, 1 percent; duck parcels, 1 percent; shrimp spaetzle, 0.75 percent.

Activa GS: 50 parts per gram transglutaminase
Ingredients: sodium chloride, fish gelatin, trisodium phosphate, maltodextrin, transglutaminase, safflower oil (processing aid)

Activa GS is used as a slurry for large amounts of butchering. It is dispersed and hydrated in a 4:1 ratio, water to GS, by weight. It should be dissolved in 70°F–80°F (21°C–27°C) water so that the trisodium phosphate will break down. Overly hot water will kill the enzyme, so you want to stay in the recommended zone. If the water is not warm, the trisodium phosphate will not hydrate, and the slurry will not work on your proteins. The trisodium phosphate is there to keep the gelatin, a protein bridge, in suspension and increase the pH of the solution so the enzyme will remain active.

To make the slurry, slowly whisk the GS into your warm water; it will begin to produce foam. At this point you can whisk harder until it looks like softly whipped cream. Let it rest at room temperature for about ten minutes. Once the foam subsides, you can use the slurry by brushing it directly onto proteins. Vacuum seal or tightly bind the proteins together with plastic wrap and let them rest, refrigerated, for a minimum of six hours so that the enzyme can take effect. The slurry itself remains active for twenty-four hours. Use it in small portions for different meat and fish dishes while keeping the remainder in the refrigerator until you are ready for it.

GS can also be used in its powdered form, sprinkled on a base and then tumbled together for five minutes before shaping and pressing. The general usage level is 0.5 to 1 percent.

SHRIMP MOSAIC

SERVES 8 AS AN APPETIZER

The shrimp mosaic can be served warm or cold. It is an unusual presentation that works nicely on the bottom of the plate with a pasta or salad built on top of it, much like a chicken paillard. We've served it with a chunky avocado salad or tucked underneath a creamy risotto. It also makes for a fine spin on the traditional shrimp cocktail.

350 grams **21–25 shrimp**, peeled

4.5 grams **fine sea salt**

0.25 gram **cayenne pepper**

3.54 grams **Activa RM** (1 percent) (see Sources, page 309)

Cut the shrimp into ½-inch (1.25-centimeter) pieces and place them in a bowl. Season with the salt and cayenne, and gently mix with a rubber spatula. Sprinkle the Activa on the shrimp and stir to coat evenly.

Place the shrimp in a 10 × 12-inch vacuum-seal bag. Vacuum the air out of the bag, then use a meat mallet to flatten the shrimp evenly and cover the interior of the bag with a uniform sheet of shrimp. When the shrimp are completely flat they will look like a mosaic of shrimp. Place the bag in the refrigerator overnight to allow the transglutaminase to bond the pieces of shrimp.

The following day, place the bag in a water bath set at 131°F (55°C) and cook for 20 minutes. Transfer the bag to a large ice bath to rapidly chill the shrimp. When they are cold, cut open the bag and remove the sheet. Lay it on a cutting board and cut into 8 rectangles.

GOAT CHEESE DUMPLINGS

MAKES 48 DUMPLINGS

This recipe demonstrates the versatility of Activa YG in a dairy system, allowing us to make a delicate dumpling without conventional binders. We use the Activa at a ratio of 1 percent of the total weight of the ingredients. In the past we've paired these goat cheese dumplings with lobster. They would also be nice with a stew of mushrooms or spring vegetables, or as a warm accompaniment to a crisp salad with a simple vinaigrette.

300 grams fresh **goat cheese**

200 grams fresh **ricotta**

2 large **egg yolks**

5.38 grams **Activa Y-G** (see Sources, page 309)

3 grams **fine sea salt**

0.25 gram **cayenne pepper**

Nonstick cooking spray

Put the goat cheese, ricotta, egg yolks, Activa, salt, and cayenne in a blender and puree until smooth. Pour the mixture into a squeeze bottle.

Spray the inside of a magnetic sphere mold or spherical ice cube tray with nonstick cooking spray and wipe it with a dry paper towel. The fine film remaining will ease the unmolding process. Close the sphere mold and fill each cavity, squeezing the cheese mixture through the top opening. Fill all the spheres and tap the mold on the counter to force out any air bubbles. If necessary, top off the mold with any remaining goat cheese. Alternatively, you could substitute small chocolate molds for the spheres. Loosely cover the top of the sphere mold with plastic wrap and refrigerate for eighteen hours.

Remove the mold from the refrigerator and carefully remove the top section. The spheres will have set and there will be a small extension on each sphere from the fill hole. Use a paring knife to cut this cheese extension off of each sphere. Gently remove each sphere from the mold and place in a shallow container.

To serve, gently warm the spheres in simmering water to heat through. When hot, remove them from the water and place them in a serving dish with the desired sauce and glaze.

TURKEY THIGH ROULADE

SERVES 4

This is a fun spin on traditional roasted turkey. It cooks evenly, slices beautifully, and cooks much more quickly than the whole bird. We've even used it on Turkey Day with great success. The Jaccard is a spring-loaded meat tenderizer that has fifteen, sixteen, or forty-eight blades, depending on the model you purchase. It creates tiny, evenly spaced holes throughout the flesh, shortening the muscle fibers. This allows seasonings to penetrate to the interior of the meat, speeds the cooking time, and helps it cook more evenly. It may seem counterintuitive, but it actually works very well. You can skip this step if you don't have a Jaccard, but we really recommend keeping one in your kitchen. It's a very handy tool to have around.

> 200 grams room-temperature **water**
>
> 50 grams **Activa GS** (see Sources, page 309)
>
> 2 **turkey thighs** (1.36 kilograms)
>
> 6 grams **fine sea salt**
>
> 2.5 grams **togarashi spice blend** (see Sources, page 309)
>
> 454 grams sliced **bacon**

Pour the water into a bowl. Slowly sprinkle the Activa over the water and whisk to combine. The mixture will begin to foam and look like lightly whipped cream. Once all the Activa is dispersed in the water, let the mixture rest for 10 minutes. The foam will subside and the GS is ready to use. Refrigerate until the thighs and bacon are ready to be assembled.

Remove the skin from the turkey. Cut out the thighbone and remove any obvious pockets of fat and sinew. Starting from the place where the thighbone was, butterfly the thighs. Cut from the center outward on each side, leaving enough meat intact to hold the pieces together. Tenderize the thighs by pressing the Jaccard evenly over the thighs to cut uniform incisions into the muscle fibers. Combine the salt and togarashi in a small bowl, and season both sides of the thighs with the spices. (You may have some left over.)

Lay the bacon out flat on a cutting board. Use a pastry brush to apply a fine layer of the Activa slurry over both sides of each slice of bacon. Brush the Activa mixture on the turkey thighs, making sure to get into all the nooks and crannies.

Lay two 3-foot (1-meter) sheets of plastic wrap on the counter. Let the sheets overlap slightly so you have a double-wide sheet of plastic. Begin laying the bacon in the center of the plastic, overlapping the slices by one-third to create what looks like a raft of bacon.

Arrange the turkey thighs on the edge of the bacon nearest you, one on top of the other and slightly offset so they form a uniform thickness. Use the plastic wrap to help lift the bacon up and around the thighs, like a giant sushi roll. Once the bacon is wrapped around the turkey, use the plastic to pull the bacon tight around the thighs. Pull and roll the plastic around the turkey bacon roll, making a tight roulade. Use another sheet of plastic to roll around the roulade one more time and squeeze it tight. Place the roulade in the refrigerator for at least 6 hours or up to 24 hours.

To cook the roulade, preheat the oven to 375°F (190°C).

Remove the plastic wrap, place the roulade on a rack set over a roasting pan, and roast for 1 hour. The bacon should be brown and caramelized. If it's not fully cooked, turn on the broiler to finish cooking the bacon. Remove the roulade from the oven and let it rest for 15 minutes. Slice and serve.

LIQUID NITROGEN

Liquid nitrogen is an incredibly cold liquid that allows us to freeze things quickly in the kitchen. It is sometimes viewed with trepidation, and understandably so. However, working with liquid nitrogen is not so different from dealing with hot oil or boiling water. But as long as you regard it with respect and handle it with care, it is relatively safe to use.

Liquid nitrogen is simply pure nitrogen in a liquid state. Daniel Rutherford discovered the element nitrogen in 1772. As a gas, it makes up 78.1 percent of the earth's atmosphere by volume. In its gaseous state, nitrogen is odorless, colorless, nonflammable, nontoxic, and largely inert. Nitrogen is found in organic materials, foods, explosives, fertilizers, and poisons. The single largest use for nitrogen is combining it with hydrogen to produce ammonia. The ammonia is then used in many different products such as nitric acid, urea, hydrazines, fertilizers, and laughing gas.

Liquid nitrogen is a relatively inexpensive cryogenic liquid. It is created by fractional distillation of liquid air. Air is made liquid by lowering its temperature to a point where it condenses. The liquid air must be stored in a vacuum container because it absorbs heat easily and will quickly revert to a gas. Fractional distillation is the process of separating chemical compounds by their boiling point. Nitrogen has a lower boiling point than oxygen and therefore can be distilled and separated out of the liquid air. Once separated, it is compressed, reliquefied, and poured into a vacuum container for storage.

Liquid nitrogen freezes at −346°F (−210°C) and boils at −320°F (−195.5°C). It will boil immediately upon contact with warmer temperatures. As it boils it evaporates into nitrogen gas and dissipates into the atmosphere. The vapor it creates is a reaction between the liquid nitrogen and water vapor in the air. The extreme cold of the nitrogen causes the water droplets in the air to condense into a liquid, creating the smoke. Inhalation of too much nitrogen can cause dizziness, nausea, loss of consciousness, and even death, so it is very important to work with liquid nitrogen in well-ventilated areas.

Liquid nitrogen is typically stored in containers called *dewars*. These cylinders are insulated, vacuum-jacketed pressure containers equipped with safety valve releases and rupture discs that release pressure as it builds up and prevent explosions. Under normal circumstances these containers will occasionally vent their contents, so it is important that they too be kept in well-ventilated areas. The extremely cold contents mean that any uninsulated metal piping on the cylinder will be at dangerously low temperatures when the liquid nitrogen runs through it and should not be touched with bare flesh for fear of freezing and tissue damage. Loose-fitting protective gloves, goggles, and face shields are generally recommended when working with cryogenic liquids.

The most common culinary use for liquid nitrogen is making ice cream. The beauty of liquid nitrogen is that you don't need to use traditional safeguards to keep the ice cream from getting too hard. Sugar and/or alcohol are generally added to the bases to keep large ice crystals from forming and to facilitate smooth, creamy textures. But when using liquid nitrogen, the ice crystals are formed so quickly and are so small that these precautions are unnecessary. Smooth ice creams are guaranteed regardless of what is in the base. You can even scoop sweetened whipped cream, with or without extra flavorings, directly into liquid nitrogen and it will set up into scoops of ice cream almost instantly.

A less common culinary use for liquid nitrogen is in grinding ingredients, particularly high-fat products, to create powders or purees. For example, fresh raw peanuts may be frozen in liquid nitrogen and put through a juicer to create a completely uncooked peanut butter that preserves all the flavor of the raw nut. Or nuts can be roasted and ground into superfine flour that will be exponentially fresher than anything you can buy at the market. Olives may be partially dehydrated, frozen, and ground into a fine seasoning powder that would not normally be achievable due to their high fat content. Cooked shrimp and other proteins may also be frozen and ground and used for various preparations.

Grinding spices and other aromatics with liquid nitrogen is wonderful. The nitrogen keeps the grinder from heating up and helps preserve the volatile aromas and essential oils, which can then be infused into other mediums.

Fruits and vegetables may be frozen instead of cooked to tenderize them. The freezing process creates ice crystals, which poke microscopic holes into the cell walls. When the ingredients are defrosted, they are slightly tenderized but still retain some of their original texture and their raw flavor. While in their frozen state the fruits and vegetables can be shattered and the pieces used for a dramatic presentation in a finished dish. They can also be pureed so that you can get a smooth texture while preserving the uncooked flavor of the ingredient.

Finally, liquid nitrogen is perfect for chilling hot preparations quickly and efficiently. This minimizes the development of bacteria and harmful microorganisms in the food. A batch of spaghetti sauce or a pot of chicken curry can go from boiling to ice cold in five minutes. In terms of food safety, this is a very good thing.

All in all, we've come to look upon liquid nitrogen as an important addition to our kitchen. It's more than just a trendy ingredient of the moment; it's become a standard in our batterie de cuisine.

NOTE: *Always use proper safety precautions (gloves and goggles) when handling liquid nitrogen and work in a well-ventilated area.*

POWDERED LARDO

MAKES 2 CUPS

Small Styrofoam coolers are a wonderful tool when working with liquid nitrogen because they are insulated and relatively deep. This minimizes splashing and keeps the nitrogen from evaporating too quickly. Plastic coolers tend to crack upon exposure to the extreme cold, and glass bowls will shatter, so look for sturdy Styrofoam coolers with smooth inside walls.

This recipe takes an earthy, full-flavored fat and transforms it into something light and delicate. Powdered lardo is wonderful spooned on grilled crusty bread or folded into raw-fish tartares. It can be used as a finishing touch on roasted vegetables or salads, or anywhere you might use a full-flavored olive oil. This same technique may be applied to butter and other high-fat ingredients.

> 4 liters **liquid nitrogen** (see Sources, page 309)
> 250 grams **lardo**

Pour the liquid nitrogen into a Styrofoam container and slide the lardo into the nitrogen using a slotted spoon or skimmer. The nitrogen will boil furiously. When the lardo is frozen solid and the bubbling subsides, use a slotted spoon to transfer the lardo to a plastic blender top.

Turn the blender on low and gradually increase to high speed, grinding and pulverizing the lardo into a fine powder. Use a rubber spatula to scrape the frozen powder into a resealable plastic bag. Place in the freezer until ready to use.

POPCORN GELATO

MAKES 1 LARGE BOWL OF "POPCORN"

This ice cream is just fun. We use the natural starch in the popcorn to thicken the ice cream base; then we use a whipped cream canister to create small popcornlike bites in the liquid nitrogen. You can serve the popcorn ice cream in a bowl (with spoons on the side, of course), and watch grown-ups revert to childhood as they discover your secret.

> 1,530 grams **whole milk**
> 225 grams **butter-flavored Orville Redenbacher microwave popcorn** (3 bags), popped
> 200 grams **white chocolate**
> 5 grams **fine sea salt**
> 4 liters **liquid nitrogen** (see Sources, page 309)

Put the milk and popcorn in a pot set over medium-high heat. Bring the mixture to a boil, turn off the heat, cover the pot, and let the mixture steep for 30 minutes. Strain through a fine-mesh strainer, pressing on the solids with the back of a ladle. The strainer will catch the coarse corn particles while allowing the milk and the broken-down popcorn solids to pass through. Discard the residue in the strainer and reserve the popcorn milk (you should have about 1,030 grams).

Put the white chocolate in a Mason jar and lightly screw on the lid. Place the jar in a pressure cooker and add water to fill the chamber by one-quarter. The water creates steam in the chamber and forms a double-boiler pressure cooker. Seal the pressure cooker and bring up to high pressure. Cook the chocolate on high pressure for 30 minutes. Let the pressure dissipate naturally. Carefully remove the jar and let it cool. When the jar is cool enough to handle, remove the chocolate from it by running a butter knife or small offset spatula along the inside of the jar and gently shaking the chocolate out onto a plate. Alternatively, place the white chocolate in a heatproof bowl in a 250°F (120°C) oven for 45 to 60 minutes, stirring occasionally, until it turns a deep golden brown. Let cool. Reserve the caramelized white chocolate. This step can be done in advance. The cooled caramelized white chocolate can be wrapped in plastic and kept at room temperature for up to a month.

Chop the caramelized white chocolate into small pieces and put them in a blender. Prepare an ice bath.

Pour the popcorn milk into a medium pan set over medium-high heat and bring to a simmer. Pour the hot milk over the chocolate. Turn the blender on low. Sprinkle in the salt and increase the speed to high. Puree the mixture for 1 minute. It should be smooth and creamy. Strain the mixture through a fine-mesh sieve into a bowl and cool the mixture in the ice bath. Refrigerate the ice cream base for at least 4 hours. Place a bowl for the gelato in the freezer.

Fill a Styrofoam container halfway with liquid nitrogen. Pour the ice cream base into a whipped cream canister. Charge it with two nitrous oxide charges, then extrude the base in short bursts into the nitrogen. Use a slotted spoon to remove the gelato, which will now look like popcorn. Place the frozen popcorn pieces in the frozen bowl and set them in the freezer for 10 minutes. The gelato is too cold to eat when it first comes out of the liquid nitrogen and would cause frostbite on the inside of your mouth. It has to "warm up" in the freezer for 15 minutes to become edible. Alternatively, you can freeze the base using a traditional ice cream maker. It will keep for up to 1 week in the freezer.

CARBON DIOXIDE

Joseph Priestley was an Englishman born near Leeds. He was a Presbyterian minister, schoolteacher, philosopher, and scientist. Among his scientific achievements, Priestley is cocredited with the discovery of oxygen. He established the law of inverse squares, which states that the attraction or repulsion between two electric charges is inversely proportional to the square of the distance between them. Priestley was the first to identify plant respiration and photosynthesis. As his lasting culinary achievement, he created carbon dioxide and nitrous oxide in his laboratory and pioneered the first version of manmade carbonated water.

Priestley lived next door to a brewery and observed that the gases given off by the fermenting vats of liquid floated to the ground. This told him that the gas was heavier than air. He also noted that it extinguished fire. He named this gas "fixed air" and later discovered that it was carbon dioxide. After he suspended a bowl of water over one of the vats, he tasted it and discovered that it had a pleasant tangy flavor. Later he devised a method of dripping sulfuric acid on chalk to produce carbon dioxide and then dissolved the gas in water by shaking them together in a closed vessel. He published a treatise on the subject titled "Impregnating Water with Fixed Air."

Carbon dioxide is a chemical compound formed when two oxygen atoms form a covalent bond with one carbon atom. It is an acidic oxide, meaning that it reacts with water to produce an acid. It is colorless and odorless at low concentrations. Carbon dioxide is a compressed gas. This means that it exceeds 40 psi (pounds per square inch) at 100°F (38°C). It can displace oxygen in air and at high concentrations can be toxic, causing dizziness, headaches, sweating, and disorientation. CO_2 gas is commonly used in carbonated beverages; in food packaging as a preservative; in aerosol cans as a propellant; in chemical processing, especially for methanol and urea production; as a shield gas in welding; for pH control in water treatment; and in oil and gas recovery systems.

Carbon dioxide can be compressed into a liquid at very low temperatures. Liquid CO_2 can only be formed under pressure, at 5.11 atm (atmospheric pressure) at −70°F (−56.6°C). It is used mainly as a refrigerant or as a solvent.

Carbon dioxide in its solid form is known as dry ice. It is formed by chilling carbon dioxide gas under pressure to its freezing point of −109.3°F (−78.5°C). It is produced either as large blocks or as small pellets. The solid CO_2 sublimates at normal atmospheric pressure, changing directly from a solid to a gas. This produces a characteristic "smoking" that is often used for artistic effect. It is extremely cold and should never be handled with bare hands. Because the gas is heavier than air, dry ice should only be used in well-ventilated areas to avoid toxic concentrations. It is used heavily in shipping and manufacturing for its cooling properties. It can usually be found at your local supermarket in the summertime to help frozen foods make it home without melting. Dry ice is also used for blast cleaning, a method of abrasive blasting with a stream of pressurized air and dry ice, because it leaves no chemical residue behind.

Interestingly, scientists have never really understood how we taste carbon dioxide. Although we tend to assume that the prickle on our tongue is caused by the action of the bubbles, carbonated drinks tasted in a vacuum chamber where the bubbles don't exist create the same sensation. The sensation of drinking carbonated liquids—actually, the sensation of eating and drinking anything—is a combination of activated taste receptors and somatosensory cells. The somatosensory system is a network of sensory cells throughout the body, on skin, in bones, muscles, joints, internal organs, and the cardiovascular system. The cells react to different stimuli and transfer information to the brain via sensory nerves and the spinal cord. That information determines our perception of different sensations like temperature, pressure, pleasure, and pain.

In October 2009 researchers at the National Institute of Dental and Craniofacial Research, part of the National Institutes of Health, and their colleagues from the Howard Hughes Medical Institute at the University of California, San Diego, reported that they had discovered that, in mice, an enzyme known as carbonic anhydrase 4 facilitates the taste of carbonation. This enzyme catalyzes carbon dioxide into carbonic acid, which quickly ionizes into a proton and a bicarbonate ion. This process makes it easier for the body to process acids. The carbonic anhydrase 4 is connected to sour taste receptors in the mouth, which explains the tart flavor of seltzer water. When the enzyme's activity is inhibited, it results in a decreased ability to taste carbonation. Although researchers are not exactly sure how the sensation is fully processed, locating the enzyme and determining its role is a good beginning to understanding how and why we taste CO_2.

Of course, our favorite use for carbon dioxide is the creation of fizzy beverages. There are several different pieces of equipment you can buy to achieve this effect, from an iSi canister that comes with CO_2 chargers to an entire rig based around a CO_2 tank for serious enthusiasts. The benefits of carbonating at home are that you can control the level of carbonation in the beverage and you can carbonate anything you want. The classic cherry lime rickeys never had it so good.

Fresh juices and cocktails are wonderful with a bit of a spritz. A classic egg cream is made with chocolate syrup, milk, and soda water. Specialty markets charge a premium for sparkling lemonade; with a carbonation system you can make one at home that suits your exact taste for a fraction of the cost.

In addition to beverages, carbonated liquids are wonderful for making batters. Beer and tempura batters are known for their light, crisp texture. This is because the CO_2 in the liquid adds instant leavening. Now imagine that you can add CO_2 to any flavored liquid to use in your batter—sparkling ranch dressing consommé as part of the batter for chicken fingers, or sparkling cinnamon tea as part of the batter for apple fritters. The possibilities are endless.

These batters usually call for a 1:1 ratio of flour and liquid, with additional seasoning to taste. You can also aerate the buttermilk in your pancake batter for lighter, fluffier results. Remember that most chemical leaveners are there to provide aeration in the form of carbon dioxide gas. When we add aerated liquids, it's simply a shortcut to the same results.

COFFEE ONION RINGS

SERVES 4 AS A SIDE DISH

These onion rings are extra light and crispy because we carbonate the batter. If you don't have a home carbonation system, you can substitute seltzer water and a tablespoon of freeze-dried coffee. Simple home carbonation systems run the gamut from about $60 for an iSi carbonator to several hundred dollars for a carbonation rig and CO_2 tank. Once you start playing with one, you'll wonder how you ever got along without it. The tiny bit of xanthan gum in the recipe helps the batter stick to the onion slices and keeps it from separating. You can season the onion rings *with salt and serve with ketchup, but we think you'll find that the Beef Seasoning and smoked ketchup really take the flavor to the next level.*

225 grams **brewed coffee**

0.2 gram **xanthan gum** (see Sources, page 309)

150 grams **all-purpose flour**

1 large **egg yolk**

2 grams **fine sea salt**

1.5 grams **baking soda**

Canola oil or **rice bran oil**, for frying

85 grams **all-purpose flour**

10 grams **onion powder**

3 medium **sweet onions**, cut into ¾-inch (1.9-centimeter) rings

Beef Seasoning (page 18)

Smoked ketchup (see page 62)

Pour the coffee into a blender. Turn on low and increase the speed until a vortex forms in the center. Sprinkle in the xanthan gum and increase the speed to evenly disperse it. Reduce the speed to medium and add the flour, egg yolk, salt, and baking soda. Puree to just combine. Pour the mixture into a whipped cream canister and charge with one CO_2 charge. Alternatively, if you have a carbonation rig, carbonate the batter to 50 psi.

Fill a medium pot half full of canola or rice bran oil and heat over medium-high heat until it reaches 350°F (175°C).

Put the flour and onion powder on a plate and mix well. Dispense the coffee batter from the whipped cream canister into a bowl. Dredge the onion rings in the onion flour mixture, dip them into the batter, and immediately drop them in the hot oil. Fry 3 or 4 rings at a time, flipping them once halfway through cooking. When they are golden brown, remove the rings from the pot with a slotted spoon or skimmer and put on a wire rack set over a baking sheet to drain. Season lightly with the beef seasoning and serve with a side of smoked ketchup.

AERO CHOCOLATE

MAKES 8 SERVINGS

This recipe was inspired by the idea of Aero bars. We wanted to replicate that honeycomb texture while creating something intensely delicious. This dessert achieves that. You can serve it with cookies or blood orange compote. The light texture melts in your mouth and leaves you wanting more.

400 grams **64% cacao Manjari chocolate**

150 grams **heavy cream**

50 grams **liquid glucose** (see Sources, page 309)

2 grams **fine sea salt**

4 drops **blood orange extract**

300 grams cold **water**

2.4 grams **agar** (see Sources, page 309)

0.3 gram **locust bean gum** (see Sources, page 309)

Have ready eight 8-ounce Mason jars.

Put the chocolate, cream, glucose, and salt in a medium bowl, and heat in the microwave until the chocolate has melted. Pour the mixture into a blender and add the blood orange extract.

Pour the water into a small pot. Whisking constantly, sprinkle the agar and locust bean gum into the water and turn the heat to medium-high. Bring to a simmer and cook, stirring, for 5 minutes. Pour the agar mixture over the chocolate in the blender. Puree until combined.

Pour the chocolate mixture into a whipped cream canister. Add two CO_2 charges. Dispense the mixture into the Mason jars, filling them to the top. Screw on the lids. (Lids must be screwed on tightly so that when the mixture cools it creates a vacuum in the jar and allows the air bubbles to be captured and set in the gel structures.) Place the jars in the freezer for at least 2 hours to set the gel and make it easy to remove.

To serve, remove the aerated chocolate from the jars by running a butter knife or small offset spatula along the inside of the Mason jar and gently shaking the frozen chocolate out onto a plate. The chunks of chocolate will have a honeycomb texture and intense flavor accented by blood oranges. The aero chocolate may be plated and then brought to room temperature before serving, if desired.

ACKNOWLEDGMENTS

The decisions we make and the directions we choose in life are not as random as they may appear; we have been guided by many people. First I must thank my parents, Karen and David, for cooking so well and being passionate about food. They had me hooked on delicious from day one. Grandma Kitty and her television show, *Cooking with Kitty*, provided a playground for a toddler becoming aware of what is possible. From those early days she has always encouraged me to work hard while following my dreams. Our family friend Tom Haas was instrumental in getting me into a professional kitchen and it was Lenny Phillips who instilled the drive to succeed in the kitchen into my head. Doron Wong deserves many thanks for keeping me on the path to improve and chase perfection. It was in the kitchen of Clio working with Ken Oringer where I learned the need for continuous tasting and research. Ken pushed me to look down all avenues of food and lift every possible rock for inspirations. He also hired Aki, which allowed us to meet, and well . . . Finally, without Aunt Marie's unwavering belief in Aki and myself, many of our accomplishments would have never been possible.

—H. Alexander Talbot

As a little girl I always loved to cook. Food was my passion. Even as a child I gravitated toward books with great food from the *Little House* series by Laura Ingalls Wilder to the *All-of-a-Kind Family* books by Sydney Taylor. It was no great stretch to imagine that one day I would write books about food. I was lucky enough to be surrounded and supported by a family that loves food as much as I do and for that I thank Mom, Aunt Marie, and Uncle Steve. You were the best parents I ever could have asked for. Claire was a late entry to the family circle. In my early twenties, when I got a little distracted by life in the city, she's the one who pushed me to refocus my energy and lent me the money I needed to go to the culinary school in Vermont I had been talking about for years. A special mention for Barbara, Peg, and Bob who went out of their way to be there for us at a time when we needed them most and are always there when I need them now.

The New England Culinary Institute was a great experience for me and I have to thank both the staff of the school and the friends I made there. They were always ready to answer my questions and provide support when I needed it. A special acknowledgment has to go out to Mark Molinaro, who was my block mate both years, a good friend, and a good cook who wasn't afraid to lecture me when he felt I needed it, something I didn't always appreciate at the time. Chef David Hale was both an inspiration in the classroom and integral in helping me secure my internship at Clio in Boston, where I worked for Ken Oringer and met Alex. I learned more in Ken's kitchen than anywhere else before: that a good palate is as important as practical knowledge, that there is no substitute for hard work, that all the details matter, and that there is always something more to learn. These are lessons that have stayed with me ever since. Eddie and Steve taught me the ropes in garde manger and made me feel at home in a place where I easily could have been overwhelmed. Their willingness to share their knowledge inspired me to do the same for others.

Of course there is no book without Alex. Our greatest collaboration is our daughter, Amaya, but this book is a close second. It captures the essence of all the things we both love about food and cooking. It's always a pleasure to spend time with him, in the kitchen and out. Shared passions tend to push us to greater heights than either of us would reach alone.

—Aki Kamozawa

We both would like to thank Marco Canora and Laura Sbrana for giving us the keys to their kitchen. Those two summers proved to us that anything is possible. Beth and Warren Busteed deserve a big nod of appreciation for dealing with our youthful aspirations. Even though we ultimately had to part ways, they took a chance on us and gave us the opportunity to do things our way with minimal interference. Barbara and Alan Sackman encouraged us to push ourselves to improve constantly and gave us a wonderful kitchen in which to do so. Barbara especially was an unwavering supporter of both our food and our dreams for the future. Wylie Dufresne deserves a huge thanks for giving us our first container of meat glue, introducing us to the concept of hydrocolloids, eloquently pointing out the benefits of using a scale, and being a sounding board for ideas in the rough. Michael Chaffin is a good friend who is also a believer; he introduced us to the concept of a blog and encouraged us to pursue one of our own. Without Michael there would not be an *Ideas in Food*.

Thank you to John Mahoney for taking a chance on our writing skills and offering us an opportunity to work with *Popular Science*. There are not enough words in this space to thank our editor, Rica Allannic, for her passion and drive in this project. She never would have found us if Michael Anthony hadn't graciously pointed her in our direction. Rica introduced us to our agent, Sharon Bowers, who helped us organize our book in a smart and approachable way and then supported us through the sometimes painful process of writing and publication. Thank you to Ashley Phillips and the entire Clarkson Potter team who helped cull through all of our ideas and shape them into what this book has become. Danya Henninger helped us organize our digital vision and is still making the website look better than we ever could.

A big thank you goes out to all of the family and friends too numerous to list here. You know who you are and why we love you. Thank you to all of the cooks who have worked with us through the years; we've learned something from every one of you. Finally, a heartfelt thank you to all of the readers of our website, whose questions force us to look deeper and learn more about everything we do in the kitchen. Without the ongoing conversations with chefs, enthusiasts, idealists, and eccentrics we would not have been able to produce this book.

FURTHER READING

Aberle, Elton David, John C. Forrest, David E. Gerrard, and Edward W. Mills. *Principles of Meat Science*, 4th ed. Dubuque, IA: Kendall Hunt, 2001.

Adría, Ferran, Juli Soler, and Albert Adría. *El Bulli 2003*. Spain: RBA Libros SA and Ecco, 2005.

Alford, Jeffrey, and Naomi Duguid. *Flatbreads & Flavors: A Baker's Atlas*. New York: William Morrow, 1995.

Anderson, Pam. *The Perfect Recipe*. Boston: Houghton Mifflin, 1998.

Arbuckle, W. S. *Ice Cream*, 2nd ed. Westport, CT: AVI Publishing, 1972.

Barham, Peter. *The Science of Cooking*. New York: Springer, 2001.

Beranbaum, Rose Levy. *The Cake Bible*. New York: William Morrow, 1988.

Blumenthal, Heston. *Family Food*. London: Penguin Books, 2002.

———. *The Fat Duck Cookbook*. London: Bloomsbury, 2008.

Boi, Lee Geok. *Classic Asian Noodles*. Singapore: Marshall Cavendish Cuisine, 2007.

Brown, Amy. *Understanding Food: Principles and Preparation*. Belmont, CA: Wadsworth Thomson Learning, 2000.

Bugialli, Giuliano. *Bugialli on Pasta*. New York: Stewart, Tabori & Chang, 2000.

Carluccio, Antonio. *Antonio Carluccio's Passion for Pasta*. London: BBC Books, 1993.

Carroll, Ricki. *Home Cheesemaking*. North Adams, MA: Storey Publishing, 2002.

Charley, Helen, and Connie Weaver. *Foods: A Scientific Approach*, 3rd ed. Upper Saddle River, NJ: Prentice Hall, 1998.

Clarke, Chris. *The Science of Ice Cream*. Cambridge, UK: RSC Publishing, 2008.

Clayton, Bernard, Jr. *The Complete Book of Breads*. New York: Simon and Schuster, 1973.

Colwin, Laurie. *Home Cooking: A Writer in the Kitchen*. New York: Alfred A. Knopf, 1988.

———. *More Home Cooking: A Writer Returns to the Kitchen*. New York: Harper-Collins, 1993.

Corriher, Shirley O. *BakeWise: The Hows and Whys of Successful Baking*. New York: Scribner, 2008.

———. *CookWise: The Hows & Whys of Successful Cooking*. New York: William Morrow, 1997.

Damodaran, Srinivasan, and Alain Paraf. *Food Proteins and Their Applications*. New York: Marcel Dekker, 1997.

David, Elizabeth. *English Bread and Yeast Cookery, New American Edition*. Newton Highlands, MA: Biscuit Books, Inc., 1995.

Diggs, Lawrence J. *Vinegar: The User-Friendly Standard Text Reference & Guide to Appreciating, Making, and Enjoying Vinegar.* San Jose, CA: Authors Choice Press, 2000.

Ellis, Merle. *Cutting Up in the Kitchen: The Butcher's Guide to Saving Money on Meat and Poultry.* San Francisco: Chronicle Books, 1975.

Field, Carol. *The Italian Baker.* New York: Harper and Row, 1985.

Figoni, Paula. *How Baking Works: Exploring the Fundamentals of Baking Science.* Hoboken, NJ: Wiley, 2004.

Gunasekaran, Sundaram, and M. Mehmet Ak. *Cheese Rheology and Texture.* Boca Raton, FL: CRC Press, 2003.

Hamelman, Jeffrey. *Bread: A Baker's Book of Techniques and Recipes.* Hoboken, NJ: Wiley, 2004.

Helou, Anissa. *Savory Baking from the Mediterranean: Focaccias, Flatbreads, Rusks, Tarts, and Other Breads.* New York: William Morrow, 2007.

Imeson, Alan, ed. *Thickening and Gelling Agents for Food,* 2nd ed. Gaithersburg, MD: Aspen Publishers, 1999.

Kamman, Madeleine. *The Making of a Cook.* New York: Weathervane Books, 1971.

Kindstedt, Paul. *American Farmstead Cheese: The Complete Guide to Making and Selling Artisan Cheeses.* White River Junction, VI: Chelsea Green Publishing, 2005.

Kluger, Marilyn. *The Wild Flavor.* Los Angeles: Jeremy P. Tarcher, 1984.

Lahey, Jim, and Rick Flaste. *My Bread: The Revolutionary No-Work, No-Knead Method.* New York: W. W. Norton, 2009.

Lee, Cecilia Hae-Jin. *Eating Korean: From Barbecue to Kimchi, Recipes from My Home.* Hoboken, NJ: Wiley, 2005.

Lepard, Dan, and Richard Whittington. *Baker & Spice: Baking with Passion, Exceptional Recipes for Real Breads, Cakes, and Pastries.* San Diego: Thunder Bay Press, c. 2002.

Levinson, Leonard Leuis. *The Complete Book of Pickles & Relishes.* New York: Hawthorn Books, 1965.

Lin, Florence. *Florence Lin's Complete Book of Chinese Noodles, Dumplings, and Breads.* New York: William Morrow, 1986.

Lowe, Belle. *Experimental Cookery, from the Chemical and Physical Standpoint,* 3rd ed. New York: Wiley, 1943.

Matz, Samuel A. *Snack Food Technology,* 3rd ed. New York: Van Nostrand Reinhold, 1993.

McGee, Harold. *On Food and Cooking: The Science and Lore of the Kitchen.* New York: Scribner, 2004.

McWilliams, Margaret. *Foods: Experimental Perspectives,* 6th ed. Upper Saddle River, NJ: Pearson Education, 2008.

Medrich, Alice. *Chocolate and the Art of Low-Fat Desserts.* New York: Warner Books, 1994.

Mehas, Kay Yockey, and Sharon Lesley Rodgers. *Food Science: The Biochemistry of Food and Nutrition.* New York: Glencoe McGraw-Hill, 1997.

Migoya, Francisco J. *Frozen Desserts.* Hoboken, NJ: Wiley, 2008.

Pearson, Albert M., and Tedford A. Gillett. *Processed Meats,* 3rd ed. New York: Chapman and Hall, 1996; Gaithersburg, MD: Aspen Publishers, 1999.

Phillips, G. O., and P. A. Williams, eds. *Handbook of Hydrocolloids.* Cambridge: Woodhead Publishing Limited, 2000.

Potter, Norman N., and Joseph H. Hotchkiss. *Food Science,* 5th ed. New York: Chapman and Hall, 1995; New York: Springer, 1998.

Reinhart, Peter. *The Bread Baker's Apprentice: Mastering the Art of Extraordinary Bread.* Berkeley: Ten Speed Press, 2001.

————. *Brother Juniper's Bread Book: Slow Rise as Method and Metaphor.* Cambridge: Perseus Publishing, 1991.

Rodgers, Rick, ed. *The Baker's Dozen Cookbook.* New York: HarperCollins, 2001.

Ruhlman, Michael, and Brian Poleyn. *Charcuterie.* New York: W. W. Norton, 2005.

Silverton, Nancy. *Breads from the La Brea Bakery.* New York: Villard, 1996.

Smith, Tim. *Making Artisan Cheese: 50 Fine Cheeses That You Can Make in Your Own Kitchen.* Beverly, MA: Quarry, 2005.

Steingarten, Jeffrey. *The Man Who Ate Everything, and Other Gastronomic Feats, Disputes, and Pleasurable Pursuits.* New York: Alfred A. Knopf, 1998.

Stern, Jane, and Michael Stern. *Square Meals.* New York: Alfred A. Knopf, 1984.

Tsuji, Shizuo. *Japanese Cooking, a Simple Art.* Tokyo: Kodansha International, 1980.

Vieira, Ernest R. *Elementary Food Science,* 4th ed. New York: Chapman and Hall, 1996.

Witherly, Steven A. *Why Humans Like Junk Food.* New York: iUniverse Inc., 2007.

Wolfert, Paula. *The Cooking of Southwest France.* Garden City, NY: The Dial Press/ Doubleday, 1983.

Websites

These are some very interesting and informative websites that greatly helped increase our education and stretch our horizons.

Ajinomoto USA Inc.
(201) 292-3200
www.ajinomoto-usa.com

CheeseForum.org
http://www.cheeseforum.org

Cooking Issues, the French Culinary Institute's Tech'N Stuff Blog
www.cookingissues.com

CP Kelco
www.cpkelco.com

Discover, Science, Technology, and the Future
www.discovermagazine.com

Dow Chemical Company
www.dow.com/methocel

Eggcyclopedia
www.incredibleegg.org/egg-facts/eggcyclopedia

Food-Info
www.food-info.net/uk/index.htm

Food Politics, Marion Nestle
www.foodpolitics.com

Food Product Design
www.foodproductdesign.com

Ideas in Food
http://blog.ideasinfood.com

Khymos, Martin Lersch
www.khymos.org/

Northeast Fisheries Science Center
www.nefsc.noaa.gov

A Practical Guide to Sous Vide Cooking, Douglas Baldwin
http://amath.colorado.edu/~baldwind/sous-vide.html

Prepared Foods Network
www.preparedfoods.com

Science Daily
www.sciencedaily.com

Scientific American
www.scientificamerican.com

Umami Information Center
www.umamiinfo.com

University of Guelph, Dairy Science and Technology Education Series
www.foodsci.uoguelph.ca/dairyedu/home.html

University of Illinois, Interactive Lessons in Meat Science
www.labs.ansci.illinois.edu/meatscience/lessons/lesson1.html

SOURCES

Ajinomoto USA Inc.
(201) 292-3200
www.ajinomoto-usa.com
Activa products, soy sauces, sesame oil,
and other flavoring ingredients

All-Clad Metalcrafters LLC
(800) 255-2523
www.allclad.com
Heavy-duty cookware

Anson Mills
(803) 467-4122
www.ansonmills.com
Organic heirloom corn and rice products

Berkel
(800) 348-0251
www.berkelequipment.com
Vacuum sealers and slicers

BLiS, LLC
(616) 942-7545
www.blisgourmet.com
Artisan caviar, barrel-aged maple syrups,
and vinegars

Bob's Red Mill
(800) 349-2173 customer service
www.bobsredmill.com
Specialty grains, flours, beans, and
baking ingredients, with organic and
gluten-free products

Bradley Technologies Canada Inc.
(800) 665-4188
www.bradleysmoker.com
Electric smokers

The Chef's Warehouse
(718) 842-8700
www.chefswarehouse.com
Specialty ingredients for chefs, pastry
chefs, and passionate home cooks;
source for glucose and Valrhona
chocolate in bulk

Chocosphere
(877) 992-4626
www.chocosphere.com
A supplier of fine chocolates and cocoa
powders

Cookshack, Inc.
(800) 423-0698
www.cookshack.com
Electric smokers

iSi
www.isinorthamerica.com
Whipped cream canisters and soda
siphons

JB Prince Company, Inc.
(212) 683-3553
(800) 473-0577
www.jbprince.com
Chef tools and equipment

Just Tomatoes, Etc.
(800) 537-1985
www.justtomatoes.com
Dehydrated and freeze-dried fruits and
vegetables

King Arthur Flour
(800) 827-6836 customer service
(802) 649-3717 baker's hotline
www.kingarthurflour.com
Great flour and other baking staples

Kitchen Aid
(800) 541-6390
www.kitchenaid.com
Our favorite mixers and food processors

Kitchen Arts and Letters
(212) 876-5550
www.kitchenartsandletters.com
Arguably the best cookbook store in the
world

Korin Japanese Trading Company
(212) 587-7021
www.korin.com
Japanese knives and kitchen equipment

Le Sanctuaire
(415) 986-4216
www.le-sanctuaire.com
Purveyors of spices, spice blends
(including Vadouvan), specialty
ingredients (including hydrocolloids and
sequestrants used in the professional
section of this book), high-end china,
and equipment such as vacuum sealers
and the Gastrovac

Lodge Manufacturing Company
(423) 837-7181
www.lodgemfg.com
Cast-iron cookware

Michael's Stores, Inc.
(800) 642-4235
www.michaels.com
Their cake decorating section is a
good source for specialty pastry items
including glucose and glycerin

MULTIVAC INC.
www.multivac.com
A great vacuum sealer

New England Cheesemaking Supply
Company
(413) 397-2012
www.cheesemaking.com
Cheesemaking supplies and equipment

Oak Barrel Wine Craft
(510) 849-0400
www.oakbarrel.com
Oak Barrel Wine Craft claims to have
"everything for the makers of wine
and beer" and we would add vinegar
to that list. From starter cultures to
actual vinegar-making kits and oak
barrels for aging, this company has a
comprehensive inventory of supplies.

PolyScience
(800) 229-7569
www.polyscience.com
Makers of our favorite immersion
circulator

Taylor-Wharton-Cryogenics
(800) 898-2657
www.taylorwharton.com
Source for purchasing dewars and
information on working with liquid
nitrogen

Terra Spice Company
(574) 586-2600
www.terraspicecompany.com
Purveyors of spices, spice blends,
and specialty ingredients. They carry
birch bark, melting salts, sodium
hexametaphosphate, smoke powder, and
many of the hydrocolloids used in the
professional section of this book.

Valrhona Chocolate
www.valrhona.com
One of our favorite chocolates

Vita Mix Corporation, Food Service
    Division
(800) 437-4654
www.vitamix.com
Quite possibly the best blenders
available for the consumer today

Volcano Vaporizer
(866) 486-5266
www.thevolcanovaporizer.com
For those who want to experiment with
using a vaporizer to make aromas

Weber-Stephen Products Co.
(800) 446-1071 customer service
(800) GRILLOUT grill line
www.weber.com
Great grills and lots of information

Whole Foods Market
www.wholefoodsmarket.com
If you don't have access to a great local
butcher, we've found that Whole Foods
will cut meat to order and is a good
source for specialty cuts.

Williams-Sonoma
www.williams-sonoma.com
Source for quality cookware, bakeware,
immersion circulators, home vacuum
sealers, the Smoking Gun, and induction
burners for low-temperature precision
cooking.

Winston Industries
(800) 234-5286
www.winstonind.com
Makers of the CVap, this company has
a great website that is both educational
and will help you to find a sales
representative in your area.

INDEX

tapioca flour, 152, 169, 250
taste sensation, 297
tenderness, of meat, 215, 216, 222–25
terrine, two-melon, 254–56
thickeners. *See* hydrocolloids; *specific types*
thixotropism, 245
tofu, 283
  Cheddar tofu, 275–77
tomatoes, sun drying, 49–50
tomato stock, 211
trans fats, 183
transglutaminase, 238–39, 278–84
  recipes using, 284–88
triglycerides, 183
trisodium phosphate, 283–84
turkey thigh roulade, 287–88
twice-cooked scallops, 25–26
two-melon terrine, 254–56

vacuum sealing, 204–6. *See also* sous vide cooking
  rosemary pineapple, 207
  strawberries and syrup, 208
  using transglutaminase, 281, 283, 284
V00.......adouvan spice blend, 40
vanilla salt, 19
veal breast, braised, 228–29
vegetables. *See also specific types*
  blanching, 196–97, 199–201
  brining, 45; honey mustard brine, 26–27; roast chicken brine, 27–28
  browning of, 45, 49, 197–99
  controlled bruising, 205–6
  dehydrating, 49–50
  freezing, 43–45, 197, 291
  pickling basics, 36–37
  roasting, 217
vegetable stocks, 209
Versawhip, 248, 271
vinaigrettes, oil-free, 245
vinegar, 28–32, 216–17. *See also* pickling
  every wine vinegar, 33–34
  maple vinegar, 34–35
vitamins, in milk, 159

waffles, sourdough, 88–89
watermelon rind pickle, instant, 37–38
wheat flour. *See* flour
whey, 157, 158, 161–62, 281
whipped cherry juice, 248
white chocolate
  popcorn gelato, 293–94
  white chocolate frozen yogurt, 192–93
  white chocolate sheet, 261–62
whole wheat sweet potato bread, no-knead, 78–79
wine, corked flavors in, 267
wine vinegar, 29, 30–31
  every wine vinegar, 33–34
wine yeasts, 30
Wolfert, Paula, 231
wood smoke, 53–55

xanthan gum, 239, 243–46, 260
  recipes using, 247, 248, 270–71, 298–300

yeast breads, 65–68, 91. *See also* sourdough breads
  fail-safe bread, 68–70
  flatbreads, 90–91
  no-knead, 71–73; brioche dough, 75–76; pizza dough, 74–75; whole wheat sweet potato bread, 78–79
  salt in, 17
  sticky buns, 77
yeasts
  in breadmaking, 65–66, 67–68, 72, 81
  for vinegar making, 29, 30
yogurt, 177
  dressing, green beans amandine with, 203–4
  homemade, 179–80
  smoked, 62–63
  transglutaminase and, 282
  white chocolate frozen yogurt, 192–93
yuzu meringue, 270–71